UP FROM ZERO

PAUL GOLDBERGER

RANDOM HOUSE  NEW YORK

UP FROM ZERO

Politics, Architecture, and the Rebuilding of New York

 Published in the United States by Random House, an imprint of The Random House Publishing Group, a division of Random House, Inc., New York, and simultaneously in Canada by Random House of Canada Limited, Toronto.

RANDOM HOUSE and colophon are registered trademarks of Random House, Inc.

Library of Congress Cataloging-in-Publication Data

Goldberger, Paul.
Up from zero : politics, architecture, and the rebuilding of New York / Paul Goldberger.
p. cm.
ISBN 1-4000-6017-6
1. World Trade Center Site (New York, N.Y.) 2. Architecture—New York (State)—New York—21st century. 3. Memorials—New York (State)—New York—Planning. 4. City planning—New York (State)—New York. 5. New York (N.Y.)—Buildings, structures, etc. I. Title.
NA6233.N5W6745 2004
725'.23'097471—dc22 2004046769

Printed in the United States of America on acid-free paper

Random House website address: www.atrandom.com

246897531

FIRST EDITION

Book design by Carole Lowenstein

For Susan, Ben, Alex, Adam,
Delphine and Thibeaux, Edna and Moe,
and the memory of Ruth

Contents

Preface

Sixteen Acres

There is no instruction manual to tell a city what to do when its tallest buildings are suddenly gone, and there is a void in its heart. There is no road map to lead its officials and its citizens along the route of renewal, no guidebook to help them figure out whether renewal, in fact, is even what they want. When the twin towers of the World Trade Center—the two tallest skyscrapers in New York and each the second tallest in the United States—were destroyed on September 11, 2001, there was not only no precedent for dealing with the enormity of the loss, there was no system for figuring out what should happen next. Should the towers be put back? Should they be replaced by a triumphant substitute or by a sober memorial? Or both? Or would it be better if nothing at all were built where these buildings had been? Who should be empowered to decide all of this, and by what means? Should it be done right away, with the wounds raw, or in a few years, when people would feel different about this piece of land? And who should pay for it?

Although it took less than two hours for the towers of the World Trade Center to collapse, it has taken more than two years to figure out these questions, and some of them still have no answers. It has seemed at various times to have been an architectural debate, a political one, an economic one, and a cultural one. In truth, it has been all of these things, all of the time, played out within a context of intense emotion. How could it be otherwise, when you think of what provoked the questions? Planning is not always a particularly rational process in New York City under the best of circumstances, and these circumstances were stunningly different from any anyone had ever experienced.

A word of background, before we get into the story itself. Although the physical form of New York has always been subject to constant upheaval, we are not accustomed to the notion that portions of the skyline could disappear in an instant and by surprise. New York City has had a tumultuous history, but nothing in its past—or in the experience of any city for that matter—could prepare people to respond to the sudden and violent loss of their most prominent landmark. What happened in New York City in 2001 was not like the long and painful siege of London during World War II or the bombing of Berlin, even though the Allies' air strikes there yielded a result—a void in the heart of a great city—that might be considered similar to Ground Zero, as everyone soon after September 11 began to call the site of the World Trade Center. But the attacks on London and Berlin and other great cities during World War II, however terrible they were, were expected by the citizens of these cities, and they occurred over a long period of time. They did not come during periods of peace. The destruction of the World Trade Center was an event of stunning surprise. Few people in the United States believed that the country was vulnerable to attack, and certainly not in the form in which it came. And that it would result in horrendous loss of life and the complete destruction of a pair of buildings that were among the tallest and most celebrated in the world is an event that few Americans envisioned.

We think of the skyline as something that grows slowly, organically even. Before September 11, 2001, New York had seemed to operate with a kind of brute order: the bigger things on the skyline would always drive out the smaller ones. While we did not always like that or believe it meant that the skyline was inevitably getting better, we tended to accept it as a kind of natural precept. When something on the skyline went away, we could pretty much count on the notion that it would be replaced, relatively slowly, by something bigger. This was the order of things, and most people, even architecture critics, made a peace with it. After all, while we like to think of New York as a place that thrives on a certain kind of anarchy, the reality is that we expect it to be a controlled anarchy, a kind of contained, energizing chaos. It is not supposed to be subject to cataclysmic change. We think of it as chaotic but not as possessing true chaos. But on September 11, of course, we experienced something else: cataclysmic, instantaneous change, frightening chaos, as the biggest things suddenly became the most vulnerable. It turned the entire order of this organic skyline upside down.

No wonder, then, that we did not know what to do. Beyond the shock and horror of death and devastation, there was a sense that this event fit into no known scheme of things. It was obviously not the normal process of the city relentlessly tearing itself down and building itself up, but neither was it any kind of war that we had ever known. Nothing that city planners had studied was of much use; architects had no purpose, at least not in the immediate aftermath, and politicians were for once at a loss. It is no accident, surely, that the most effective political leader in the days and weeks following September 11 was Mayor Rudolph Giuliani, who was so caught up in the tragedy that he counseled against building anything ever again on the site. Giuliani wanted the sixteen acres of Ground Zero to be consecrated as a memorial to the victims of the attack, and for a long time the sense of shock was so great that it was hard to disagree with him. A void seemed right, and even to talk of building seemed utterly disrespectful.

Such feelings do not last, however, nor should they. As the immediacy of the attack receded in the months following September 11, there was a collective sense that a permanent void in the heart of the city, however respectful it might be intended to be, was not the way to heal New York, and that sixteen acres of emptiness might not send the wisest message to the world. But it was not going to be easy to decide what to build or to figure out how to pay for it. The World Trade Center had been built originally by the Port Authority of New York and New Jersey, an enormous and bureaucratic agency that reported to the governors of both states. The Port Authority still owned the land of Ground Zero, but earlier in 2001—only weeks before September 11, in fact—it had completed long negotiations to lease the twin towers to Larry Silverstein, a private real-estate developer. So from the beginning, the governors of two states, a quasi-public bureaucracy, and a private businessman all had an interest in these sixteen acres and a concomitant belief that they could and should determine what would happen there. Of course, the City of New York itself was hardly indifferent to what happened at Ground Zero, even though it did not, technically, control the land.

Within two months after September 11, the governor of New York established the Lower Manhattan Development Corporation, a new state agency, which he charged with overseeing the rebuilding process. The LMDC was intended not to replace the Port Authority, Silverstein, and the city but to work with them. The creation of the LMDC, however, far from simplifying the rebuilding process, only made it a more complex and confusing web of political and financial entities. And beyond all of this officialdom, there were the thousands of relatives of people who had died on September 11, and the thousands of people who had gone to work in the World Trade Center and managed to escape, and the firemen and policemen who participated in rescue efforts, and the tens of thousands of people who lived in the neighborhood, and the tens of thousands more who worked in the blocks around the site.

They all felt that they were entitled to some say in what was to be built where the twin towers had stood. They were right, of course—there was no precedent for any of this, and who could deny that all of these people had a legitimate claim to some stake in the future of the site? They certainly had a deep emotional connection to it. But then again, so did almost everyone else. Not thousands but tens of millions of people around the world had seen the destruction of the twin towers on live television. They, too, felt a sense of connection to the events of September 11, to the site itself, and to its future. It was clear that whatever was built on the sixteen acres of Ground Zero was to carry a symbolic weight far greater than that of any other building project of our time. And thus amid complex politics and a widespread sense of passion began the most challenging urban-design problem of the twenty-first century.

UP FROM ZERO

CHAPTER 1

Architecture Takes the Stage

THE WINTER GARDEN IS A 200-foot-long, 125-foot-high glass-enclosed room in the middle of the World Financial Center, a cluster of high-rise office buildings and shops in Lower Manhattan, across the street from the site where the World Trade Center once stood. It had been severely damaged in the terrorist attack that destroyed the trade center on September 11, 2001, and when it was restored the following year its reopening was taken as a welcome symbol of the renewal of the area. The Winter Garden is one of the few large, indoor public rooms that Lower Manhattan has. It is not a typical public space for New York. It has a dozen palm trees, a grand, formal staircase, and a view to the Hudson River. Most of the time, it functions like an indoor version of a public square, where visitors and shoppers and office workers mill around under the architect Cesar Pelli's spectacular arched glass ceiling or sit reading newspapers and sipping coffee on metal benches.

On the morning of Wednesday, December 18, 2002, the Winter Garden was closed to the public. The benches were organized into rows, and a few hundred folding chairs had been added to them in an attempt to make the space function in the manner of an auditorium. A makeshift stage was set up at the west end, and temporary partitions and large video screens were placed in front of the glass wall that normally offers a view toward the river. Platforms for video cameras had been squeezed in and around the palm trees, and there was a lectern, plus lots of microphones and bright television lights. All of the seats were filled, and those that were not occupied by politicians, civic leaders, and architects were taken by journalists from newspapers, magazines, and television stations around the world.

At about ten o'clock, a distinguished-looking eighty-year-old man with white hair stepped to the podium. His name was John C. Whitehead, and he had been, at various times in his career, chairman of the investment-banking firm Goldman Sachs, chairman of the Federal Reserve Bank of New York, and deputy secretary of state of the United States. Here, he was speaking in his latest role, chairman of the Lower Manhattan Development Corporation, which had been established in the fall of 2001 by the governor of New York, George Pataki, to oversee reconstruction of the trade-center site. The LMDC had gotten off to an uncertain start, and it had been through a particularly bruising period the previous summer, when it had unveiled a set of preliminary studies for the site that were universally panned by the public as dreary and unimaginative. The fiasco had a positive effect, however: it stimulated the LMDC to become more ambitious and to think of the rebuilding less as a commercial venture and more as a symbolic act, as a chance to show vision. By the middle of August, the agency had settled on a plan to revive its reputation. It issued a call to architects from around the world to submit their qualifications to craft a design for the site, in the hope of enticing some of the leading architects of the world. Nine hundred architects responded, from every continent except Antarctica. Many of them joined forces to create special partnerships for this project, so the LMDC actually had 406 teams to evaluate. The LMDC spent several weeks reviewing the submissions with the help of a panel of advisers and winnowed the pack down to seven teams, eliminating not only hundreds of unknowns but several of the most prominent architects in the world, including Robert A. M. Stern, Robert Venturi and Denise Scott Brown, Santiago Calatrava, Eric Owen Moss, and Bernard Tschumi. At the end of September, a little more than one year after the terrorist attack, the LMDC announced the seven teams, gave them each forty thousand dollars, and sent them off to spend the next few weeks designing something that it hoped would give the public the sense of vision it had found lacking in the preliminary studies.

The early studies had been done by the firm of Beyer Blinder Belle, a solid, middle-level professional firm that was best known for preservation projects such as the restoration of Grand Central Terminal, with some contributions by Peterson/Littenberg, a small, respected firm of architects and urban designers that had been serving as a consultant to the LMDC. This time around, the names were more recognizable. Richard Meier, Charles Gwathmey, Peter Eisenman, and Steven Holl, four of the best-known architects in the city, if not the nation, joined forces as one team. Lord Norman Foster, the celebrated British architect known for his skyscrapers, was another of the participants. The eminent corporate firm Skidmore, Owings & Merrill headed another team, and Rafael Viñoly led another, which became known as THINK. An exceptionally talented group of younger architects known for their work with computers—Greg Lynn, Ben van Berkel, Jesse Reiser, and Kevin Kennon—formed another group, United Architects. Daniel Libeskind, a largely academic architect who had received international acclaim for his Jewish Museum in Berlin, also participated, his firm the only one other than Lord Foster's to enter the competition without a partner. And Peterson/Littenberg, eager to distance themselves from the dreary work of Beyer Blinder Belle, had, after the other six teams were chosen, convinced the LMDC to allow them to submit an entry as well.

On December 18, the designs were ready to be unveiled, and the Winter Garden was the natural place to do it, just beside Ground Zero and possessed of a sense of grandeur befitting what had become a genuine media event. The LMDC called the work by the seven teams its Innovative Design Study, to distinguish it from the not-very-innovative study of the previous summer, but most people called it the World Trade Center competition or the Ground Zero competition, and the very word *competition* seemed to heighten public interest further. In the weeks leading up to December 18, this had become an architectural event like none other. New Yorkers had been obsessed for more than a year with the question of what would be built on the site, and the notion that some of the world's most famous architects were now competing against one another for the job only heightened the excitement. The unveiling of their designs had begun to feel more like a sports event than a cultural one: big names in architecture competing against one another for the right to decide what would go up on the most intensely watched site in the world. At stake was a prize much bigger than anything the architectural world usually gets to think about. Even though there would be no instant winner—the LMDC planned to take several weeks to evaluate the designs and then would narrow the field further—public interest was so great that NY1 News, the local all-news channel, broadcast the Winter Garden news conference live. With seven architectural firms making presentations, the whole event was expected to take three and a half hours, itself an extraordinary amount of time for any live news event, let alone one that more resembled a lecture in an architecture school than a presentation to political figures and the public. An advance minute-by-minute schedule was printed that set every participant's time and limited each architect to twenty minutes. When John Whitehead began his remarks—scheduled to start at 10:00 A.M. and conclude by 10:03—he tried to set an august tone, opening the proceedings not as if he was introducing a bunch of architects presenting some models but more as if he were addressing the United Nations.

"The original World Trade Center was more than a set of buildings. It stood for global commerce over global conflict," he said. "These teams have produced world-class work that embraces and extends the ethos of the original World Trade Center. Underlying these diverse plans is the common theme of rebirth. Beyond the powerful aesthetic statement that these designs make, they also convey powerful messages—they must speak to our children and our children's children about who we are and what we stand for."

Whitehead was followed by a series of officials: Louis Tomson, the first president of the LMDC; Joseph Seymour, the executive director of the Port Authority; and Roland Betts, a well-connected member of the LMDC's board who had played a major role in thinking up the architectural competition in the first place. Betts was a close friend of President George W. Bush, and he had already helped to focus the president's attention on New York's rebuilding needs. Now, he saw his mission as delivering a major piece of architecture as a symbol of the renewed city.

Betts began his remarks with a reference to his longtime friend. "I would like to thank President Bush for his concise counsel to me, 'Do something that will make people proud,' " Betts said. He looked at the architects assembled in the front row. "It's as if Rembrandt and da Vinci and Matisse and Jasper Johns were all drawn to the same task," he said. "What is it that we want to say about our city? What is the new face of the new New York that we want to present to the world? We know that within the next twelve hours, billions of people will see these images." Betts concluded by calling the designs "visions for an anxious world," and he said, "This day belongs to the visionaries."

It was left to Alexander Garvin, a Yale professor of city planning who had been serving as the LMDC's vice president of design and planning and who had managed the competition that Betts had helped to conceive, to introduce the architects. Garvin did it with the panache of a Broadway impresario. He had determined, pretty much at the last minute, the order of the presentations, and he decided to start off the proceedings with an architect whose work had interested him from the beginning, Daniel Libeskind. Libeskind almost had not been in the competition at all. Garvin had wanted him to serve on the advisory panel he was putting together to help the LMDC narrow down the submissions and figure out just who should be invited to produce the master plan, but Garvin had insisted that panel members commit to coming to New York for a series of meetings in September, and Libeskind was tied up on the dates that Garvin had selected. Almost as an afterthought, Libeskind said that if he could not be part of the panel, maybe he would just put his name in for consideration for the competition itself. So he did.

Libeskind is short and memorable in appearance. He usually dresses all in black, sometimes with the accent of a red scarf, and he wears heavy, squarish, black-rimmed eyeglasses and black cowboy boots. It is an odd combination for an architect who was born in Poland and grew up in the Bronx, but Libeskind has never been a particularly easy figure to pigeonhole. His work over the previous few years had straddled academic architecture and intense, real-world politics. His most important buildings—the Jewish Museum in Berlin, which was finished in 1999, and the addition to the Victoria and Albert Museum in London, which had not yet begun construction—each took years of lobbying to win approval.

Libeskind went up to the lectern. His first words were not about architecture at all. "I believe this is about a day that altered all of our lives," he said. And then he went on to describe his own arrival in the United States forty-three years earlier. "I arrived by ship to New York as a teenager, an immigrant, and like millions of others before me, my first sight was the Statue of Liberty and the amazing skyline of Manhattan," Libeskind said. "I have never forgotten that sight or what it stands for."

He went on to describe his proposal, which he called Memory Foundations. Libeskind's design had one particularly striking element: he wanted to expose the slurry wall, the concrete retaining wall that had served as a portion of the original World Trade Center foundation and kept the Hudson River out of the trade center's basement, as a monument. Libeskind described it as "the great slurry wall, the most dramatic element which survived the attack, an engineering wonder constructed on bedrock foundations and designed to hold back the Hudson River. The foundations withstood the unimaginable trauma of this destruction and stand as eloquent as the Constitution itelf asserting the durability of democracy and the value of individual life."

It was a clever idea, not only because the wall could serve the purpose of a ruin but also because exposing the wall meant that the whole area facing it, the "footprints" of the twin towers, would have to be below street level, and it seemed somehow right that people who came to mourn and to honor would step down into the earth. Going down to the footprints seemed to connect to an almost visceral feeling. "We need to journey down into Ground Zero, onto the bedrock foundation, a procession with deliberation into the deep indelible footprints of tower one and tower two," Libeskind told the audience.

Libeskind wanted to place cultural facilities, such as a museum of September 11, in glass buildings around the footprints that he designed in his characteristic angular manner, like crystalline forms. For the rest of the sixteen-acre site he suggested a mix of office buildings, public plazas, and retail stores, as well as a train station that would unify the various subway and transit lines in the area. And at the northwest corner of the site he proposed what he called, at first, the Gardens of the World, a 1,776-foot spire that would contain hanging gardens and would be tied to a seventy-story office building that would help to provide its structural support.

Libeskind did not talk about square footage or economics, and he barely used an architectural term in his presentation. He talked about commemoration, memory, mourning, and renewal, and he did it with the zeal of a preacher. "Life victorious," were his final words, to sustained applause. Libeskind told the audience very little about how his architecture would directly achieve the emotional goals he sought, but his rhetoric—he wanted to call one of his plazas the Wedge of Light, and another, the Park of Heroes—suggested that he knew far better than most architects how to communicate with a traumatized public.

Libeskind was followed by the one architect who might be considered more suave in presentation manner than he was, Lord Foster. Foster's style was completely different from Libeskind's, however. Instead of an earnest appeal to the emotions, Foster delivered crisp, self-assured professionalism. Everything about Foster's manner, like his buildings, seemed to embody sleekness and confidence. He stepped to the podium clad in a black turtleneck, and, unlike Libeskind, he spoke without notes.

"Architecture is about needs—the needs of people—and this project starts with the needs of the local community, and it moves outwards to the city of which it is a part, and then finally to a global dimension," Foster said. "How do you measure dappled shade in a park?" he continued. "How do you measure intangibles? How do you measure emptiness? Loss? Memories? How do you balance that against life and regeneration?"

Foster's solution was to focus almost entirely on the new. He would provide a bold and enormous new skyscraper that resembled a pair of torqued, or twisted, towers based on the geometry of the triangle, a kind of variation on the original twin towers, updated to become more sculptural, more visually exciting, and more technologically advanced. "Two towers which kiss and touch and become one," Foster said of his building, which he asserted would be "the tallest, the greenest, the strongest, and the safest" skyscraper in the world.

Foster, whose wide-ranging architectural practice has produced not only the new London City Hall, the Great Court of the British Museum, and the new Hong Kong airport but several of the most striking and innovative skyscrapers of the last generation, spoke almost as if he felt his impressive body of work had earned him the right to the project. He addressed the audience with the air of a man who was accustomed to having boards of trustees, chief executives, and public officials treat him with deference, whereas Libeskind was constantly trying to please by tugging at the heartstrings. Foster was not without his own insecurities, however. One of the oddest aspects of his presentation was the frequent mention he made of specific subway lines that crisscrossed the area of Ground Zero—the 1 and 9, and the N and the R—and also the PATH trains, as if he worried that the one thing that could keep him from winning was a perception that he was too much of an outsider, and so he had to prove that he could drop New York references like a native. And he included a somewhat cloying section of his presentation in which he showed images of a young girl, dressed in orange, exploring the completed project.

Foster's towers, however, were magnificent, and at first glance they seemed to have the almost miraculous ability to satisfy two conflicting groups. Foster's proposal could comfort both the small but vocal cadre lobbying for the twin towers to be rebuilt—something Foster was not proposing, but his design did make certain allusions that came closer than any other project to satisfying that impulse—and those who wanted a bold, new skyscraper that would represent the most advanced architectural ideas and technological systems of the twenty-first century. From the reception he got in the Winter Garden—not as overwhelming as Libeskind's but more than respectful—this is exactly what he had managed to do, and it was no small achievement.

Next, Garvin announced the consortium of Richard Meier, Charles Gwathmey, Peter Eisenman, and Steven Holl. Meier, Gwathmey, and Eisenman had been part of the Five Architects group, along with John Hejduk and Michael Graves, who became prominent in the early 1970s for their neo-Corbusian modernism; Holl, slightly younger, was an equally impassioned advocate of a largely cerebral, austere modernist design. The architects were somewhat different in their approaches, although they were all confirmed modernists, and for years they had practiced in generally friendly, sometimes wary, competition. This was the first time that they had collaborated.

Meier, who had designed the largest cultural project of modern times, the Getty Center in Los Angeles, and who was as accustomed as Foster to speaking to high-profile, powerful clients, was the team leader, and after Alex Garvin gave him the floor he introduced the group. In spite of his experience, he seemed unsure of himself beside Foster and Libeskind. "We're the New York team—some say we're the dream team," he said. The joke fell flat, and instead of seeming funny Meier seemed to have failed to honor the dignity of the occasion or perhaps shown a degree of presumption that exceeded even Foster's. He went on, more earnestly this time: "This is our city, this is our home. We are proud and honored to take part in what is the most meaningful architectural project in the city's history." And then Meier showed his team's project, which was a surprise, even to people who knew the individual members' work well. The Meier team had proposed a tower in the form of a huge grid, like a vast tic-tac-toe board in the sky. There were other elements to the project, including a moving and powerful idea to memorialize the original towers and the people lost in the terrorist attack by creating two pierlike structures that would extend out into the Hudson River in the location of the shadows of the twin towers. But the enormous grid was so powerful an image, not to say so bizarre, that it overwhelmed everything else the group was trying to do. Both Meier and Eisenman at various points described it as resembling fingers connecting or reaching out to touch, a diversion into the somewhat sappy language favored by Libeskind that did little to make the odd shape seem more comprehensible.

The other architects both spoke briefly, and they seemed more effective the less they talked about their own project. "Our idea is to express the sublime," Holl said. Eisenman identified himself as the only architect there who had attended the 1939 New York World's Fair and then said of Ground Zero, "This is not a World's Fair. I believe that all great monuments are remembered not for the architects but for the greatness of place that they make. The place came first, the architecture second. We have tried to meld together four architects who have known each other for forty years. This has to be a place that examines daily life, not a place of business as usual. Our architecture acts as a background for reflection and hope."

When Eisenman did turn to the strange tower, he fell into architectural jargon. The group had created, he said, "a new typology of horizontal and vertical space" that, by being a grid, would be "part of the typology of New York City." (Probably never has the word *typology*—architect-speak for *type*—been uttered so many times at a public event in New York City.) None of the architects ever managed to explain, however, why it made sense to turn the idea of the New York City street grid into a three-dimensional tower, or whether doing so could actually yield a building that would be practical and usable.

Rafael Viñoly came up next, representing THINK, which had been permitted by the LMDC to present three different schemes. Viñoly, who established a large and successful practice in New York in the 1980s after emigrating from Argentina in 1979, has managed, more successfully than many of his peers, to produce big and complex projects such as stadiums, convention centers, and concert halls while still being considered an architect who produces cutting-edge design. Viñoly speaks rapidly in accented English, and he was so concerned that his three designs not be confused with one another that he spent most of his time trying to present them separately instead of pointing out that all three expressed a similar underlying idea, which is the notion that a public commemorative structure should be created first around the footprints of the original twin towers and that conventional, profit-making development should fill the periphery only later. All of THINK's schemes—one with a large, multileveled, ramped park, one with a huge, glass-enclosed room, and one with a pair of skeletal towers rising to the height of the original trade center—focused on symbol and commemoration, not on commercial space. Viñoly did not so much want to ignore the value of commercial space as make the point that the architect of the master plan did not have to spend all his time thinking about it. Let the developers do it themselves, on their own schedule and in their own way, Viñoly implied. His three plans offered different ways of making some kind of public commemoration, and they ranged from the somewhat practical in the case of the ramped park to the highly visionary—the great, square Eiffel towers that would have had cultural facilities set into the frameworks, small buildings set into the large skeletonlike drawers. Viñoly's goal, as he explained it when he presented his third scheme, which he called the World Cultural Center, was "the public component of the project." He wanted to echo the images of the original towers in a way that would be "larger, emptier, and extending vertically the public realm" in the form of "an enormous scaffolding." The project would represent the symbolic takeover by culture of the commercial ideas of the original trade center. The idea, Viñoly himself said, was "a little extreme."

Viñoly's presentation seemed somewhat rushed and almost disheveled, since the LMDC granted his team the same twenty minutes it gave all the others, even though he had three projects to explain. He was followed by Greg Lynn, who the United Architects group had decided would make its presentation. Lynn was the least known of any of the presenters so far—he is an architect celebrated for his innovative use of the computer as a design tool, and his reputation, at least at that point, was mainly among students. Lynn, a big, amiable man with long black hair, was wearing a dark suit and a tie, and he seemed to be making a special effort to appear serious. Most people who knew his group's work expected that this presentation would be the most arcane so far, the one that relied most completely on jargon and seemed the most disconnected from the issues the public cared about. Instead, Lynn's presentation turned out to be clear, straightforward, and organized, and he managed, more than any of the others, to strike a balance between talking about general emotional issues surrounding Ground Zero and describing the specifics of his group's project in a way that made sense to an audience of nonarchitects.

The United Architects scheme was daring and bold; it probably went further than any of the designs, including Foster's, in rethinking the idea of the skyscraper for the twenty-first century. The group proposed what was really a megastructure, one of the world's biggest buildings. It looked like a set of vast, X-shaped towers, mounting toward a high center point; several of the sections rose on the diagonal, and while from some angles the building would be quite graceful on the skyline, from others it would appear to have a huge, bulging midriff. The tallest sections would rise to 1,600 feet, and at the sixtieth floor a five-story-high space would join all of the towers horizontally. Lynn called this "a five-story city in the sky, a new kind of urbanism." He described the huge, triangular gateways under the Xs as "sacred, cathedral-like spaces," although it was difficult to tell whether they would have inspired respect or, at their enormous scale, fear. "We wanted to think of the memorial sequence not only of going down, but as going up, of looking up to this vast, cathedral-like space, and finally up to a sky memorial," Lynn said. Because all of the architects in the United Architects consortium were active in computer-generated design, it was not surprising that they invited Imaginary Forces, a computer-graphics design firm, to join their team, and IF produced an excellent short film that Lynn showed at the end of the presentation, which used computerized imagery to show a group of tourists walking around the completed buildings, looking up at the colossus in awe.

Lynn presented a vision of the future that was one part Paolo Soleri, one part *Blade Runner,* and if the sensibility of the consortium of young architects was humanistic and rational, the image of their huge megastructure was nonetheless somewhat overwhelming. The next presentation could not have been more different. Steven Peterson and Barbara Littenberg, husband and wife, had been friends and colleagues of Alexander Garvin on the faculty at

Yale, and they had worked together on several projects. They were impassioned New Yorkers who believed, as Garvin did, in the importance of New York's streets and its traditional building types in establishing the city's underlying identity, as well as in the wisdom of basing new projects on some of the urban-design principles that had proved so effective in the past. As consultants to the LMDC, they had earlier helped Garvin produce the studies that led, in part, to the development corporation's request that the architectural competitors consider putting back some of the streets that had been eliminated back in the 1960s in the original design of the World Trade Center, which had turned the whole sixteen-acre plot into one enormous "superblock." Garvin continued to believe strongly in the importance of restoring streets to the huge Ground Zero site, even though he had come in the months since those early studies to be skeptical of a design that felt too traditional in its architecture. But once Peterson and Littenberg began to work fully on their own on the problem of designing Ground Zero as competitors in the LMDC design exercise, they seemed to become more convinced than ever that the solution lay in creating something that closely resembled the kind of urban fabric that had been there before the World Trade Center. Although they did not think of themselves as conservative, as the competition proceeded it seemed inevitable that they would end up playing the conservative role, if only by default.

And so they did. Steven Peterson began his presentation with a swipe at the Meier team. "Those guys said they were the New York team, but we have the New York project," he said. "This is not Houston or Dallas—it is New York. The essence of New York is a grid—rectangular, multiplicity, diversity. New York is a city of towers, and we have the opportunity to make towers from space."

Peterson and Littenberg's plan contained several delicate and subtle urban-design gestures, including a memorial that consisted of a large garden around the footprints of the twin towers, surrounded by the walls of medium-rise buildings, as if Turtle Bay Gardens, the common backyard amid a block of brownstones in the east forties, was raised to monumental scale. The footprint of one tower would be a reflecting pool, and the other would be an amphitheater with nearly three thousand seats, each one commemorating one of the people who died at the trade center. But the architecture, which included a pair of fourteen-hundred-foot skyscrapers that looked roughly like the Empire State Building, seemed tame by comparison to everything else. Peterson and Littenberg seemed to be offering Brooks Brothers when all the other architects came selling Prada. Although the Peterson/Littenberg plan contained several exceptionally sophisticated urban-design gestures, it was doomed to be remembered not as creative but as the retro entry in the competition.

It was well after noon when Peterson and Littenberg began their presentation, and several people, including Larry Silverstein, the seventy-one-year-old developer who held the lease on the original World Trade Center, had departed for lunch meetings uptown. Silverstein played a large public role in the days immediately following September 11 and then had fallen somewhat from public view, but he always maintained that a decision about what should happen on the site was largely up to him since his lease on the twin towers, in his view, required him to rebuild. He had nothing to do with the LMDC's competition, but his presence in a prominent seat in the front had been noted, and when he slipped out before the proceedings were finished, that was noted, too.

By the time Garvin introduced the final presentation, which was a team led by Skidmore, Owings & Merrill, several of the powerful real-estate people and politicians in the audience had also departed. Although the Winter Garden hardly felt empty—it was still crowded with journalists, LMDC officials, citizens' groups that had been advising the LMDC, and members of numerous independent civic groups that were watching the redevelopment process closely—it was not hard to feel a slight drop in voltage.

The Skidmore presentation did not do much to raise the energy level. David Childs, the firm's most prominent partner, who had been Larry Silverstein's architect since before the twin towers fell (Silverstein had hired him in the summer of 2001 to study ways to improve the old complex), did not step up to the podium, although he was only a few feet from the stage, in the audience. For months, Childs had been designing various Ground Zero towers for Silverstein, and he had gotten the LMDC's approval for his firm to enter the competition on the condition that he put aside his work for Silverstein during the competition period to avoid a conflict of interest.

He did so and helped a younger colleague, Roger Duffy, assemble a group of other architects and artists to collaborate with the firm. It was Childs's and Duffy's idea that Skidmore, with its expertise and experience in large-scale skyscraper design, would act as the convener and senior partner of a consortium of younger, more avant-garde designers. But the collaboration, which included the Los Angeles architect Michael Maltzan and the artist Ellyn Zimmerman, among others, was never smooth. Some of the participants dropped out, and as the scheme evolved it seemed to move farther and farther away from anything that Skidmore itself would be likely to produce. It certainly bore no relation to the projects Childs had been sketching for Silverstein. Childs distanced himself from it and essentially turned it over to Duffy.

Duffy is a talented designer who had chosen a career in a large, corporate firm, where Childs had given him frequent opportunities to stretch the firm's boundaries. He is slim and soft-spoken, and his low-key manner stood in marked contrast to that of most of the other architects who showed their work in the Winter Garden. Duffy explained the notion of the Skidmore project, which consisted of nine wavy towers of identical height, filling the Ground Zero site as a statement "intended to demonstrate how an increasingly densified city can be a better place to live and work." There were gardens at high levels within the towers, and the project was intended to demonstrate a considerable degree of environmental sensitivity. It was an intriguing conceptual exercise. But the series of matching, flat-topped towers, none of which reached significant height, would have appeared as a blur on the skyline, with none of the memorable elements many of the other projects had. Beside most of the other projects, the Skidmore effort seemed ponderous and preachy. Ultimately, it gave the impression of being designed purely to make a conceptual point. And while it may have had certain practical elements in its high level of environmental sustainability, its lack of aesthetic appeal doomed it from the start. If anything had become clear, it was the extent to which the LMDC expected the architects to make a powerful aesthetic statement at Ground Zero.

Duffy's presentation ended the day on a relatively quiet note, but it mattered little either to his powerful firm, which seemed to have treated the competition as something of a lark, or to most of the other architects, who had always expected that if Skidmore, Owings & Merrill ended up working at Ground Zero, it would be because Larry Silverstein wanted it to, not because it won a competition. The day seemed to belong, as Roland Betts had said, to the visionaries, and most of them had performed well and had taken advantage of their moment in the spotlight. But no one really knew at that point what winning the competition would actually mean. It would be several weeks before the LMDC figured out which of the architectural teams would be designated as the official master planner of Ground Zero, and the agency was making no promises to actually build the design of the team that was selected. The Port Authority and Larry Silverstein still had to weigh in, and the LMDC itself might come up with plenty of other ideas as the planning process evolved, so in reality the competition was more of a starting point than a conclusion. What was clear is that its result would be to choose an architect much more than to choose an actual design. And even though every one of the architects who participated showed elaborate designs for actual buildings, the competition was to create a master plan for the site, not actual pieces of architecture, a fact few people focused on at the time but which meant that it was possible that an architect could win the competition and still never see the buildings he had shown at the Winter Garden actually built. LMDC was making no promises here, either. One thing everyone knew was that the project would take at least fifteen years to complete, and more likely twenty or more, and it would cost billions and billions of dollars—nobody could even begin to figure out how many.

It was close to two o'clock when the program finished and the crowd began to scatter. As workmen started to remove the chairs, reporters and photographers crowded the architects' models that had been lined up on the podium. One journalist asked Lou Tomson, who was then the president of the development corporation, what he thought of what had happened that morning.

"These are among the greatest minds in the world," Tomson said. "To reject what they've offered is to say the problem is insolvable."

CHAPTER 2

Rockefeller's Vision

The Original World Trade Center

ON THE DAY THAT IT FELL, THE World Trade Center seemed to embody the image a great many people had of New York and, indeed, of the United States. It was tall, very tall, and even those who did not admire it as a work of architecture did not doubt that it seemed imbued with solidity and power. To many people, the twin towers of the trade center were also excessively simple, almost reductionist—the world's biggest metal boxes. If the buildings seemed to some people to imply an aesthetic banality and a tendency on the part of architects to put too much faith in simple solutions, to others they represented a sense of liberation from the tiresome, cluttered debris of earlier times. For better or for worse, the trade-center towers represented modernity to almost everyone. Whether or not you liked them, the towers seemed to embody the belief that western might and the latest technology would yield a fresh solution to the problems of making civilizing urban places that had been so vexing to previous generations. Many New Yorkers found their boxy, identical forms a bit prissy and dull, hardly the equal of their city's beloved icon, the Empire State Building, but the very height of the trade center and the novelty of its two identical towers were inspiring to visitors. The buildings were never officially named the twin towers, but the phrase, conferred by visitors, quickly entered the urban lexicon. For many people around the world, it was not the Empire State Building, the Statue of Liberty, or Rockefeller Center that was New York's most potent symbol; it was the towers.

That the towers loomed so large in the world's imagination was something of a paradox, since they had never sat particularly comfortably with New Yorkers. The buildings had a strange history. Although construction of the towers did not begin until 1968, and they were not completed until 1973, their origins, in a sense, went back to the 1940s, when a complex of buildings serving businesses involved in world trade was first proposed as a way of energizing the commercial environment of Lower Manhattan, which had been in decline since the 1930s, when businesses had first begun to move away. They left mainly for Midtown Manhattan, which was much more accessible from most suburban residential districts. Lower Manhattan was the city's historical core and its longtime financial center, but that was hardly enough to sustain it in the face of competition from places that were easier to reach from Greenwich, Scarsdale, Locust Valley, or most other towns that bankers and stockbrokers tended to live in—including, for that matter, Park Avenue, since part of the paradox of Lower Manhattan is that it is not even all that easy to reach from the rest of New York City, requiring either a long subway ride or an even longer taxi ride down the length of Manhattan along crowded streets. The exodus from Lower Manhattan was modest in the years before World War II, but it accelerated thereafter as more and more workers moved to the rapidly expanding suburbs, and the problem of getting to a central business district that was not very central and had little suburban train service began to affect a far greater number of people, including many of the executives who made decisions about where banks and law firms were located. Once, it had seemed essential for them to have their offices near the New York Stock Exchange, at the corner of Wall and Broad streets in the heart of Lower Manhattan. As the new, postwar city evolved, such propinquity seemed less necessary. The world was spreading out, and businesses could spread out with it. To make Lower Manhattan's problems more severe still, it was losing other industries even faster than it was the financial industry. Once, the commercial waterfront was a major source of employment, surrounding the financial district in the core of Lower Manhattan with piers on both the Hudson River and the East River. But these were being supplanted by other ports in Brooklyn, New Jersey, and other regions of the country.

By the late 1950s, Lower Manhattan's most prominent booster, David Rockefeller, the vice chairman of Chase Manhattan Bank, feared that the neighborhood around Wall Street would decline to the point that it could no longer justify its historic role as the nation's financial center. Chase Manhattan's chief rival, First National City Bank of New York, was moving uptown to Park Avenue, and Rockefeller, determined to counteract the trend, commissioned the architect Gordon Bunshaft of Skidmore, Owings & Merrill to design a new headquarters for Chase in the heart of the financial district, just a block north of Wall Street. It was Rockefeller's hope that 1 Chase Manhattan Plaza would turn around the neighborhood's fortunes.

It did not. The eight-hundred-foot-tall glass and aluminum Chase building was a distinguished example of modern architecture, and it gave Lower Manhattan a glittery and elegant new symbol, but its success—it quickly became a prized address for several venerable law firms—had little effect on the larger issues affecting the area's economy. The problem was that it did nothing to address the area's real shortcomings: a nearly total lack of housing, stores, entertainment, culture, or almost any kind of urban amenity at all. Lower Manhattan was famous and historic, but it was dull, and there was almost nothing about it to persuade anyone to visit it who did not have to go there to work. Rockefeller and the Downtown–Lower Manhattan Association, the area's business group, asked the Skidmore firm to prepare a broader plan for the east side of Lower Manhattan, and Skidmore revived an old idea for an international trade center that had been proposed a decade before. The firm's suggestion was that it go on a thirteen-acre site along the East River at the east end of Wall Street. The site was just below the

Brooklyn Bridge, one of many waterfront areas that were increasingly quiet as Manhattan's port continued its decline, losing business both to other regions and to New Jersey. On this fallow land beside the financial district, Skidmore's architects thought, the trade center could rise.

Rockefeller's brother Nelson, who was the governor of New York, was sympathetic to the idea, and he asked the Port Authority, the bistate agency in charge of bridges, tunnels, and airports, to look into building it. Rockefeller's decision to turn the trade center into a Port Authority project made considerable sense. The Port Authority had great engineering expertise and experience with huge infrastructure projects, and the project was too large—and too risky—to be taken on by a private developer. Moreover, turning the World Trade Center over to the Port Authority also meant that Rockefeller did not have to carry the enormous cost of the project on his state budget. This decision was to have tremendous implications, however, for the building of the center, for its operation, for its eventual ownership, and, ultimately, for its replacement after September 11. Back in the early 1960s, Rockefeller alone could not ordain the Port Authority's involvement, even though Austin Tobin, the executive director of the authority and a man who was as quietly eager for power as legendary city shaper Robert Moses was conspicuously so, was more than willing to take on the project. But the authority was controlled jointly by New York and New Jersey, and the governor of New Jersey had as much right as Nelson Rockefeller to tell it what to do. Robert Meyner, the governor of New Jersey, saw no particular reason to go along with Rockefeller's trade-center project to save Lower Manhattan unless there was something in it for him. What was in the project for Meyner turned out to be what real-estate people would call the only thing about any piece of property that really matters: its location.

While both David and Nelson Rockefeller had been thinking about a massive building project as a way of reviving Lower Manhattan, Robert Meyner had been worrying about a small, nearly bankrupt commuter railroad, the Hudson and Manhattan, that brought commuters from New Jersey to the Wall Street area. Known as the Hudson tubes, the railroad had limited routes connecting Newark and the Hoboken and Jersey City waterfront to Lower Manhattan and Herald Square. It was more like a glorified subway line than a real train line, but it was the only direct train route into Lower Manhattan for New Jersey commuters, and the prospect that it might go out of business did not please the large number of New Jersey voters who worked in New York City. They wanted their state to buy the railroad. Meyner realized that there was another way he could assure that the railroad kept going: the Port Authority could buy it, saving the state the expense and providing the same benefit. He let it be known that if the Port Authority would take over the tubes, he would consent to Rockefeller's trade center.

It took months of negotiations and special legislation in both states, but eventually the deal was struck, and the Port Authority was in the mass-transit business for the first time. It renamed the line the Port Authority Trans-Hudson—PATH. And then it began to examine what it had acquired, which turned out, in addition to the lines themselves, to be a huge, somewhat derelict office complex over its Lower Manhattan terminus on Church Street. The buildings, which dated from 1908, would be expensive to restore. Why not tear them down instead and put the World Trade Center there? And so the trade center, which had not yet been designed, was moved from the east side of Manhattan to the west. The location of what was to become the largest skyscraper project in the history of New York was determined not by any master plan or even by any city planner's recommendation but as the result of a political deal struck by two governors to save a railroad.

As the project moved forward, Austin Tobin assumed a larger role. Skidmore, Owings & Merrill stepped aside in favor of an architect chosen by the Port Authority. Guy Tozzoli, an engineer from the authority staff whom Tobin had put in charge of the project, oversaw a search that led, eventually, to a curious choice: Minoru Yamasaki, a modernist whose work was characterized by an entrancement with romantic, often delicate forms. Yamasaki, who was based in Detroit, was not a conventional, commercially oriented skyscraper architect (although he had designed a few medium-sized office towers), nor was he considered one of the great artistic leaders of the profession. If he was in the vanguard of anything, it was in his strong reaction against the coldness of so much modernist architecture. Many of Yamasaki's buildings had details such as neo-Gothic arches set in front of glass walls, which was his way of using traditional decoration as an antidote to what he believed to be modernism's excessive harshness. Yamasaki's soft-edged modernism did not win much favor with critics, though he was far from indifferent to design. He presented himself as an aesthete—it is just that his aesthetics seemed to appeal only rarely to more sophisticated clients. Paradoxically, for an agency like the Port Authority, which was dominated by engineers, Yamasaki represented an advanced, almost daring choice, even though much of the architectural world thought of his work as being just this side of kitsch.

Yamasaki was hired in 1962, and he spent more than a year studying various ways of responding to the Port Authority's program for the trade center, which continued to expand until it reached a request for ten million square feet of office space. The agency seemed uninterested in including much of anything except office space; the things that Lower Manhattan really needed to transform itself—housing, cultural facilities, lively restaurants, and retail establishments—were not on the agenda at all. Curiously, the Port Authority seemed intent on repeating the mistake that Rockefeller had made when he envisioned the new Chase Manhattan tower as a panacea for Lower Manhattan's ills—the belief that office space alone could fix what was wrong with the neighborhood. But this time the mistake was being replicated at vastly larger scale, with far more serious implications. And even though the Port Authority had agreed to take over the Hudson and Manhattan railroad, there was no discussion of trying to find a way to make Lower Manhattan easier to reach from other suburbs or other parts of New York City. No one seemed to realize that a sense that the neighborhood was inconvenient and difficult to get to was at the heart of the migration of offices away from downtown, and building more office space where there was already more than the market wanted was not going to solve the problem at all—it was only going to make it worse.

Yamasaki did not see it as his role to challenge the program but merely to give it some architectural form. He considered spreading the ten million square feet of office space across three or four identical towers, as well as numerous schemes with multiple buildings of different heights. He continued to try to simplify his plans, and eventually he reduced the scheme to a pair of identical towers, each roughly eighty stories high. Yamasaki presented this version as his favorite but acknowledged that there was a problem: a pair of eighty-story towers could not yield quite as much space as the Port Authority wanted. Tobin and Tozzoli liked the twin towers as much as Yamasaki did, and they asked him why he couldn't simply make the buildings taller. They did not mind, they told him, if they rose higher than the Empire State Building—in fact, they rather liked that notion.

The problem, Yamasaki understood, was not bruising the ego of the Empire State Building, which at that point was only a little more than thirty years old. It was that skyscrapers did not make much economic sense when they got taller than eighty stories. Engineers could build much taller towers, but they could not figure out ways to make them profitable. Supertall skyscrapers are astonishingly expensive, and not only because they require enormous amounts of structure. There is a more subtle but ultimately more difficult problem: when buildings become exceedingly tall they require so many elevators that most of the space on the lower floors is taken up by elevator shafts passing through to reach the upper floors. At somewhere around eighty stories, further building is rarely practical, since there is so little space left to rent on the lower floors, and even the highest floors are unlikely to command the kinds of rents that are needed to pay for the entire thing. (Even the Empire State Building, which is officially 102 stories high, is really more like eighty-four stories—its top floors are no more than tiny spaces in the missilelike crown, and for all practical purposes the eighty-sixth-floor observatory is on the roof.)

The Port Authority's engineers came up with an economically justifiable solution. They suggested dividing the building into vertical thirds, in effect piling three identical buildings of about thirty-five stories on top of one another. A system of huge express elevators would carry passengers from the ground to "sky lobbies" one third and two thirds of the way up the tower, where people would transfer to local elevators to reach their own floors. The plan permitted the local elevator banks to be stacked on top of one another, occupying the same vertical space, freeing up enough space on the lower floors to make the building profitable, at least theoretically.

The other important innovation in the trade-center design was the work of John Skilling and Leslie Robertson, structural engineers who had been hired along with Yamasaki. Most skyscrapers of this time were not supported by their outside walls but by steel or concrete "skeletons," frames of columns and beams put together into a three-dimensional grid running all the way through the building. The invention of the steel skeleton made the first true skyscrapers possible in the 1880s, since exterior walls alone could not bear the weight of a very tall building—they would have had to be dozens of feet thick at the bottom. But with steel and later concrete frames the weight could be carried on a light structure that was no bulkier at the bottom than at the top. By the middle of the twentieth century, the aesthetics of the modern skyscraper had developed to the point where the exterior walls were often made of nothing but glass—curtain walls hung on the skeletal frame.

But the skeletal system is not without disadvantages. Since the frame fills the entire volume of the building, it requires a lot of structural material, and the interior space is frequently interrupted by columns. Robertson was an early proponent of an alternative structural system, known as the framed tube, a kind of web of metal that formed so tight a latticework on the exterior that it could support the weight of the building by itself. (It is something like a gigantic version of a wire-mesh litter basket, which is an exceptionally strong piece of street furniture.) The tube was the most advanced form of skyscraper construction in the 1960s, and before the World Trade Center it had been tried on a limited basis, including Yamasaki's own small IBM building in Seattle, finished in 1964. Building the World Trade Center as a tube represented a striking irony, since by having the exterior walls bear the weight of the building, the tallest skyscraper in the world would have a closer kinship in some ways to old-fashioned buildings with load-bearing walls than to other skyscrapers. But unlike traditional load-bearing masonry walls, framed tubes were light, often requiring as little as half the material needed to support a conventionally framed skyscraper of the same size. In an age when the goal of technology often seemed to be to find a way to make everything lighter, from airplanes to cars to household products, this seemed like a virtue.

When the buildings were hit by airplanes, of course, their lightness seemed less assuredly a positive element, though there is no certainty that another structural system would have performed all that differently under the tragic circumstances of September 11. Such catastrophic events were not envisioned when the towers were designed; indeed, until very recently structural engineers have considered wind to pose the greatest threat to skyscrapers. Other than keeping tall buildings standing, bracing them against the wind has usually been the primary goal. The dense latticework of the tube provided good wind bracing, especially in concert with the floor slabs, huge squares that were anchored to the tube and served to provide horizontal stability from top to bottom. The weakest part of the design, in a sense, was the core of the building, the central area containing the stairs and the elevators, since it was not a part of the main structural support, and it was made largely of drywall, which provided no resistance at all to the force of the airplanes that hit the towers.

But when the towers were being designed, Yamasaki and the Port Authority were thinking mainly of what kind of office space they would contain, and from this standpoint the tube system was only to the good, since it allowed the World Trade Center's enormous floors to be largely open and free of columns, exactly what tenants liked. The structural system pleased Yamasaki for another reason: he was nervous about heights and uncomfortable in buildings with wide expanses of glass on the upper floors. The tight mesh of the tube structure meant that the offices would have to have narrow windows. Yamasaki, believing that there was psychological comfort in windows that were narrower than his own shoulder span, ended up reducing the width of the windows to twenty-two inches, beyond even what the engineers required. The result was that windows took up only 30 percent of the facade of the trade-center towers, as compared to 50, 60, or 70 percent on many other modern skyscrapers. So slender were the windows that from a short distance away Yamasaki's towers seemed almost to be made of solid metal.

When they were completed in the early 1970s, the towers were an architectural misfit: the tallest buildings in the world and among the largest, their architecture was delicate, almost dainty. Yamasaki had put neo-Gothic arches at the bases of the towers and at the top, which he thought would give the buildings a humane air but served only to make them seem fussy. The buildings represented an extraordinary technological leap in skyscraper design, but their aesthetic seemed to deny the engineering innovations that the towers embodied, and when the World Trade Center opened it was thought of more as backward looking than as avant-garde.

But there was a more important problem with the design, beyond the aesthetic of the towers themselves. From the standpoint of urban planning, the notion of a pair of towers sitting in an enormous paved plaza was utterly rearguard, having already gone out of fashion by the 1970s. When the trade center was built, the streets that ran through its sixteen-acre site were obliterated in favor of a huge superblock, essentially a podium on which the structures were set. Retail space was not in storefronts but underground so as not to disturb the prim perfection Yamasaki aspired to. The overall design was more of an abstract composition than a functioning piece of the city; indeed, like so much urban renewal from the 1950s and 1960s, the very basis of the design was a rejection of the traditional form of the city.

It may seem odd, given that these were the world's tallest skyscrapers, to say that their design was antiurban, but in a way that is precisely what it was. The layout of the trade center embodied a planning theory that viewed the complex, disorderly form of the city mainly as a nuisance, as a mess to be cleaned up and replaced with gleaming new abstract objects. It is not surprising that the Port Authority paid little heed to the protests of the merchants whose shops made up one of Manhattan's more vibrant small commercial districts, the blocks of electronics stores known as Radio Row, which lay under the footprint of the proposed trade center. It was inconceivable to the Port Authority that there could be anything worth saving in this messy mix of old buildings. Sweeping away the old and providing a clean slate for the new was the highest and best calling of city planning, or so the Port Authority seemed to believe.

The Port Authority was hardly alone. The conviction that bigger and bigger doses of American power and know-how could solve any problem had plenty of other manifestations in American culture in those years, many with more serious consequences than the destruction of older neighborhoods for gigantic buildings that did not seem to belong there. But as this view was beginning to be questioned in the political sphere, it was coming increasingly to be challenged in the realm of planning and design as well. By the time the trade center was under way, it seemed out-of-date as a piece of urban planning, where the freshest thinking, inspired by such writers as Jane Jacobs, was moving toward a greater respect for the complex and subtle fabric of real streets, older neighborhoods, and smaller scale. The gigantism that was beloved by the Port Authority was rapidly losing its appeal, and in New York the Landmarks Preservation Commission was firmly establishing itself as a force moving the urban culture in a different direction. The historic-preservation movement, which was in its infancy in the 1960s when the old Pennsylvania Station was demolished, had grown into a substantial cultural force by the mid-seventies. Not only were important buildings like Grand Central Terminal and the Plaza Hotel declared official city landmarks, neighborhoods made up of more anonymous older buildings that constituted a coherent whole were designated as historic districts.

Thus, the finished trade center seemed to flaunt a view that had become determinedly reactionary. By the time the trade center opened, Radio Row might well have qualified as one of the landmarks commission's historic districts, along with Greenwich Village, SoHo, and Brooklyn Heights. It was not surprising that less than a decade after the World Trade Center was completed, the master plan for Battery Park City, a complex of housing and commercial buildings on landfill in the Hudson River adjacent to the trade center (landfill that came mainly from the trade center's excavation), made much of the fact that it would have "traditional" streets and blockfronts like the rest of the city, as if in deliberate rebuke to Yamasaki's plan.

Back when the trade center was still in the planning stages, several New York real-estate developers, claiming to share the views of preservationists, formed the Committee for a Reasonable World Trade Center, to push for a smaller project that would not destroy Radio Row or rise so high. In fact, their real concern was less the small merchants of Radio Row as the competition that ten million square feet of office space would pose for their own buildings. They got nowhere against the political forces lined up in favor of the trade center, but they need not have worried. There was not much of a market for all that new space, and commercial renting went so slowly that before the buildings were finished the Port Authority announced that it would fill much of the north tower with its own offices, and the State of New York said it would take much of the other. (It eventually occupied fifty floors of the south tower.) The public agencies never admitted it in so many words, but they moved in themselves because there were not enough commercial tenants who wanted to be in Lower Manhattan.

Great height was itself beginning to go out of fashion when the trade center opened, at least in the United States. The World Trade Center towers were the tallest buildings in the world for only a short time after their completion—the Sears Tower in Chicago, only slightly higher, took the title in 1974. Not a lot of extremely tall skyscrapers went up in the late seventies and early eighties as the economy struggled, and when it rebounded, most American developers had lost interest in the notion of going still taller. They understood that supertall buildings, even with structural innovations like the ones at the trade center, are rarely the most profitable kinds of buildings to build. Their value is as signboards, as advertisements and symbols, more than as conventional real estate. And so it was not surprising that when the Sears Tower was surpassed as the world's tallest building in 1996, it was not by another American structure but by the corncoblike Petronas Towers in Malaysia, which rose to 1,476 feet. Asian countries, newly strutting their presence on the world economic stage, took over the quest to build ever-taller towers. After Petronas, buildings were designed for Shanghai that went still higher.

The shift in sensibility that made the trade center out-of-date as a piece of urban planning when it opened had an even more powerful effect on the perception of the buildings as architecture. By the

1970s, boxy steel and glass skyscrapers no longer seemed like fresh and exciting presences in the cityscape. There were too many boxes, and they were too much the same, so much so that many people dismissed the best examples of modernism, like the Seagram Building, along with the worst, like the buildings that filled Third Avenue. When the World Trade Center was finished, the only skyscrapers New Yorkers seemed enthusiastic about were the old ones, buildings like the Woolworth and the Chrysler and Rockefeller Center: people delighted in their shapes, their decoration, and the ways in which they seemed full of emotion. Next to these buildings, Yamasaki's flat-topped towers seemed, if not mean-spirited, at least lacking in imagination. (I wrote then that they were "boring, so utterly banal as to be unworthy of the headquarters of a bank in Omaha," and I meant it.) The towers seemed an occasion to mourn not just for the skyline, which they transformed so utterly, pushing the center of gravity downtown but also throwing its balance off-kilter; in their very flatness and bluntness the towers seemed to dare us to react to buildings with emotion and to taunt us for thinking of skyscrapers as potential objects of affection.

But there are many phases to the relationships we have with buildings, and almost invariably they come around to acceptance. Long before September 11, the World Trade Center had begun to seem more palatable. Like all architecture, it is there, and you cannot avoid it the way you can choose not to listen to a piece of music you dislike or not to attend a play that you expect will make you uncomfortable. Buildings are present in a way that no other form of art is, and that requires us to adapt ourselves to them. We can walk on another block to keep some buildings out of our field of vision, but that technique was of little help with the World Trade Center, since it was visible from almost everywhere in and around the city. It became, for many people, an orienting device, the campanile of the huge city, and thus its enormity served, curiously, to make New York feel smaller, for when you saw the trade-center towers and because of them knew where you were, then the city was more manageable. It is one of the paradoxes of the trade center that its vastness could in this way confer intimacy, but so it was, and that made acceptance easier, less grudging.

Popular culture began to embrace the towers long before high culture did. While Dino De Laurentiis never achieved much success with his remake of *King Kong,* despite the striking image of King Kong straddling the two towers, Superman seemed entirely at home flying beside the towers, and the towers began to appear almost everywhere that an iconic view of the skyline was called for—covers of *The New Yorker,* television commercials, travel posters, and little souvenir replicas. (Before September 11, however, miniature trade centers never outsold little Empire State Buildings, perhaps because they looked too much like tiny boxes.) There was a whole different level of acceptance for people who used the World Trade Center towers, and as the years passed the nature of the uses within the buildings changed. In 1976, Windows on the World, the extraordinary, splashy, sprawling restaurant on top of the north tower, opened, and that brought a sense of indulgence to buildings that, for all their size, seemed until then to have a kind of puritanical restraint. Philippe Petit, the aerialist who walked between the towers, and George Willig, the climber who crawled up one of them, made the architecture the setting for performance art, and added a level of glee that Yamasaki surely never dreamed of. Petit and Willig enlisted the towers as co-performers, and humanized them. Things were not the same after Petit and Willig. They were better; their escapades made the towers relax.

The construction of Battery Park City and its centerpiece, the World Financial Center, helped, too. Cesar Pelli, the architect of the financial center, said that he thought of his four squat towers as foothills to the mountains that were the trade center's towers, and he did what had seemed impossible, which was to bring Yamasaki's huge buildings into some kind of urban context, at least from the riverfront and the west. When Battery Park City and the World Financial Center were constructed, the trade-center towers no longer stood aloof; these buildings that had tried to stand apart were embraced by neighbors that brought them visually into a larger composition.

All of these events—the performances of Petit and Willig, the architecture of Pelli—coincided with the beginnings of an upturn in the city's economy and with the gradual shift in the tenancy of the towers toward the financial companies and trading organizations for which they had been intended. It was not until the mid-1990s, however, as the financial-services industry entered its largest boom, that the towers were filled almost entirely with higher-paying commercial tenants. By then, the state offices and many of the Port Authority offices had moved elsewhere, the restaurants and shops in the underground mall had gone through several cycles of tenancy, and the place had begun to take on the qualities of a medium-sized city that was neither newly ascendant nor in decline but entering a kind of self-satisfied middle age. Its complacency was shattered in 1993 with the first terrorist attack, in the form of a bomb set off in a truck in the underground parking garage, which resulted in significant property damage but miraculously little human cost. The terrorist event was shocking to the people who lived through it, but to the city at large it seemed less like a warning of worse things to come than a welcome opportunity to spruce up a piece of real estate that was, by then, a good two decades old.

The trade center had begun to seem more benign from the outside as well as from within in the years before the 1993 bombing, and it is hard to tell, looking back, how much of this is a matter of becoming continually more accustomed to its presence, and how much it is a matter of changing attitudes toward architecture in general. As the trade center's image as a work of architecture suffered at the beginning from being out of cycle with architectural fashion, it appeared in a different light a decade or so later, as the architecture world became less willing to be seduced by the idea of faux Art Deco, faux Gothic, and faux classical towers (or perhaps bored by an excess of them), and began to look with new respect toward modernism. Crisp metal boxes did not seem so harsh, and sometimes they even seemed refreshing. The particulars of Yamasaki's design—the plainness, the bluntness, of the buildings—began to seem like a virtue. And the facades did, after all, emphasize the vertical, as if Yamasaki had heard Louis Sullivan's famous exhortation—"the skyscraper must be tall, every inch of it tall . . . every inch a proud and soaring thing, rising in sheer exaltation that from bottom to top it is a unit without a single dissenting line"—and tried to interpret it as best he could. That the surfaces were mostly of metal and not of glass may have made the towers less than exhilarating to be in—it had to have been frustrating to have an office seventy or eighty or ninety stories above the greatest urban view in the world and never see a panorama of it—but Yamasaki's metallic facades made the buildings seem far less brittle than glass. The towers did wonderful things in the light. They did not glare, like glass, but they did not absorb all the light either, the way stone or brick buildings often do. They reflected it back, softly, with a gentleness that belied their size.

The towers had always done that, of course, but when they were new you did not see it, blinded by the very fact of the buildings' existence. But then it became clear that Yamasaki, trying to get away from what he thought was the harshness of modern architecture, had actually designed one of the greatest pieces of modern, minimalist sculpture of all time. Yamasaki had been right: two of them was exactly the right number. One would have been deadly dull, and three would have been a cluster. Two identical towers, set 130 feet apart, corner to corner, could play off against each other, their masses not as inert as they looked, since each shape was engaged with the other. Your eye went back and forth, always seeing each tower in relationship to its twin, and you could feel now, more than ever before, how the surface made the towers seem solid enough to function as minimalist sculpture yet soft enough to be decent to the eye. Strangely, the buildings came, over time, to have the appeal of quietness. The buildings that once seemed to be the most arrogant intrusions into the cityscape became, in spite of themselves, almost like background architecture.

Still, the urbanistic values represented by the World Trade Center—the role of the twin towers as a piece of urban design, the qualities they possessed not as a pair of discrete objects but as a part of the larger organism of the city—could not have been more distant from the values that had come to prevail by the time of their destruction. Whatever their other virtues, the towers were the apotheosis of a certain way of making cities, an attitude that viewed buildings as pure, abstract objects and viewed streets largely as anachronistic irrelevances. They also embodied an attitude toward the making of large-scale projects that considered public opinion to be essentially a nuisance. Austin Tobin was no more interested in participating in any kind of public process than his great rival as a builder of public works, Robert Moses, was, and while Moses became better known for a kind of "public be damned" attitude than Tobin, Tobin was probably more effective at having his way and not having to make compromises as the result of public opinion.

If you were seeking a project that represented the absolute opposite of Jane Jacobs's worldview, then, you could not do better than the World Trade Center—and it was Jane Jacobs who had won the battle for the hearts and minds of most New Yorkers, not Minoru Yamasaki. However much some people were prepared to confer martyr status on Yamasaki's buildings (and thus, in a sense, to render any architectural criticism of them irrelevant), it was Jacobs's view of the city, not Yamasaki's or Austin Tobin's or Robert Moses's, that eventually prevailed in New York and in much of the rest of the country. It had become the common wisdom, long before the towers were destroyed—so much so that it is hard to believe that the twin towers could have been built as they were had the project begun only a few years after it did. It is unlikely that all the streets in the sixteen-acre site would have been eliminated; it is unlikely that the efforts to preserve Radio Row would have been so completely ignored by public officials; and it is unlikely that Yamasaki's design would have been considered exempt from public review. In the months after September 11, as the process of planning for the future of the site began to gather steam, the belief that the World Trade Center represented an outdated and untenable vision of the city was to have significant implications.

CHAPTER 3

Reclaiming the Skyline

The Decision to Rebuild

IN THE IMMEDIATE AFTERMATH of the tragedy of September 11, almost no one was talking about rebuilding. Mourning the dead, comforting their survivors, and observing the painful process of searching for human remains and clearing the site—not to mention recovering from shock—was preoccupation enough for most people. Even those who did not lose friends or family in the World Trade Center felt as if they had experienced a great trauma, and a sense of catastrophe is not particularly conducive to planning for the future—especially if you were unsure, as many people were in the autumn of 2001, as to whether there should be much of a future for this piece of land at all, at least in the conventional sense. It was common in those early months after September 11 to hear suggestions that the land remain forever empty, since many people believed that to build anything at all other than a memorial would be disrespectful to the lives that were lost there. For many of the survivors, Ground Zero was the burial ground of their husbands or wives or parents or children, and they did not feel as if they were asking for anything special when they said that you do not build on a burial ground. Mayor Rudolph Giuliani, whose strong leadership was a critical factor in helping New York recover, argued strongly against any kind of civic or commercial development of the site. Giuliani thought the entire site should be a memorial, and he advocated transferring the development rights on the site to some other part of the city. Giuliani felt so strongly about this that he devoted his final speech as mayor, in December 2001, to a call for a "soaring memorial" to be the only thing that would be where the World Trade Center had stood.

One person who held a very different view was Larry Silverstein. Silverstein had lost not only the trade center, which he had leased from the Port Authority only weeks before September 11—indeed, the lease was so recent that the insurance documents had not yet been finalized, a fact that made for significant complications—but also the adjacent forty-seven-story slab known as 7 World Trade Center. Number Seven, which housed, among other tenants, the City of New York's emergency-management control center, was not part of Yamasaki's original design. It had been constructed by Silverstein in 1987 on space he leased from the Port Authority over a service area just north of the main trade-center complex. (The site contained a truck loading dock providing underground access to the complex and an electrical substation that powered the trade center.)

Silverstein wanted to rebuild and rebuild fast. He issued a statement not long after the buildings came down proclaiming his right and his intention to reconstruct the World Trade Center—indeed, he presented it almost as if it were his obligation. He was not insisting on reconstructing the towers as they were, and he said he would be quite happy to consider other architectural options, such as four towers of about fifty stories each. Silverstein did not care so much about the height; the important thing, for him, was to start building again, so that the ten million square feet of office space that the twin towers and their surrounding buildings contained could be put back on the site as quickly as possible. "It would be the tragedy of tragedies not to rebuild this part of New York," Silverstein told *The Wall Street Journal*. "It would give the terrorists the victory they seek."

Silverstein called the trade center the symbol of the city and called the day he acquired it "the crowning moment of my life." But for all its fame, the World Trade Center had not been among Lower Manhattan's more prestigious pieces of real estate. It may have been high, but it was not considered high-end. For years, it was occupied largely by its own builders, the Port Authority and the government of the State of New York, since there was not enough demand in the private market to fill the huge amount of office space the towers contained. (The original notion, that the trade center would be occupied by businesses active in international trade, never really took hold, the name notwithstanding.) During the boom of the nineties, however, the economics of the trade center began to change. The enormous expansion of the financial-services industry created such a drastic need for office space in Lower Manhattan that the twin towers began to fill with brokerage firms and other financial organizations that were willing to spend far more for office space than the state government or the Port Authority had been. Gradually, two decades later than expected, the towers turned into profitable commercial space. As the complex became more valuable, the Port Authority considered selling it but decided that a sale was so complicated that it would be better advised to lease the trade center to a private developer. The authority called for bids on a ninety-nine-year lease of the property, and early in 2001 its attorneys were deeply involved in negotiations with Vornado Realty Trust, the high bidder. Vornado's bid had been accepted, but the Port Authority had trouble finalizing the terms of the lease with Steven Roth, Vornado's chairman, a famously tough-minded negotiator.

After long and trouble-ridden negotiations failed to conclude a deal, Vornado and the Port Authority parted company, rather like a couple that splits up just before marching to the altar, and the authority turned to Larry Silverstein, whose $3.2 billion bid had been the runner-up. Silverstein, then a seventy-year-old developer who had built a substantial fortune by acquiring numerous older buildings in both Lower and Midtown Manhattan as well as building several others, was a well-known figure within the New York real-estate industry, but his name was not particularly prominent outside it. While many of his properties were highly profitable, he had never owned a building with a famous name or even one of the city's celebrated landmarks, unless you considered 120 Broadway, the venerable Equitable Building of 1915, to be in that category. The Equitable was the bulkiest office building in New York when it was completed, and its huge mass provoked such an outcry that it led to the passage of the nation's first zoning laws, in 1916. The Equitable thus represents one of the earliest, not to mention one of the most dramatic, examples of overreaching by the New York real-estate industry; as one of the city's historic monuments to greed, it may not be quite the best building a real-estate developer would want his name to be associated with.

If Silverstein kept a somewhat lower profile than some New York real-estate moguls, he was hardly a secretive figure. In fact, he seemed eager to be seen as a solid citizen. He and his wife, Klara, were active presences in the city's social and philanthropic circles—he was a generous supporter of New York University, among other charities—though he spent many of his weekends sailing his large yacht off the coast of Florida. His greatest professional pleasure lay in the making of deals, and like many of his colleagues in the real-estate industry he tended to see buildings less in terms of their architectural design than in terms of their cash flow. It was not surprising, then, that Silverstein was known more for the success of his business than for the specific buildings that he owned. But that was about to change. Silverstein was to acquire the property that would make him more famous than he had ever imagined, though it happened almost by accident, on the rebound from the Port Authority's failed deal with Vornado.

However well-known the trade center was and however high the hopes Silverstein had for it, he recognized that in 2001 it had only a handful of prestigious tenants. The exterior of the twin towers may have been in millions of tourists' snapshots, but the inside was occupied mainly by second-tier brokerage houses and financial firms, or by back offices of large companies like Morgan Stanley, the executive offices of which were elsewhere in Manhattan. The trade center required burnishing, and Silverstein knew that if he was to make enough money to justify the ten million dollars per month he was to pay the Port Authority as rent, he would have to upgrade the center to attract more corporate tenants who would view the place as a headquarters building and pay rents to match. During the summer of 2001, as he was finishing up the details of his lease, Silverstein hired Geoffrey Wharton, an experienced real-estate executive who had successfully helped Tishman Speyer upgrade Rockefeller Center, in the hope that Wharton would help him do the same thing at the trade center. And he made another hire that would end up being far more important than he could have realized, which was the architect David Childs of Skidmore, Owings & Merrill, whom Silverstein asked to try to improve the public space of the twin towers and make some proposals for cosmetic improvements that would give the buildings an aura that would make them seem more like upscale properties.

Childs hadn't gotten very far by September 11, but his work over the summer at least had made him familiar with the complex and its shortcomings. When Silverstein spoke shortly after September 11 to express his eagerness to build again quickly, he asked Childs to begin drawing some plans for a new trade center, and Childs was ready to start working as soon as he could get back into his office at 14 Wall Street, in the old Bankers Trust building just a few blocks from Ground Zero. Silverstein thought that his statement and his charge to his architect were positive responses to the tragedy. He was, after all, a devoted, civic-minded New Yorker, and he had suffered a horrendous loss himself. What could be better than looking forward and promising the city that he was ready to rebuild, better than ever? It was the spirit that moved Chicago to come back after the great fire of 1871, and Silverstein wanted to apply the same kind of gumption to New York. He was not prepared for the fact that his remarks would generally be received not as benign civic boosterism but as intemperate—and that some people would go further and see them as greedy and insensitive to the loss of life.

The reaction to Silverstein's suggestion was so negative that he never released Childs's early plans, which were never fully developed. Silverstein, advised by the public-relations guru Howard Rubenstein, began to maintain a lower profile. More important to Silverstein's public image, however, was the advice he received not from Rubenstein but from his lawyer, Herbert Wachtell, who insisted that he take a highly aggressive position toward the insurance companies that had insured the twin towers. Only by stating his intention to rebuild all of the office space lost in the terrorist attack could Silverstein receive the maximum insurance benefit, Wachtell argued, and he helped Silverstein devise a claim based on the assertion that the events of September 11 constituted two discrete terrorist acts, not one, and that he was therefore entitled to a double payment—roughly seven billion dollars instead of three and a half billion. It was something of a Talmudic argument—were there two incidents because there were two planes, each hitting a different tower, or was it one incident because it was part of a single attack? Whatever the rightness or wrongness of Wachtell's argument from a legal standpoint, it had the effect of making Silverstein look even greedier in the eyes of the public. While Rudy Giuliani was talking about how the land had become sacred ground and had to be kept free of building, Larry Silverstein was talking about money—and asking for double the usual insurance payout, to boot.

If Silverstein's first comments after the terrorist attack seemed rash and inappropriate, the fact is that no one really knew what to say in those painful weeks after September 11. No one was in charge, and Silverstein understandably believed that as the leaseholder he had the right to decide what to do. Silverstein's assertive position was in sharp contrast to that of the agency that owned the property that he had leased, the Port Authority, which was in considerable trauma in the aftermath of the terrorist attack. The authority had lost its headquarters, which had been in the north tower, as well as seventy-five employees, including its articulate, energetic executive director, Neil Levin. It had been something of an accomplishment for the Port Authority to establish itself in temporary offices on Park Avenue South within a few days after September 11 and resume its normal business of overseeing bridges, tunnels, and airports. The Port Authority had not been particularly known for demonstrating vision under the best of circumstances, but immediately after September 11, when it was a shaken bureaucracy without a leader, directing the rebuilding process was more than the agency could even attempt. And Mayor Giuliani, for all the strong leadership he had shown in overseeing the rescue and recovery operation at the trade-center site, was a lame duck, only three and a half months away from the end of his second term as mayor. His focus was on the physical management of the effects of the tragedy and on the needs of the families of the dead, not on the future of the site, which he would not be in office to oversee in any event. And since most of the high officials in the city government were appointed by Giuliani and would be leaving when he did, they had no incentive to think in terms of planning for the future, either. Giuliani and his administration were, for all intents and purposes, disengaged from the issue of rebuilding. It was not their problem, and most of the constituency Giuliani cared most about at that point, the family members of the victims, did not want to see anything built anyway.

There was one public official who had both the means to push the rebuilding process forward and a political reason to do so, and that was the governor of New York, George Pataki. Pataki controlled the Port Authority in tandem with the governor of New Jersey, and as a result he was in a position to have far more influence on the future of the site than any mayor, lame-duck or not. It was a paradox that for all that the World Trade Center was seen as an icon of New York City, the Port Authority's ownership meant that the city government had little control over these sixteen acres—indeed, the governor of New Jersey was in a position to have more say over the future of Ground Zero than the mayor of New York. And Pataki had a couple of other cards to play in addition to the Port Authority. The Empire State Development Corporation, a quasi-public agency charged with undertaking major projects around the state, which had both the power to issue bonds and the right to override local zoning laws, reported to him. And, since federal disaster funds generally flowed through the state government, not the city, Pataki could have some control over the spigot of federal money, giving him a further means of exerting influence over what was to happen at Ground Zero.

In the dark weeks following the terrorist attack, Pataki said relatively little about the future of the site. He let Giuliani set the theme, and he kept the public discussion focused on honoring the dead, supporting their families, and generalized talk about the necessity for some kind of memorial. But Pataki never shared Giuliani's preference to see the entire site restricted as a memorial, and he tried to balance his public support for the concerns of the victims' families with a private recognition of the fact that some kind of building was inevitable and might eventually be seen as desirable. There were some people who would never want to see any building again on the site, just as there were others who, like Larry Silverstein, thought the best response to the terrorist attack was to build immediately, and boldly. But Pataki's political instincts led him to realize that the great majority was probably somewhere in between. When the sense of mourning and tragedy began to recede—and no one knew whether that was weeks, months, or even years away—the public would be far more receptive to building. Pataki himself had an election to face, but his was not a few weeks after September 11, when the mayoral election would occur, but a year later, timing that was more favorable to him, since the wounds would not then be so raw. But then again, by election day 2002, Pataki would also be judged on how much he had accomplished in giving Ground Zero a future.

On the second of November, less than two months after September 11—and just a few days before a mayoral election that most people expected would be won by Mark Green, a Democrat who had long been an opponent of Rudolph Giuliani—Pataki announced his intention to create a new public agency, the Lower Manhattan Development Corporation, to oversee the reconstruction of the trade-center site and to coordinate planning and recovery efforts downtown. The LMDC would be a division of the Empire State Development Corporation, which meant not only that Pataki would control it but that it would not need any new legislation to enjoy the powers of its parent corporation. Creating an entirely new agency, even if it reported to Pataki, would require the approval of the Democrat-controlled state assembly, and Pataki did not want to engage in a political negotiation over the terms of rebuilding. Sheldon Silver, the speaker of the state assembly, was a downstate Democrat whose district included Lower Manhattan, and he was in a position to demand a significant role in the rebuilding process. Thus, Pataki all but cut Silver out of the decision-making loop, in effect bringing a new governmental unit into being by decree.

Giuliani joined with Pataki to announce the formation of the LMDC, and he agreed with the governor's plan to give six of the nine seats on the new organization's board of directors to the governor's appointees. Giuliani seemed to be selling the city short in favor of the state, but with Mark Green as the likely new mayor both Giuliani and Pataki wanted to keep the rebuilding process firmly out of Democratic control. By the time the governor was ready to announce the composition of the board, however, the mayoral election had concluded with an unexpected outcome: Michael Bloomberg, a billionaire businessman running as a Republican, had defeated Green. At the end of November, Pataki, Giuliani, and Bloomberg appeared together to announce the initial composition of the board, which they had expanded to eleven members, four appointed by Giuliani and seven by Pataki. (Later, the board was quietly expanded still more, to give the mayor four additional appointees, allowing Bloomberg to have nearly as much influence over the makeup of the board as Pataki did.)

The most important announcement, at the outset, was the name of the new organization's chairman, John C. Whitehead. The seventy-nine-year-old former cochairman of Goldman Sachs, Whitehead was one of the few elder statesmen of Wall Street, and while he had no experience in building or city planning, his career had cut a wide swath through both business and public service, and his presence appeared to give the LMDC immediate gravitas. Pataki also appointed Frank Zarb, the former chairman of NASDAQ; Lewis Eisenberg, a former Goldman Sachs partner who gave up the chairmanship of the Port Authority's board of commissioners to join the LMDC board; Ed Malloy, head of the Building and Construction Trades Council of Greater New York; Deborah Wright, the chief executive of the Carver Savings Bank, one of the few black-owned banks in the city; Madelyn Wils, chairman of Community Board 1, the local advisory planning board for Lower Manhattan; and the man who would end up to be Pataki's most significant appointment, Roland Betts, chairman of Chelsea Piers, the enormous athletic complex on the Hudson River. Betts, a lawyer, former teacher, and classmate at Yale of George W. Bush, was the lead owner of the Texas Rangers when Bush was the team's managing partner. As one of the president's closest personal friends in New York, Betts had spoken often to Bush about the future of the city in the weeks since September 11. Betts socialized with the president at the White House and Camp David but had chosen not to join the Bush administration, preferring to exercise his influence behind the scenes. He was seen not only as the board's unofficial liaison to the White House but as a devoted architecture buff and a passionate builder. He was expected to be the rebuilding project's strong advocate.

Giuliani named to the board Paul Crotty, a former New York City corporation counsel who was a top executive at Verizon; Howard Wilson, chair of the New York School Construction Authority; Robert Harding, the deputy mayor for economic development; and Dick Grasso, who was the chairman of the New York Stock Exchange. Grasso was to resign from his post at the stock exchange in 2003, after an outcry over his lucrative pay package, and some weeks after that he left the board of the LMDC also.

In the fall of 2001, as the LMDC was getting organized, it was impossible to know how much influence it would have, or how it would work with the Port Authority, with Larry Silverstein, or with the city government. The LMDC was supposed to be the "official" voice of the planning process, but whether that meant it would have total control over what would happen or that it would be nothing more than a bureaucratic fig leaf to allow Silverstein or the Port Authority to do whatever they pleased was a mystery.

What was clear was that there were plenty of interested parties—indeed, almost everyone seemed to want to have a say in what happened and to demand to be heard. The families of the victims of the terrorist attack were increasingly vocal, and as they emerged from their immediate mourning they began to organize themselves. Monica Iken, a statuesque young blond widow whose husband,

Michael, had been a trader with Eurobrokers on the eighty-fourth floor of the south tower, formed a group called September's Mission, which was devoted to the establishment of a memorial. Iken quickly became one of the most prominent spokespeople for the families, and she argued initially against development of the site and later for a more prominent presence for the memorial component. Another group, Families of September 11, which included members of the families of people who had died in the planes as well as of the families of those who had been in the trade center, was somewhat broader in its mission, serving as a clearinghouse for information and support as well as advocacy. The 9-11 Widows and Victims Families Association, on the other hand, was made up primarily of firefighters' and policemen's widows, and its prime mission was to argue not only against redevelopment but also for the continued recovery of victims' remains and for a memorial to the rescue workers. There were numerous other groups as well, including a group made up only of families connected to Cantor Fitzgerald, the brokerage firm that had been at the top of the north tower and had lost 685 employees, the greatest single loss of any organization. But if the families were organized, they were also somewhat factionalized, since the interests of the firefighters' widows were not always the same as the interests of the relatives of the bond brokers or the bankers. Some were more concerned about insurance proceeds or the building of a memorial than any new development. Some were determined that nothing ever be built; others were inclined to consider it, but not for a long time. A handful of family members, such as Tom Roger, an executive in a construction firm whose daughter died in one of the planes that crashed into the towers, and Nikki Stern, the widow of James E. Potorti, an executive of Marsh & McLennan, were sophisticated about design and planning issues (Stern had spent much of her career as a public-relations executive in an architecture firm), but most of the relatives knew little about how large-scale urban projects come together. Still, a great many of the family members, understandably enough, believed that they had a justifiable right, or even an obligation, to have a major say in the future of the site.

The family members were not the only people other than public officials who expected to have a say in the planning process. When the World Trade Center was built, almost no one lived in Lower Manhattan; but by 2001, thousands of people did, in several distinct residential areas surrounding the site. There was Battery Park City, with blocks and blocks of new high-rise apartments facing a riverfront promenade; Tribeca, to the north of the trade center, where old warehouses and industrial buildings had been converted into residential lofts; the financial district to the east and southeast of Ground Zero, where numerous old office buildings had been converted into hundreds of new apartments; and Chinatown and the South Street Seaport district to the northeast. All of the residents of these areas had been shaken by the terrorist attack, which kept them from their homes for days, weeks, or in some cases months. As full-time residents and, in many instances, property owners, they felt that they had at least as much long-term interest in the future of the neighborhood as the survivors of the dead, many of whom lived in distant suburbs. So, too, with business owners in Lower Manhattan, who were inclined to feel that they had an investment in the area that made their interests important.

The residents were, at least technically, represented on the LMDC board by Madelyn Wils. Representing business owners was Carl Weisbrod, a lawyer who formerly served as president of the New York City Economic Development Corporation and now ran the Downtown Alliance, the largest privately funded business-improvement district in the country. Weisbrod eventually won a seat on the LMDC board as well, but for the moment he was an outside advocate who had exceptionally good political connections. But probably the most powerful businessperson in the area was a lawyer and real-estate entrepreneur who tried hard to avoid playing a public role in the rebuilding process: John Zuccotti, chairman of Brookfield Properties, Larry Silverstein's biggest competitor in the downtown real-estate market. Unlike Silverstein, who knew only the rough-and-tumble world of New York real estate, Zuccotti had begun his career as a lawyer, and he had served as chairman of the New York City Planning Commission in the 1970s. At the end of 2001, he had two jobs. He was a partner in the influential law firm Weil, Gotshal & Manges, and he was the head of Brookfield, which controlled the World Financial Center. Zuccotti's buildings, which had become unusable on September 11, housed the headquarters of Merrill Lynch, Dow Jones, and Deloitte & Touche, among other companies. Even before the terrorist attack, the World Financial Center had felt like an island, separated from the rest of Lower Manhattan by the trade center and also by West Street, which was as wide as an interstate highway. Zuccotti was concerned that he would not be able to attract companies back to his huge complex once the buildings were repaired, and he took it upon himself to commission a plan to rebuild Ground Zero and the surrounding area from the architect Alexander Cooper of Cooper, Robertson & Partners, who had been a codesigner of the master plan for Battery Park City. At first Zuccotti, Cooper, Silverstein, and David Childs considered working together to create a single privately sponsored plan, but Childs and Cooper did not agree on many aspects of the redesign of the site, and their clients had different priorities in any event: Silverstein wanted Childs to facilitate the rebuilding of the office space on the site quickly, whereas Zuccotti wanted a plan that would reduce the isolation of the World Financial Center. The landlords and their architects soon went their separate ways and continued to prepare separate plans—neither of which, of course, had any official standing.

The final constituents, beyond public officials, families, residents, and business owners, were New York City's myriad civic groups, and they did not waste a moment in asserting their role in the rebuilding process. Several new organizations sprung up, such as a group that called itself R.DOT, which stood for "Rebuild Downtown Our Town" and was run by an architect, Beverly Willis, and the editor of a design publication, Susan S. Szenasy of *Metropolis,* and had many local residents as members. Somewhat larger was New York New Visions, a coalition of 350 architecture and design professionals that studied the site in the context of Lower Manhattan and suggested guidelines for its development. But the strongest voice, at least on the civic front, seemed to belong to Robert Yaro, president of the Regional Plan Association, a venerable civic group whose interests spanned the tristate area but which, in 2001, had been widely perceived as old and out of touch with current concerns. Yaro saw in the aftermath of September 11 an opportunity both to fill the void left by the absence of strong governmental leadership and to renew his own organization, which had not been in the forefront of the civic dialogue since the creation of its second regional plan for the New York area in the 1960s. (The RPA's third plan, released in 1996, had minimal impact.)

Yaro realized that rebuilding the trade-center site, whatever form it took, would have regional implications—just as the commuters who had worked in the World Trade Center had come from dozens of city neighborhoods and suburban towns and villages across the tristate area, so would any new structure be important, not just symbolically but in real economic terms, to people far beyond Manhattan. He thought that the Regional Plan Association, as the only planning and civic group that reached across state lines, was ideally suited to coordinate an effort to combine the civic voices in the region. He convened a whole consortium of civic organizations, including New School University, the Pratt Institute, the New York chapter of the American Institute of Architects, and the Municipal Art Society, into something he called the Civic Alliance to Rebuild Downtown New York. Yaro made the argument that New York was so full of civic groups of all kinds that even the most articulate of them would not be heard on its own in the cacophony following the terrorist attack; if they wanted to have any influence over the planning process, the groups had to join forces and speak with one voice. The Civic Alliance began meeting within weeks of the attack, and the group formulated a set of principles for the future of the site. It called for an open planning process with significant public participation—in effect the opposite of the process by which the original World Trade Center was planned—and for the effort to encompass all of Lower Manhattan, not just the sixteen-acre site. The alliance also called for sustainable, environmentally friendly development and for attention to the needs of a wide range of economic groups, not just the financial community that had traditionally been Lower Manhattan's primary business. "Lower Manhattan can become the world's first twenty-first century city, incorporating the best practices in urban design, green buildings, and technology, transportation and economic development," the initial "vision statement" of the Alliance said. "It is altogether fitting that Lower Manhattan show the way to a new urban future, in much the same way that a century ago it became the first great twentieth-century high-rise city built around a modern metropolitan transportation system."

New York New Visions, for its part, tried to focus on some of the more specific issues of urban design. Several of the city's well-known architects participated, including Hugh Hardy, Eugene Kohn, David Rockwell, and Marilyn Jordan Taylor of Skidmore, Owings & Merrill, who as David Childs's partner was also working for Larry Silverstein, which put her in a somewhat awkward position. Taylor was working pro bono to devise recommendations from the architectural profession for the trade-center site, but she was being paid to do what Silverstein wanted, which might or might not agree with what her colleagues believed was in the public interest. And Taylor, along with Childs, would be asked to advise Silverstein as to whether or not the recommendations made sense.

In fact, they made a great deal of sense. The New York New Visions planning team, under the leadership of Mark Strauss, in February 2002 issued a set of seven basic principles that were intentionally general. The architects understood that specific designs were premature, and they probably could never have agreed on any actual building schemes anyway—being architects, they would all have had their own ideas, which could wait, or so they believed. One of the problems throughout the early stages of the planning process was the extent to which some members of the public hungered for real designs. They craved pictures of buildings, even before the rebuilding process was set or anyone had determined what functions the new structures would serve. Many architects themselves drew up versions of new skyscrapers or memorials or other projects for the site. Confusion about just how you go about a building project was rampant in the fall of 2001—the emotions surrounding the sixteen acres were so intense that it was easy to forget that it was still necessary, even in these extraordinary circumstances, to figure out a process and a program before designing a building.

The notions the New York New Visions group set out, though so broad as to be almost vague, were nonetheless to define a great deal of the planning process, and they were an early hint at a consensus that ultimately emerged. Mindful that mourning the dead was still paramount in the minds of almost everyone and not just the families of those who died, the group urged as its first principle "a formal, transparent and open process to determine the nature and location of memorials." But the architects made it clear that they did not support the notion of devoting the entire site to a memorial, since the second principle was a call for a mixed-use future for Lower Manhattan, in effect endorsing the notion that the neighborhood, as well as the site, could not be only a financial district but should continue to include housing, cultural facilities, and retail space. The third principle encouraged improved transportation access, and the fourth called for a stronger relationship between Lower Manhattan and the tristate region, in effect echoing Robert Yaro's theme. The fifth principle, "Design Excellence and Sustainability," called for high-quality architecture and environmental sensitivity, and the sixth was a call for an inclusive planning process.

The group was not inclined to trust the Port Authority or the governor to demonstrate that the age of Robert Moses and Austin Tobin had passed in favor of the age of Jane Jacobs, and it called both for a "transparent and open process" and for a high level of public involvement, although the architects put their call for public participation near the end of their list, as if they did not want to make the point too emphatically. The final principle was called simply "Immediate Action," and it emerged from the architects' recognition that whatever happened, it was likely to be years before any permanent memorial and new construction was built—a fact that few members of the public seemed at that point to understand—and therefore it was urgent that certain short-term, temporary improvements to the site be made as soon as the work of rescue and clearing of debris was concluded. People and businesses would be making decisions fairly soon about whether to remain in Lower Manhattan, the architects observed, and "a sense of predictable and continuous improvement in the public environment is essential to retaining residents and office workers and to addressing the needs of visitors." In other words, the neighborhood was in a desperate state, and it needed not only a long-term plan but all the help it could get right now.

CHAPTER 4

The Future of Memory

Finding Common Ground for Money and Culture

GIVEN THE NUMBER OF PEOPLE who hoped that nothing would be built at Ground Zero because they believed that building any structures would violate the sacred precinct that the site had become, as well as those who, like Larry Silverstein, were willing to consider having almost anything built so long as it restored the amount of office space that had been blown apart, it was easy to think of the dilemma about what to do at Ground Zero as yet another confrontation between God and mammon. But there were plenty of other ways of looking at the site that did not fall neatly into either of these camps.

For many people—myself included—building nothing made sense at the outset, because it was impossible to know quickly what the right thing to do was, and this was too vast a decision for a traumatized city to rush into. You could believe that a void could be the right short-term solution—indeed, even a necessary short-term solution—without believing that it would be the correct thing in the long term, because perceptions of the site and, indeed, of the entire meaning of September 11 change over time. For a while, a void was exactly what was needed. But what was right for the end of 2001 or the beginning of 2002 would not be right three or four or ten years on. When people looked downtown and still felt a sense of shock or surprise at the absence of the towers, it was clearly not yet time to build again, or even to know precisely what to do. But that feeling would ebb, month by month, and there would come a time when most people were no longer shocked at the void, when they would feel no surprise that the towers were not there, when they would expect to see nothing there except a hole—when Ground Zero would feel less like a place of death and more like a construction site. For those whose families died there, such a time may never come, of course, and that is reasonable. But the power of the site to suggest death continued to fade over time, at least somewhat, as if, like uranium, it had a half-life, losing its potency in stages, though it would never disappear completely. And as that happened, people moved gradually toward thinking that the ways in which they might respect the lives of those who died there and the ways in which they might respect the future of the city and build toward it need not be entirely incompatible.

Not everyone, of course, understood the values of uncertainty or the virtues of moving slowly. One of the most striking events in the first few months after September 11, at least so far as architecture was concerned, was the exhibition at the Max Protetch Gallery in Chelsea of some sixty design proposals for the site by leading architects from around the world, which Protetch, whose gallery sells architectural drawings, had commissioned. Protetch viewed the exhibition as a way of demonstrating his, and the architectural profession's, desire to "make a positive contribution" in the aftermath of the terrorist attack. "I couldn't deny an irrepressible interest in what would replace the World Trade Center," Protetch wrote.

> I knew most architects and many others were thinking along similar lines, though they probably felt, as I did, that such thoughts were unseemly given the horrible circumstances of that day. However, I realized that in four months' time there would be a great deal of pressure on those who

would have the power to control the future of the World Trade Center site, and that the drive to maximize commercial square footage might lead to knee-jerk responses. I felt moved to utilize my experience in a way that would allow me to help prevent the sacrifice of great architectural opportunities in the name of "business as usual."

Not all the architects Protetch approached saw the exhibition as an opportunity. He invited 125 to participate, and more than half turned him down. It took, in Protetch's words, "some major arm-twisting" to fill out his show's roster. To many architects, it felt inappropriate to be drawing up new designs while Ground Zero was still being cleared.

Protetch was certainly correct in realizing that there was plenty of pressure to do something ordinary at Ground Zero—indeed, the coming months were to show that the greatest conflict was not between those who wanted to build and those who wanted the site to remain empty but between those who saw the priority of new construction on the site as primarily commercial and those who saw it as primarily symbolic and cultural. Would the site be developed like most pieces of New York real estate, in which maximizing profit is the only serious goal, or would the extraordinary circumstances make for something bolder, something different, something more memorable?

The problem with Protetch's project was not that it encouraged architects to demonstrate vision, which was certainly going to be needed. It was more that Protetch's architects, unfortunately, demonstrated nothing but vision, most of it utterly disconnected from reality. In January 2002, when Protetch mounted his show, there was only the beginning of a process—the board of the LMDC had not yet even had its first meeting—and there was certainly no clear program for the site. Without a process and a program, the designs the architects came up with were not much more than entrants in a beauty contest, in which each of them paraded their favorite shapes before an eager public. It was a beauty contest with an eager audience, to be sure—Roland Betts paid a visit to the gallery before the official opening—and the night the show opened, there was a line all the way down the block, and the crowd jam-packed into the room included several television reporters covering the event for the evening news. The exhibition opening had the air of a high school science fair with the architects, like eager students, standing proudly behind their models, showing off projects that had very little to do with what grown-up scientists were doing in their laboratories.

Not that the grown-up architects, if that is the role that David Childs and Alexander Cooper had been cast in, were demonstrating much vision themselves: they were working for real-estate developers, and while they were producing master plans that aspired to do more than cram ten million square feet of office space onto the site, nothing that either Childs or Cooper had produced for Silverstein and Zuccotti could be said to stretch the boundaries of architectural imagination. And there was a genuine craving for an architectural response to the crisis, for creative designs that would somehow manage to demonstrate the ability of architectural aesthetics to heal a broken world. It is something that architects often dream of and rarely achieve, but the Protetch exhibition, if nothing else, proved how fertile the hope for architectural solutions continued to be.

As to the specifics of the schemes, almost all of them provided more enlightenment about their architects than about the problem of rebuilding Lower Manhattan. Michael Graves, for example, proposed the reinstatement of the original grid of city streets that had been obliterated by the superblock of the World Trade Center and the development of the blocks essentially as if the trade center had never been there. Hugh Hardy, like Graves an architect who frequently sought in his work to emulate certain qualities of buildings of the past, envisioned a forest of decorated tower tops, like those of the buildings of the 1920s. Richard Gluckman wanted to replicate the original profiles of the twin towers but sheathed in a newer, slicker, multimedia skin. Foreign Office Architects of London and NOX of Rotterdam each came up with variations on the old towers in the form of undulating or torqued towers, eight of them in the case of Foreign Office. There were numerous other towers, too, most of them swirling or looking vaguely anthropomorphic, as if in deliberate contrast to Yamasaki's boxy forms. Paolo Soleri proposed what he called a "secular cathedral," looking something like the swooping forms of buildings from the 1960s, and Michael Sorkin offered what was probably the only truly thoughtful plan for rethinking Lower Manhattan as a work of urban design, with an improved transit hub, a tunnel replacing West Street, new green space, and links between various academic institutions in the area. Sorkin, a teacher, writer, architect, and urban planner, did not want to build tall at all—he envisioned the dispersal of the trade center's office space around the city and the preservation of the site of Ground Zero as a memorial and public open space. There were several other memorial proposals, most of them self-indulgent in a way that Sorkin's disciplined scheme was not.

Quite a number of the architects who answered Protetch's call for designs saw it as an opportunity to rethink the form of the skyscraper. It was an understandable response, not only because of the likelihood that Silverstein and the Port Authority's desire to build commercial office space would prevail. There was also a symbolic justification: the skyscraper is the ultimate American building type, the most important contribution of American architecture and American technology to world building, and where better to conceive of the next generation of skyscrapers than in America's greatest city, on the very site in which American culture had been so ruthlessly attacked? If it was not easy to see many of these designs as pointing the way clearly to the future of the skyscraper, it was certainly logical and natural to think of Ground Zero as an architectural laboratory in which experiments on the skyscraper form could be considered a central mission.

Most of the skyscrapers dreamed up by the architects who participated in Protetch's show were flamboyant, even narcissistic, but some of them resonated months later. Daniel Libeskind, for example, came up with a startling, sculptural form that looked like a series of shards slicing into the sky. Its most impressive aspect was the thoughtful text Libeskind wrote to accompany it. "The real question is about memory, and the future of that memory is what remains paramount," Libeskind wrote. Whatever is built, he said, "must be a response that takes into consideration the relationships between the uniqueness of a site and its global significance; fragility and stability; stone and spirit." Libeskind's short text, far more than his design, foresaw the essential conflict between the need to remember and the need to rebuild the functioning city.

If many of the architects' skyscraper designs seemed disconnected from reality, for plenty of people any tall building of any kind, whatever it looked like and however it was designed, made no sense. For everyone who felt that the most important response to the terrorist attack was to build tall once again and reclaim the skyline, there seemed to be another person who felt that anything tall on this site would make it a target, that to put another very tall building at Ground Zero would be tantamount to daring the terrorists to do it again. Real-estate executives doubted that anyone would want to rent space on a very high floor, especially in that location, and believed that the economic prospects of such a building, however beautiful or innovative it might be, would be grim.

Indeed, in the months following September 11, despite the proclivity of architects to conceive of new forms that skyscrapers might take, it was common to hear that very tall buildings were dinosaurs, not just at Ground Zero but everywhere. They had come to symbolize fear as much as romance, danger as much as excitement, and in any event who could afford them? The antiskyscraper crusaders forgot that the very tallest buildings had rarely made economic sense, that they were generally exercises in vanity as much as profitability, and that there hadn't been a supertall office building put up in the United States since the Sears Tower, in Chicago, was finished in 1974. Since then, the only buildings to reach a hundred or more floors had been put up in places like Kuala Lumpur and Shanghai, Asian cities that were less interested in the economics of supertall buildings than they were in their role as icons. Building the world's tallest tower was a perfect way for a city eager to strut on the world economic stage to be noticed. Long before September 11, it had become clear that the future of skyscrapers in the United States, such as it was, was going to be in new designs for buildings of forty, fifty, or perhaps seventy-some stories, not towers of ninety or a hundred or more floors. American developers had been quite happy to concede to Asians the megaskyscraper category, realizing that there was far more money to be made in building lots of medium-sized towers than a handful of supertall ones. If the United States had largely given up on very tall buildings before September 11, the notion of building such towers was even less appealing after the terrorist attack, when the fear that supertall towers would become targets was added to the economic uncertainty that they represented.

But another thing was different in the period after September 11, beyond this new fear. In an age of terrorism, what had once been a goal of corporations in search of efficiency, to have as much of their high-level staff physically together as possible, no longer seemed viable. Indeed, a centralized operation was risky, since it meant that if one building or even one city became a target, then an entire global operation might cease to function. Shortly after September 11, the financial-services giant Morgan Stanley, which had its headquarters in a pair of skyscrapers at Times Square in Midtown Manhattan and was preparing to move many of its employees into a brand-new building across the street that it envisioned as the final element in a three-building urban "campus," abruptly reversed course and put the new building up for sale before a single employee had moved in. Morgan Stanley (which also was the largest single tenant in the World Trade Center, where it occupied relatively low floors and thus had few casualties) bought the former headquarters of Texaco in Westchester County and moved its overflow staff there on the theory that it was safer now to decentralize. Morgan Stanley sold the new building to Lehman Brothers, which had been a tenant in the World Financial Center and whose leaders decided that they had no interest in returning to Lower Manhattan, especially not to a site across the street from Ground Zero. The impulse to decentralize and spread corporate staffs across wide geographic areas—an impulse made vastly easier by contemporary communications technologies, of course—did not bode well for the skyscraper, which is a means of keeping people close together, not spreading them apart. Skyscrapers exist to get more people onto a single piece of land, and the pressure after September 11 was to do exactly the opposite.

Those who feared that a very tall building would continue to be a natural terrorist target found allies in a group of victims' family members that crusaded for improved safety standards in skyscrapers. The Skyscraper Safety Campaign, created by Sally Regenhard, the mother of a probationary firefighter who died in the rescue effort, had the ostensible mission to fight for greater safety in tall buildings, and its members complained bitterly about the Port Authority's exemption from New York City building codes. The twin towers originally had no sprinkler systems, although they were added later; however, in many ways the buildings met or exceeded building codes, despite the Port Authority's legal right to depart from certain code requirements. The lack of a concrete core in the towers is one factor that probably contributed to their collapse, although there is no certainty that any other form of skyscraper design could have withstood the impact of a Boeing 767 jet filled with twenty thousand gallons of kerosene fuel and the intense fires it ignited. A report on the catastrophe by the Federal Emergency Management Agency noted that the structural system of the twin towers was strong enough to have kept one of the buildings up for well over an hour after the impact of the jet, and the other for slightly under an hour, time enough for thousands of people to have fled to safety. Many other structural systems would have performed less well, the report observed.

While building codes and fire codes had been toughened considerably since the trade center was built, the Skyscraper Safety Campaign sometimes seemed to be pressing not for further improvements but for giving up on the idea of tall buildings altogether. Monica Gabrielle, whose husband, Richard, worked in the trade center and died in the attack, and who serves as cochairman of the group with Regenhard, wrote in a letter to *The New York Times* that "the rebuilding of 10 million square feet of office space is ludicrous. Who would want to go back into one of the world's tallest buildings after experiencing death knocking at the door? What incentives will lure tenants again? Are we going to allow another World Trade Center to be built on the ashes and remains of our loved ones? Are we going to let greed dictate what we, the families of the victims and citizens of New York City, will have to endure? When will we wake up and realize that our most important goal must be not to repeat history?"

There was one other group making its voice felt in the first few months, and its members had no patience for those who rejected tall buildings, for those who wanted to see the site kept free of buildings, or for those whose interests lay in using Ground Zero to further the bounds of architectural creativity. It was the small but vocal cadre that wanted to do precisely what Monica Gabrielle crusaded against, which was to "repeat history" literally by putting the World Trade Center back, just as it was. These people believed that the only proper response to the terrorist attack was to fix the city so it would look as if September 11 had never happened. Some of these people were motivated by a genuine love for the original towers, others by a certainty that any significant change in the city's skyline would be seen by the world as a capitulation to the terrorists. They organized themselves into numerous groups with names such as Build the Towers, Restoring the Twin Towers, and Build a New WTC. The most prominent group eventually took on the name Team Twin Towers, and it had an elaborate website that promoted the Yamasaki buildings as "a national monument, just like the White House, Capitol, Statue of Liberty and many other unique places in the US." The site went on to suggest that the World Trade Center towers should be considered in the category of great cultural artifacts, and it stated that "without exception, most people would argue that any national monument destroyed should be rebuilt and restored like the original. Even Afghanistan is restoring its national monuments . . . the giant statues of Buddha destroyed by the Taliban not that long ago."

The advocates of rebuilding thus cast the buildings as a quasi-religious symbol, the reconstruction of which could be justified on spiritual as much as patriotic grounds. But the people behind Team Twin Towers, whose spokesman, Jonathan Hakala, later appeared at public hearings and stated his intention to lease space on the seventy-seventh floor of a reconstructed tower, viewed the towers not only as international symbols. The site also presented the towers as urban magicians, which had rescued Lower Manhattan from a run-down, dreary state. Indeed, Team Twin Towers went so far as to claim that the World Trade Center not only was responsible for the revival of Lower Manhattan but that it should be thanked for the technological developments that brought about the boom of the nineties. "Until the Twin Towers were built, Lower Manhattan was a depressed slum. Today, it is a high-end, gentrified area populated by stock brokers, investment bankers, lawyers, accountants, and IT professionals. Not bad for a pair of buildings," the website proclaimed.

There are literally dozens of reasons why the pleas of Hakala and his cohorts were never to amount to much. From the standpoint of architecture, for all that the towers were indeed icons (if never so beloved as symbols of New York as the Empire State Building or the Chrysler Building), their aesthetic shortcomings as well as their urban-design failings are well documented. They hardly had the positive effect on Lower Manhattan that the rebuilding advocates claimed—indeed, in some ways the towers were a regressive force, not enabling the urban regeneration that later took place in Lower Manhattan neighborhoods like Tribeca but acting as a brake on it. To rebuild the buildings as they had been before September 11 would be to suggest that the architects of the twenty-first century had learned nothing since Yamasaki designed the trade center in the 1960s, and that you could do no better than to repeat the mistake of an earlier age.

The most important reason not to rebuild the original towers, however, was that while the families of the victims of the terrorist attack did not agree about everything, few of them wanted to see replicas of the buildings in which their loved ones had died. To people who were uncomfortable enough with the idea of anything built on the site, the notion of putting back the buildings as they had been seemed tasteless, even grotesque. But the very notion of a replica was itself bizarre, even to people who had lost no one on September 11. It had an unreality about it, as if New York were not a living, changing city but a kind of enormous theme park, in which make-believe buildings took precedence over real ones.

It is true that in 1902, the campanile of St. Mark's Cathedral in Venice collapsed and was rebuilt, precisely as it had been. But no one was killed in that collapse; it was a harmless, if startling, event, and it carried few other meanings with it. Putting things back so that they looked as if nothing had happened made some sense in Venice, largely because by the beginning of the twentieth century Venice had already assumed its identity as primarily a city of tourism—a city that was, for all intents and purposes, a vast and intricate stage set. If a piece of the set crumbles, you fix it and get on with the play. But New York City is not a stage set; it is a city in which real lives are led, and it is a city that cannot afford to mask the reality of the cruelest day in its entire history behind the facade of a replica of a pair of skyscrapers designed forty years ago. There is an understandable allure to performing a kind of cosmetic surgery at urban scale. But however much the purpose of architecture and urban design is to give pleasure, they cannot exist only to cover wounds or to deny that history happened. In Venice, the collapse of the St. Mark's tower was a minor event, a tiny footnote in the larger history of the city, and there is no great distinction between life in Venice during the period of the original campanile and the period of the replica. The building itself was more important than the event of its collapse, in other words. The terrorist attack on the World Trade Center on September 11, 2001, on the other hand, was a cataclysmic event, far more important to history, really, than the World Trade Center itself ever was. In New York, history is divided between the period before September 11, 2001, and the period after it. Putting the buildings back as they were would turn this equation upside down and pretend that an earth-shattering event barely occurred. If it is reasonable to say that leaving the entire site empty would make the pain of history all too present and would get in the way of the process of healing and of renewing the ongoing life of the city, then it is surely the case that replicating the twin towers would have the opposite effect—it would cause history to all but disappear.

CHAPTER 5

Listening to the City

What Matters and Who Decides?

JOHN WHITEHEAD MADE IT CLEAR to anyone who asked him in the fall of 2001 that, in his view, the Lower Manhattan Development Corporation had no preconceived agenda. Although Whitehead had spent much of his career in public service, he understood from the outset that negotiating treaties as a deputy secretary of state or discussing exchange rates as chairman of the Federal Reserve Bank of New York were not quite the same as negotiating with the myriad of different "stakeholders," as the various groups with an interest in the future of Ground Zero were coming to be called. And nothing in Whitehead's years at the helm of Goldman Sachs or his work as a philanthropist or his avocation as a serious art collector (his elegantly furnished office in a midtown skyscraper had paintings by Pissarro, Renoir, and Matisse, as well as a roomful of art-auction catalogs) fully prepared him for the task of figuring out what should be built on the site, either. Whitehead, for all his sophistication, knew relatively little about architecture and city planning. But he was a loyal and devoted New Yorker who had a visceral understanding of the virtues of urban life. He knew that an energetic street life was better than empty sidewalks, that city neighborhoods have a way of encouraging public life in a way that suburban towns rarely do, and that culture thrives in an urban environment and brings with it lots of beneficial economic activity. Whitehead did not share the feeling of Mayor Giuliani and many of the families that nothing whatsoever should be built on the trade-center site, but he knew that, whatever happened, the site could not appear to be an ordinary commercial development. He realized that his greatest challenge would be to assure that any memorial have pride of place and that it somehow be balanced with commercial buildings—in effect, making harmony between the sacred and the ordinary.

Whitehead sensed that his lack of knowledge of the development process might, under the unusual circumstances, actually be an asset. He was not a real-estate developer who, believing himself to know everything about building in New York, would be tempted to plunge ahead too fast, without engaging in long consultation with the various stakeholders, a part of the process that, however frustrating and time-consuming, would be absolutely essential politically. And neither, of course, was Whitehead an architect who might quickly develop a conceptual vision for the site in his mind and be tempted to push to realize his vision, whether or not it was in accord with the wishes of the public. The extraordinary history of Ground Zero and the unusual number of stakeholders made it clear that the planning process was not going to proceed in a normal fashion no matter who was in charge, and someone with little experience in planning would at least have the advantage of not being tempted to do things as they had been done in the past. If nothing else, Whitehead would not rush ahead. He had to learn the ropes, and the time it would take for him to do that might be a blessing, since it would slow down the process and assure that the LMDC would at least listen to the families, the residents of Lower Manhattan, and the general public before articulating any vision of its own.

Whitehead decided that the first order of business for the LMDC would quite literally be to listen. He organized several advisory councils, each containing one or more board members and representatives from various stakeholder groups: a family advisory council, a neighborhood residents advisory council, a council of small businesspeople in the area, one made up of representatives of professional firms, and another devoted to arts, education, and tourism. There was also a council on transportation and commuters, acknowledging the development corporation's intent to open the planning process to people who did not have either homes or businesses around the Ground Zero site.

Whitehead said that he did not want the board even to begin to think in terms of actual plans for the first few months. "This board is in a listening mode, and we will be until March 15," he said at the first public meeting of the board, which he convened at eight o'clock on a late January morning a few blocks from Ground Zero. The board met in a third-floor classroom in Borough of Manhattan Community College, a sprawling modern building redolent of the failed ambitions of architecture from the 1970s.

Whitehead reported to the public on the initial work of the advisory councils and asked Roland Betts and Deborah Wright, members of the LMDC board, to report on a trip they had just taken to Oklahoma City to see the recently completed memorial to the victims of the bombing of the federal building there, the 1995 event that, until September 11, had been the most devastating act of terrorism in the United States.

The design for the Oklahoma City memorial, which consists of both a museum tracing the history of the event and an abstract memorial of which the centerpiece is a series of bronze chairlike forms, each one representing one of the victims of the bombing, was selected after an architectural competition. "We had the highest praise for the inclusiveness of the process—everyone in the city could participate, and a lot of what happened is applicable to New York City," Betts said. Wright, however, pointed out how different the scale of Oklahoma City was and how much more limited the task. "They didn't have the task we had of redevelopment," she said.

"They had a unanimous vote—that's one of the things that doesn't apply here," Betts broke in.

"As to the specifics of any memorial park, I think it would be good for the public to realize that it does take a long time and not to be critical of the time it takes to develop," Whitehead said. "Major national memorials have always taken a long time. If the park is to be created on top of the actual site of the twin towers, as many feel it should be, that is on top of an excavation. If we have an international competition of architects, we must allow time to do that. If the crowds that come now are still coming in a few months, we must allow for that in our planning. It is an important place for visitors from around the country and around the world. As I observe, I see at least a third of the people are speaking other languages. This will become a place where people go, like the Statue of Liberty."

Whitehead, unlike many of the politicians speaking about Ground Zero, took pride in asking people what they thought and in walking around the site himself, unrecognized. He strolled the blocks around Ground Zero, dressed in a business suit and a beige raincoat. As he watched the tourists and eavesdropped on their conversations, he increasingly came to realize the complexity of the problem he faced. "It is extremely important that there be a time of listening before decision making," Whitehead concluded in his remarks to the board, "so that we can come up with a plan that, if it will not make everyone happy, will at least make everyone potentially happy."

Potentially happy is not the sort of phrase politicians use—they are more inclined either to promise total happiness, without qualifications, or to avoid the subject of emotions altogether. But it captured Whitehead's sensibility perfectly. He did not want to promise more than he could deliver, and what he wanted to deliver more than anything to the process of rebuilding was an air of reason, moderation, and rational judgment.

Reason, moderation, and rational judgment are not qualities often evident in the building process in New York City, however, and they were hardly visible at all at an event a few days after the board meeting, a public hearing on the future of the site organized by Community Board 1 along with the Civic Alliance, the Downtown Alliance, and the LMDC. The hearing was held in the auditorium of Stuyvesant High School in Battery Park City, the enormous public high school for gifted students that is almost adjacent to Ground

Zero. Stuyvesant had been evacuated on September 11 and had reopened only a few weeks before; although its building suffered no damage, it was one of those institutions that by their very proximity were closely identified with the terrorist attack. The community board was less interested in symbolism, however, than in the fact that Stuyvesant was the only public building close to Ground Zero with a large auditorium, and its nine hundred seats were filled on the night of January 29, 2002.

Madelyn Wils, the chairman of the community board who also was a member of the LMDC board, introduced the hearing. "You have a lot of ears tonight—you are going to be heard," she told the audience. She was seated on the stage, along with Robert Yaro, Carl Weisbrod, Louis Tomson of the LMDC, Ric Bell, the head of the New York chapter of the American Institute of Architects who was there to represent the New York New Visions group, and Beverly Willis, the architect who had started Rebuild Downtown Our Town. Also there "to listen" were Roland Betts; Mayor Bloomberg's deputy mayor for economic development and rebuilding, Daniel Doctoroff; C. Virginia Fields, the Manhattan borough president; Geoffrey Wharton, Larry Silverstein's executive in charge of rebuilding the trade center; and Paul Goldstein, the manager of Community Board 1.

The hearing never lost its decorum, but it quickly turned into a rambling, unfocused shopping list of desires for the site. The audience consisted largely of Community Board 1's constituency, Lower Manhattan residents, and if they had anything in common, it was a desire to express the feeling that the neighborhood belonged to them at least as much as it belonged to office workers, the families of the victims, or the rest of the world. Typical was one of the first speakers, a man who lived on Franklin Street in Tribeca. "My strong feeling is that the neighborhood needs more green space, more ball fields," he said. "I feel a memorial needs to include large areas of land in which we can all reflect on what happened."

A woman who said she had lived at the corner of Harrison and Greenwich streets in Tribeca since 1975—long before that neighborhood began to gentrify—said, "Those of us who live and work in the city have never had the luxury of shopping malls, and the World Trade Center is where we went [to shop]. We need some small place where we can pretend we are not just trapped in New York." She concluded, to applause, by calling for "a minimall." Another neighborhood speaker called for "mixed use—stores, museums, etc.," and one woman said, "We don't want it to be just a giant memorial that will mean nothing to our kids. They have to enjoy what's down there. I'm in favor of a memorial on part of the space, but my feeling is not to go crazy and use, like, eight acres and take away from what the residents of Lower Manhattan want."

Several people asked for the restoration of Greenwich Street, the important north-south street that had been cut off by the superblock of the original World Trade Center and further blocked by the placement of the slab of 7 World Trade Center like a wall across it. Offsetting their comments, however, were those of a few representatives of the "put it back the way it was" faction, whose advocacy of rebuilding the twin towers was greeted with a combination of applause and jeers. For a few minutes during the hearing, it seemed as if what all of the speakers wanted was to see the clock turned back at Ground Zero and that they differed only on which period of its history they preferred to return to—the pre–World Trade Center neighborhood with its grid of tight, narrow streets and small blocks or the World Trade Center itself and its gargantuan superblock.

A lone progressive voice was Michael Sorkin, the architect, teacher, critic, and writer. Sorkin offered the most articulate argument in favor of avoiding commercial development with alternate plans that would benefit the city more in the long run. "I believe Ground Zero is sacred ground, not a place to build," he said, and explained his rationale for dispersing the commercial development that had been on the site to other areas around the city that were in need of commercial regeneration. His thoughtful idea seemed to go over the heads of most of the crowd, just as it was too visionary and impractical for most public officials. Sorkin was followed by a speaker who lived in Battery Park City who said, "I wish they would build the World Trade Center again, as tall or taller—otherwise there will not be closure, and we will not stand up to what has happened."

There were calls to devote the site to institutes for world peace, to put a pair of sequoias in the place of the towers, to build three

110-story towers rather than two, and to turn the site into a meadow. The tone of the hearing seemed to have been captured, inadvertently, by a woman from the land-use subcommittee of Community Board 1 who said, "There are no good or bad ideas."

One of the only speakers who seemed to capture the crowd's attention was Monica Iken, who had been assuming a larger and larger public profile in recent weeks as a spokesperson for the families of the victims. "Their souls cry out, you can't build there, it is hallowed ground," she said. "What message do we send to our children? We care about our people, not about the money. Those towers are gone, and they are not coming back. We should not rebuild on their remains—think about what message that will send to the world."

While he listened passively at the Community Board 1 hearing—presumably trying, like the other officials on the stage, not to look too bored by the long train of earnest speakers—Robert Yaro had been working on plans for another kind of event that he hoped would better gauge the real public sentiment about Ground Zero than an old-style public hearing. There would be plenty of other hearings—the Lower Manhattan Development Corporation, as a public agency, would be required to hold them—but Yaro realized that such events were usually as rambling and unfocused as this one; while most of the speakers were well-intentioned, they were not always the most thoughtful citizens or the most articulate ones. Yaro and his colleagues at the Regional Plan Association and the Civic Alliance conceived of a project that came to be known as Listening to the City, which would ultimately come to have a powerful, even profound, effect on the Ground Zero planning process, if not on the entire direction of American urban planning itself. Listening to the City was conceived as a modern-day variation on the public hearing—a long, highly structured information session under the direction of a trained facilitator who would encourage citizens to express their thoughts about Ground Zero in a coherent fashion and would ask questions that the group could answer using electronic polling technology. With the help of the Rockefeller Brothers Fund, which gave the Civic Alliance several hundred thousand dollars, and the Milano Graduate School of New School University, Yaro organized Listening to the City, a series of events run by an organization called AmericaSpeaks, which specializes in running technologically advanced public meetings.

The first Listening to the City event took place on February 7, 2002, at the South Street Seaport, just south of the Brooklyn Bridge, the very site designated in the original World Trade Center plans. Despite the irony of its location, the event did not resonate with a sense of history; in fact, it was relatively low-key and offered little hint of how great the impact of Listening to the City would eventually come to be. The event was held in a large hall that had been built by the Rouse Company as part of an urban shopping mall, and it had been filled with round tables. The six hundred registrants, who were a mix of Lower Manhattan residents, members of civic organizations from around the metropolitan area, foundation executives, civic activists, and politicians, were organized into small, diverse groups at each table. After a word of welcome from Bob Kerrey, the former senator from Nebraska who had recently moved to New York to become president of New School University, the assemblage heard from Yaro, who said, "This is your day—we've all heard from the pundits and the experts, and now it is your turn to generate ideas for the world's first twenty-first century urban center." Yaro then pointed out the presence of officials from the Metropolitan Transportation Authority, the Port Authority, the Lower Manhattan Development Corporation, and other agencies who, he told the audience, "are all here to listen."

It was hard to be certain whether the point of the event was really to generate ideas or just to create the impression of democracy, since the officials in charge seemed inclined to pander to the public, congratulating themselves for listening so carefully to the citizenry, even before the event began. They seemed almost to want to give the impression that they believed city planning to be some kind of referendum, as if the best way to build a city is by popular vote.

Charles Gargano, a close colleague of Governor Pataki who is the head of the Empire State Development Corporation, spoke after Yaro. "New York has always been a unique city in which everyone has always had a right to speak out and all opinions count,"

Gargano said. "Because of you, New York is regarded as the preeminent city of the world. Your remarks will matter as we make a triumphant space weaving in with a great memorial."

Gargano was also vice chairman of the Port Authority, and thus he was the only public official other than the governor himself whose job encompassed both the Lower Manhattan Development Corporation—technically a division of the Empire State Development Corporation—and the Port Authority. He was also, among all the speakers here, the ultimate insider, the one who was most accustomed to making decisions behind closed doors. Gargano rarely spoke in public, and his presence seemed, if nothing else, to suggest that he had decided that it was politically useful to appear supportive of public involvement in the planning process and that Listening to the City was the right vehicle with which to do this.

Gargano was officially John Whitehead's boss, although that was something of a technical distinction, since Whitehead's high public profile allowed him to function with a fair degree of independence. Gargano was essentially a political operative for Governor Pataki, whereas Whitehead, perhaps alone among the people in charge of the Ground Zero process, owed the governor little. It would probably be more accurate to describe Gargano as Whitehead's opposite number, a powerful functionary whose name was little known to the public, whereas what power Whitehead had in the planning process came largely from his public identity.

Gargano ended his remarks with a word of praise for Larry Silverstein, who had announced his intention to begin construction on a new office tower to replace the destroyed 7 World Trade Center. While Silverstein's new building, which was being designed by David Childs, did not have to go through as elaborate a planning process as the buildings that were technically on the Ground Zero site itself, it would still have to be reviewed by the LMDC. "Mr. Silverstein's plan to not hesitate in rebuilding Number Seven is a beginning of this process," Gargano declared, but many people were not entirely sure that they were prepared to endorse Silverstein's plan before they had even seen it.

As soon as Gargano finished speaking, Marilyn Jordan Taylor, David Childs's partner and one of the most active members of the

New York New Visions architects' group, left the meeting. Many other prominent people also slipped away as the morning went on; as the formal program began, it took on more of the feeling of a large-scale encounter group. It was run by the head of America-Speaks, Carolyn Lukensmeyer, a patient, forceful woman who seemed to address the group as if it were a large junior high school class. She frequently used words like *visioning* and *dialoguing* and asked the group as a whole to applaud different subgroups in the room. She began by asking the audience to identify themselves racially by pushing buttons in the electronic control panels at their seats, and a few seconds later the instant polling equipment revealed that the group was 71 percent Caucasian. Forty-five percent of the participants turned out to have annual incomes of more than one hundred thousand dollars.

Lukensmeyer asked the participants why they had decided to come to Listening to the City. It turned out that 4.7 percent were relatives of victims of the terrorist attack. "Will you please give a round of applause for family members," Lukensmeyer said. Another 16.3 percent survived the attack themselves, and 25 percent had been near the World Trade Center on September 11, 2001. The instant survey also revealed that 4.5 percent of the participants were rescue workers, who received a spontaneous round of applause before Lukensmeyer could ask for it, and 19.6 percent lived in Lower Manhattan. Architects, planners, and other people involved in the rebuilding effort made up 52.8 percent of the participants, and 19.6 percent of the participants worked in Lower Manhattan. Almost 60 percent of the participants were there, they said, simply as "interested citizens," with no formal connection to Lower Manhattan.

"Let's have a round of applause for all of our reasons for being here," Carolyn Lukensmeyer said.

At that point, she asked the participants at each table to begin working with the facilitator who was seated with them. The groups, which consisted of ten to twelve people, were intentionally diverse—Eli Evans, the head of the Charles H. Revson Foundation, a New York City–based charity with assets of hundreds of millions of dollars, found himself seated with a woman who had been an office cleaner at Cantor Fitzgerald in the north tower; firemen shared tables with liberal activists, architects with financial analysts, Chinatown activists with Upper West Side liberals. Each group was asked to think first in terms of the most important issues that planners had to face and to come up with some suggestions, which the facilitator would transmit by laptop computer to a central clearing point in the room. "We will see where this converges, where we have a shared vision," Lukensmeyer said. "When we do, the computer operator will tap it in," she said, and then, as if to anticipate criticism that consensus would not always yield the best ideas, she added, "if there is a strongly held idea, it will not be lost."

"Now, get out of the conversation mode, take a couple of deep breaths," Lukensmeyer said. "I want you to actually imagine it's 2012, and Lower Manhattan has been rebuilt in the best possible way. Take the next three, four, or five minutes to express your values, your vision, about what Lower Manhattan should be like ten years from now."

Out of all of this, not surprisingly, nothing particularly fresh or different emerged. The groups favored mixed-use, lively neighborhoods and attention to both the commemorative aspects of a memorial and the commercial aspects of the city. The conclusions of Listening to the City were earnest and well-meaning, if unexceptional, but the event did help to move public sentiment closer to a compromise between the extreme voices that had predominated earlier in the process, when the discussion was polarized between those who wanted Ground Zero to be entirely a memorial and those who felt that restoring the city's commercial life was the only priority that mattered on the site. The New York New Visions group had already rejected both of these extreme views, and so had the LMDC, and a compromise was inevitable. But that idea had not gotten through to many members of the public, however, and this event helped in that process.

It served another worthwhile function as well. However much the tone of the event felt like a soft, even touchy-feely, encounter-group session, it helped wean the public away from the notion of expressing its vision for Ground Zero in terms of an actual building design. AmericaSpeaks and Carolyn Lukensmeyer did not confuse program and process with architecture, as Max Protetch and the architects who had participated in his show a month earlier had done; they knew that program and process had to come first, and they asked the public to think in those terms. As a result, the Listening to the City event recommended such things as a new transportation hub for Lower Manhattan, greater pedestrian amenity in the area, improved local services, more public open space, more cultural facilities, distinguished architecture, and a memorial that honored all of the dead and would speak clearly to the living as well. These conclusions may have been vague and general, but many of them pointed the way to the conclusions the LMDC was to reach in the months to follow.

The one issue on which the participants on February 7 seemed to differ significantly was that of the skyline. They all mourned the loss of an iconic symbol, but they disagreed as to whether restoring a tall skyline element should be a first priority of any new plan. Some people felt strongly that any plan for Ground Zero had to include a building or a tower as tall as or taller than the twin towers, and others believed that building tall was too great a risk both in economic and safety terms and that New Yorkers were wisest to accept the loss of a punctuation mark on the skyline as a price of living in the twenty-first century.

CHAPTER 6

Fitting It All on Sixteen Acres

Alexander Garvin had been trained as an architect at Yale, but after a year in Paris and a brief period working in Philip Johnson's office in the late 1960s, he decided that buildings did not interest him as much as the cities they were in. When Garvin was twenty-seven, he started teaching city planning at his alma mater, and he developed a course that had an unusual slant. Unlike many professors of city planning, Garvin did not view cities mainly in terms of their physical layout. He focused less on teaching students about the form of cities as on the process by which they come together. Garvin understood that cities are rarely pure works of design and that they take shape as the result of a myriad of political, social, economic, and aesthetic forces. He also realized that architecture students, especially at institutions like Yale, are rarely encouraged to think about any aspect of city planning except the aesthetic—or, when they are, it is usually by people who are interested only in politics and economics and the technical side of real estate and construction and have so little understanding of the aesthetic side of architecture that they can never explain how all of the different forces that shape cities interact with one another. Garvin had no desire to denigrate aesthetics. But he wanted to figure out a way to teach architecture students to understand and respect the realities of real-estate development that would not ignore aesthetics but simply put pure design in perspective and acknowledge how much of a role it does, or does not, have in the real world.

Garvin is hardly a philistine. He has lived in New York for most of his life, spends the majority of his free evenings at the opera, and prowls the museums on his free afternoons. When he began his teaching career, his favorite twentieth-century architects were Le Corbusier, Mies van der Rohe, and Frank Lloyd Wright, and his favorite nineteenth-century architect was John Nash, who designed many of the terraces and great blocks of row houses in Georgian London. Garvin wanted to teach students how to make the system work so that there would be more distinguished architecture built, not less. He realized that there would never be many architects so brilliant that they could completely transcend political and economic realities the way that Le Corbusier and Wright so often managed to do, but there were plenty who could produce better architecture if they understood how to maneuver within the worlds of real estate and politics. Teaching students how to do that, Garvin decided, would be his mission.

He invented a course called the Study of the City, and the basis of it was a series of games he devised, in which students spend the term playing out a scenario of a real-estate development—development of a suburban shopping center, perhaps, or an urban redevelopment project, or the conversion of an abandoned industrial area to new uses. Each student is assigned a role: one might be a commercial developer, for example, and others the architect, a public official charged with giving the project approval, a citizen leading an organization that was challenging the project's validity, a union leader eager for the jobs the project would provide, an environmental activist, and a banker who had put up money for the project. Garvin set some parameters that gave each student's role a logical starting point—the project might be for much-needed subsidized housing units yet in an environmentally sensitive area, for example—and had the students research their roles. Several weeks into the course, students assumed their roles and began to struggle over the fate of the project.

For most of his career, Garvin was known mainly at Yale, even though he held various other jobs, including a long stint in New York City government as a deputy commissioner of housing and urban redevelopment in the 1980s. His reputation expanded to a somewhat wider circle in 1996, when his book, *The American City: What Works, What Doesn't,* was published. The book is very much like Garvin himself: straightforward, sure of itself, no-nonsense, and not suited for any neat ideological package. It isn't prodevelopment, it isn't antidevelopment; it isn't quite in the mold of Jane Jacobs, but it is hardly anti-Jacobs, either, since more of Garvin's values parallel those of Jacobs than depart from them. Garvin never mentions the World Trade Center in his book, but he is highly skeptical about the benefits of large-scale skyscraper developments that obliterate the existing city in favor of superblocks, as the trade center did. "Their most serious error was to assume that a new city could be created one superblock at a time," Garvin wrote. "The cultural and consumer activities needed by any successful city require a critical mass. . . . It is also a misunderstanding to equate spacious public open spaces and shiny glass towers with urban renewal." One of the projects Garvin reviewed in detail in his book was Constitution Plaza in Hartford, a complex of glass office buildings he describes as "an independent enclave built on a platform that covers a 1875-car garage. . . . [It was] an enclave that was designed to be separate from the rest of downtown Hartford. Workers and visitors can park in the project and go directly to their offices without having to set foot in the city." Constitution Plaza was conceived in the mid-1950s as one of the first large-scale urban-renewal efforts directed at improving a troubled downtown and was completed in the early sixties, just as the World Trade Center was being designed. Garvin's view of it said a great deal about how he would view Yamasaki's towers in New York.

Yet Garvin believed that even if many of the large-scale, overbearing interventions of the Robert Moses era were wrongly conceived, that did not mean that planners should retreat and do nothing. Some things, Garvin believed, have to be done by the public sector, and the goal of urban development should be not to have the government try to do everything but to target key public investments so that they will inspire private development to follow. "Urban planning should be defined as *public action that will produce a sustained and widespread private market reaction,*" Garvin wrote in his book. "While urban planners are in the change business, it is others who will make that change: civic leaders, interest groups, community organizations, property owners, developers, bankers, lawyers, architects, engineers, elected and appointed public officials—the list is endless."

Over the years, Garvin taught several people who came to assume prominent roles in city planning, such as Con Howe, who became the head of planning for the City of Los Angeles, and Joseph Rose, whom Rudolph Giuliani appointed as chairman of the New York City Planning Commission. The rise to prominence of many of Garvin's students affected his own career. Rose engineered his appointment to the New York City Planning Commission in 1994, and then, in 1996, Garvin met Daniel Doctoroff, who was to have a profound effect on the rest of his life.

Doctoroff, a wealthy, self-made investment banker, was a passionate civic activist, and he became obsessed by the notion that New York was capable of hosting a Summer Olympics. He called Garvin to ask his view of the viability of this, and after Garvin told him he thought it was a good idea, Doctoroff said that almost everyone else he had approached thought he was crazy. He asked Garvin how he would go about laying out the facilities. "I haven't a clue," Garvin told him, but Doctoroff, far from being dismayed by Garvin's candor, took it as a sign that the two could work together. He hired Garvin to put together a small staff to oversee planning for a bid for the 2008 Olympics, which evolved into a larger organization that prepared a bid for the 2012 Olympics. Garvin figured out a plan by which the Olympic athletes could be housed in a geographically central location on the Queens waterfront and could travel by ferry or train to the locations of athletic events around the region. The main pattern was like a huge, distorted X—one arm of it was the East River, and the other the train lines crossing from New Jersey to

Sunnyside, Queens—and so Garvin named his plan the Olympic X. It was adopted and became the centerpiece of the New York City bid that late in 2002 was designated by the United States Olympic Committee over bids by San Francisco, Washington, and Houston as the American proposal to the International Olympic Committee.

When Michael Bloomberg was elected mayor at the end of 2001, Doctoroff was named deputy mayor for economic development and rebuilding. As the official who would oversee the city's planning efforts, Doctoroff tried to engineer Garvin's appointment as chairman of the City Planning Commission, where he would have replaced his former student, Joseph Rose. Garvin was deeply disappointed when the job went instead to another commissioner, Amanda Burden, a good friend of the new mayor. It turned out, however, that Garvin was lucky. In January, he got a call from Stefan Pryor, an associate of John Whitehead, asking if he would meet with Whitehead and Louis Tomson, the Pataki operative whom the governor had named president of the Lower Manhattan Development Corporation. The new body needed an experienced planner to serve as vice president for design and planning, and Whitehead wanted to know if Garvin was interested. It was a job that had the potential to be a great deal more influential than the city-planning chairmanship. Since the development corporation had not yet determined any real course of action—it was still very much in what John Whitehead had defined as the "listening mode"—the chief planner was in a position to have an enormous amount of authority over the direction that the Ground Zero planning process took. Garvin set only two conditions: he said he wanted to be able to continue teaching part-time at Yale, and he wanted to be free to advocate a major new rail station for downtown, which he was convinced had to be a part of any renewal plan. When Whitehead and Tomson agreed, Garvin did not hesitate to say yes. It was in some ways the job he had spent his lifetime preparing for.

Garvin reported for work in the second week of February in the LMDC's temporary offices at 1 Liberty Plaza, a huge, boxy office tower overlooking Ground Zero that happened to be owned by John Zuccotti's company, Brookfield. While the corporation waited for its offices on the twentieth floor to be pulled together, the small staff worked in somewhat grander space upstairs that it borrowed from Cleary Gottlieb, a large law firm that occupied most of the building's upper floors and had a few offices to spare.

"I arrived here Monday morning—I have no staff yet, no real office, no phone, and everybody wants a plan finished instantly," Garvin said two days after he started work. "I've got to find a way to implement everybody's agendas—the city government, the state government, the residents, the families. How you do this, I don't know, but part of my job will be to figure out the alternatives."

As he spoke, it became clear that Garvin had already thought a great deal about the process. "I see our job as doing five things," he said.

> First, we need to create such a magnet in Lower Manhattan that it becomes the place everybody wants to go. Second, we need an appropriate memorial for the people who perished, and that cannot be done without an international competition of sorts. Third, we need to reconnect Lower Manhattan to the Ground Zero site, and I don't think it is as simple as saying that the nineteenth-century street grid has to be repeated. We have to remember that Lower Manhattan wasn't a very pleasant place in 1932. Fourth, we have to expand the market area for Lower Manhattan—it is connected to New Jersey by the PATH trains and to the city by subway, but what about Westchester and Long Island? And fifth, what are the things we have to do to help local businesses in the rest of Lower Manhattan?

Garvin switched into his teaching mode. "I have a model in mind, for a war memorial that changed a major world city," he said. "Do you know what it is? In 1859, Milan held a competition to make a war memorial, and it led to the Galleria. If we can do as well as they did, I will be very happy."

Garvin's initial assignment was to work with David Childs and Larry Silverstein on the design of 7 World Trade Center. Childs had been working on designs for some time for a new "Number Seven," and it was clear that the key issue was going to be how slender the tower should be. Nobody, not even Silverstein, wanted to put back the building as it had been—the forty-seven-story, beige granite slab of the original, designed by Emery Roth & Sons, was not only dull but too bulky by far. The old Number Seven seemed less like a building than a gargantuan wall across Greenwich Street. Before Number Seven went up, there were still open views down through the World Trade Center site, even if there was no real street. The blocked view mattered especially to residents of Tribeca, the old industrial and warehouse neighborhood that had gentrified completely in recent years. When Number Seven went up, there were not enough people living in Tribeca to mount a serious opposition to Larry Silverstein's decision to wall off the street, but by 2001 the situation was entirely different. Greenwich Street was an important north-south artery, filled with restored lofts and several new apartment buildings; their occupants did not want to see it blocked off by an office tower.

Putting Greenwich Street back had come to symbolize a reversal of the superblock notion of planning that had motivated Minoru Yamasaki and the Port Authority in the 1960s. If anything could stand for the triumph of Jane Jacobs's view of the city over Robert Moses's, it was putting back the streets that had been arbitrarily taken away more than thirty years before. And no street seemed more ripe for return than Greenwich, which during the years of the World Trade Center's existence had been divided into two disconnected segments: a short, stubby Greenwich Street that extended for a few blocks south of the trade-center site, and a longer section that began just north of the trade center and went uptown to Gansevoort Street in the West Village.

David Childs was trying to figure out how to reconcile Larry Silverstein's demand for a significant amount of office space in the new Number Seven with the need to make a thinner tower if Greenwich Street were reopened. There was another complication as well. The site of Number Seven was above a Con Edison electrical substation that had ten transformers, and not only was the utility resistant to moving, it was under pressure to restore the substation as soon as possible. Design decisions were going to be made for the base of Number Seven that affected the possible position and size of the tower itself, and Con Edison could not wait indefinitely while Silverstein and Childs mulled over their options or negotiated with the neighborhood.

Childs knew that he wanted to have what architects call a view corridor down Greenwich Street, and he first designed the building as a fairly large slab with an open archway at the base, a kind of modern version of the arch at the eastern end of Chambers Street in McKim, Mead & White's Municipal Building just a few blocks away from Ground Zero. Childs soon realized that there was little point to this idea, since from a few blocks north on Greenwich Street—which is where most residents of Tribeca would see it from—Number Seven would still look like a big slab. He tried another version, with a wide glass tower cantilevered over a narrow, stainless-steel base. Silverstein was pleased with this version, but Childs was still uncomfortable with it, since from a block or two uptown it would still seem to sit in the middle of the street, obstructing the view nearly as much as the old Number Seven had. The more Childs thought about it, the less sure he became that simply opening up the bottom of the building solved the problem.

Childs found an unexpected ally in Garvin. "I was on the subway going uptown to meet Silverstein for the first time, and I realized that I had to think of Number Seven as a test case," Garvin said. He got off the train at Grand Central, walked to Silverstein's office on Fifth Avenue, and told the developer and Childs that the LMDC would not be likely to approve the design unless the building was reshaped to allow Greenwich Street to run unobstructed through the Ground Zero site. The unspoken implication of Garvin's statement was that if the developer did not cooperate with the LMDC's requests now, things would not get any easier for him when he sought to win approval for buildings on Ground Zero itself, where the stakes were much higher. Opening Greenwich Street would take more than pressure from Garvin, however. If the restored street ran through the site and Number Seven became smaller, then the Con Edison power station would have to be smaller as well, and Garvin had no sway with Con Edison. He had to ask his boss, Lou Tomson—who as a longtime colleague of Pataki's was widely known to speak for the governor—to intervene with the state-regulated utility to accommodate a rearrangement of the transformers. Before this happened, Garvin and Tomson had to learn something about how much space electric transformers need. It turned out that they do not all have to be placed together, but Con Edison did not, at first, volunteer this information to the planners. The ten transformers in the power station could be split into two groups of five, which Childs could place on opposite sides of the building, allowing room in the middle for the lobby and the elevator core.

"Planning in the city is not as simple as a set of urban-design principles," Garvin said later, "and electric power in Lower Manhattan is more important than a view corridor. But why can't we have both? If you push hard enough, you can find a way."

Garvin, some time later, recalled how much the process had been like the games he devises for his students. "I am now living in the middle of the most complicated game of all," he said. "Never in my wildest dreams did I imagine a game that would be like this one."

Childs produced a tower in the form of an elegant, slender glass parallelogram as the new 7 World Trade Center, and he took particular pride in convincing Silverstein to commission the artist Jenny Holzer to design an art piece for the lobby and the artist Jamie Carpenter to design a sculptural form in glass that would cover the vents of the Con Edison substation. Childs saw the new building as a symbol of a more sophisticated attitude on Silverstein's part that he hoped would extend to whatever bigger structures were put up on Ground Zero itself.

It would be a long time before there would be any designs for buildings on Ground Zero, however—or at least before there would be designs with any kind of official standing. Numerous civic groups, including the Civic Alliance, openly questioned Silverstein's determination to rebuild ten and a half million square feet of office space in Lower Manhattan at a time when the area was hardly any longer the city's sole financial district. Many of the businesses that had always been the neighborhood's mainstay were increasingly choosing to disperse their staffs throughout the region. Some of the major New York–based banks had moved to Midtown Manhattan decades ago, long before the events of September 11 began to focus vorld's attention on the state of that part of the city, and most e financial services companies that had chosen to remain own, such as Merrill Lynch, had placed most of their back-office and data-processing facilities in less costly locations in New Jersey and Brooklyn. Who was going to occupy these millions of square feet of expensive real estate? Wasn't office space in Lower Manhattan a declining asset even before September 11?

No one had a clear answer to those questions except to remind doubters that nothing was going to be built quickly, that even if more than ten million square feet of office space were constructed it would not be all at once but in stages over ten to twenty years, and that real estate had always involved a certain degree of risk. In reality, the optimists had no data. They could offer only their hope that the market would grow in time and that the restoration of Lower Manhattan as an appealing neighborhood would serve to reverse the forces that had been leading businesses away from Lower Manhattan for more than half a century.

None of this served as much of an answer to those who preferred other kinds of uses on the site—housing, for example, for which the demand in Lower Manhattan only seemed to grow. The increased interest in living in Lower Manhattan on the part of young professionals, many with families, was obviously all to the good in terms of the neighborhood's future, but it made the Port Authority and Larry Silverstein's insistence on seeing Ground Zero mainly as a site for enormous office developments seem all the more curious. They appeared determined to build not the housing that the market wanted but the office space that it did not. The only plausible justification for choosing offices over housing lay in the hope that since much of the new housing downtown in recent years has consisted not of new construction but of conversions of old office buildings into apartments, a continuation of that trend would eventually squeeze out many businesses that wanted to stay in the financial district, who would become prime candidates to occupy new buildings. It was a pleasing thought, since the transformation of obsolete office buildings into new residences has been one of the best things to have happened to Lower Manhattan in the last generation. But the fact is that while the trend is likely to continue, many of the old office buildings best suited to be turned into housing had already been converted, and there were hardly enough office tenants in other old office buildings to fill the millions of square feet of new space that Silverstein planned to build.

In the earliest months of the planning process, when there was still strong pressure for leaving the entire site empty, it seemed difficult to imagine that people would actually want to live on Ground Zero. Not only was it sacred ground, it was too close to the horror, a constant reminder of death. Who could want to go to sleep every night knowing that they were on the very plot of land on which thousands perished?

The connection between the site and catastrophe grew considerably weaker as the months passed, fading as the clearing and recovery efforts turned Ground Zero into something that looked more like a construction site than a place of apocalypse. But it remained strong enough to discourage serious talk of putting housing there in the early months of 2002, which is probably when an effective argument to replace some of the office space with housing would have had to have been made.

A further factor that discouraged the planners from putting housing into the program for Ground Zero was an amendment to the Port Authority's charter, negotiated by Austin Tobin when the World Trade Center was being planned, that barred it from developing housing. While there was some question as to the interpretation of this restriction—it might not have prevented the agency from allowing others to put housing on land that it leased to them, for example—no public official seemed particularly eager to challenge the Port Authority on this front, not even Mayor Bloomberg, who at one point early in the planning process had called for putting housing on the site. "A forty-year-old deal between Austin Tobin and Nelson Rockefeller is shaping the future of Lower Manhattan," Robert Yaro said. "If we feel that housing is appropriate, we ought to be able to have it there."

Indeed, the Port Authority initially resisted suggestions that Ground Zero be used for anything at all other than the functions that had been there before September 11, arguing, as Silverstein himself did, that the lease was a contractual obligation to replace what had been on the site. But the Port Authority did not challenge the notion that a memorial to the victims of the attack would have to be built, even though there was no mention of a memorial in the lease. Neither did the Port Authority express any objection to improved transit connections, since that would benefit its own PATH trains and could also be justified as an economic-development tool for the area.

The agency was also prepared to have plenty of retail shopping on the site. That, too, qualified as a preexisting use. There had been an enormous shopping complex underneath the World Trade Center, which was originally intended for commuters but which came, over time, to function as a kind of mall for residents of Tribeca and Battery Park City, who subsequently missed the presence of large national chain stores when they returned to their homes after September 11. Actually, the Port Authority had little choice about including a substantial number of retail stores as a component in the rebuilt Ground Zero, since at the same time it made the deal to lease the twin towers to Larry Silverstein it had concluded a companion deal that gave control of the retail area to Westfield America Trust, an Australia-based owner of suburban shopping malls. Westfield's lease gave it the right to rebuild in the event of loss, as Silverstein could do. Westfield had something more, however. Its lease was written in anticipation of an expansion of the retail component of the World Trade Center to some portion of the street-level plaza in front of the twin towers, and so it permitted Westfield to expand the existing retail space by several hundred thousand square feet. At the time the towers were destroyed, the underground retail space netted about nine hundred dollars per square foot, which made it one of the most profitable malls in the United States. The Lowy family, the eastern European immigrants who built Westfield into a multinational real-estate power, were not eager to give up such a lucrative franchise.

The Lowys had made their fortune with suburban malls, however, and they tended not to think in the kind of urban-design terms that Alexander Garvin and David Childs did. They wanted to build something as close to a suburban mall as possible at Ground Zero, and they had little interest in the notion of restoring streets to the site. If the streets had to come back, the Lowys argued, they should not be required to line them with shops but instead should be permitted to bridge them with a huge, enclosed mall. Even Larry Silverstein, who was not always particularly attuned to urban design but had a good sense of the shifting political currents in New York, came to agree with Childs and Garvin about putting streets back and was comfortable with placing retail storefronts along the restored streets, much as they would be in a traditional New York street like Madison Avenue. The Lowys objected strenuously. They rejected Childs's plans for the site even after they had been approved by Silverstein, and for a while in the beginning of 2002 Westfield was in a deadlock with the other parties in the rebuilding effort.

The dispute over what form the shopping area would take became quite bitter—Childs, who prided himself on getting along with almost everyone in the process, gritted his teeth and changed the subject when the name of Frank Lowy, Westfield's chairman, came up—but it was something of a sideshow, since the main issue was still office space. On that question, the Port Authority was inclined to agree with Larry Silverstein. The agency had counted on the income from the site, and it had no desire to find another source of the ten million dollars per month in rent that Silverstein was paying. The Port Authority's view was that Silverstein had a lease, and the lease entitled him to rebuild; the only questions from the agency's standpoint concerned what the site should eventually look like and how to integrate a memorial and an improved transit hub with the office buildings.

Garvin did not fight the Port Authority, at least not on the matter of office space. Neither did Roland Betts, who had taken charge of the LMDC board's planning committee and was rapidly assuming a more active role in the design process. "It's the Port's site from an ownership standpoint—and what's the point of developing a whole plan and getting into a pissing contest with the Port because they don't like it?" Betts said. Both he and Garvin started out believing that if the Port Authority had the right to determine the program for the site—that is, what functions would occupy the land and how much space would be devoted to each—the LMDC would have the right to figure out what the whole thing would look like. Don't challenge the Port Authority too much on its program, and it won't challenge you too much on the architecture, went the reasoning. It was a modus vivendi that seemed to make sense also because the Port Authority had a poor record of architectural patronage and was not noted for its receptiveness to current planning ideas. It probably would not want to interfere too much with architectural design as long as its cash flow was guaranteed. Betts and Garvin also knew that even in its shaken, post–September 11 state, the Port Authority was still large and powerful and that they had to pick their battles. Convincing the agency that it should agree to put housing on the former site of the World Trade Center was not a fight Garvin felt he had a chance of winning, especially if his bosses, John Whitehead and Lou Tomson, not to mention Betts, were disinclined to fight on that score themselves. So Garvin, too, accepted the Port Authority's program and took it as a given that the site would have to contain ten and a half million square feet of office space. The challenge was to fit it all in along with new elements such as a memorial and some improved transit facilities.

To help him do this, Garvin asked several architectural firms in the middle of March 2002 to submit proposals to serve as consultants to the LMDC. They would help the corporation study various design options for accommodating the Port Authority's demands. The Port Authority objected strenuously, however, to the fact that Garvin had acted unilaterally, arguing that the development corporation seemed to be presuming a total authority over design that it had never been given. In what was the LMDC's most embarrassing setback to date, Garvin was forced to rescind his request for proposals shortly after he issued it. A couple of weeks later, the request was reissued by the Port Authority in a more bureaucratic-sounding version, with responses to be reviewed by the Port Authority as well as by the LMDC. The message was perfectly clear: the Port Authority was in charge. Garvin and the LMDC could not even hire Ground Zero's architect on their own. The presumption that if the LMDC left the program intact the Port Authority would not challenge it on design matters was wrong.

Lou Tomson and Joseph Seymour, the executive director of the Port Authority, negotiated a memorandum of understanding in which the LMDC agreed not to attempt to unilaterally impose a plan for the World Trade Center site. The memorandum was not, however, completely one-sided. The Port Authority, for its part, agreed to give up the total independence with which it had traditionally operated and to work with the LMDC. The memorandum also formalized the Port Authority's commitment to set aside some of Ground Zero for a memorial, and it contained two significant new concessions: the Port Authority agreed to include some cultural facilities on the site as well as to accept the potential reopening of some of the streets that had been removed when the trade center was built. Both ideas had been widely discussed for months, but until the memorandum was negotiated the Port Authority had not agreed to either one of them.

Although Roland Betts clearly believed that the LMDC would, in the end, prevail—"the Port Authority acknowledges that the ultimate authority is the LMDC," Betts said—the areas of cooperation were minor compared to the areas in which the Port Authority seemed to have the upper hand. The single most important aspect of the rebuilding process—the Port Authority's insistence on rebuilding all of the lost office space, as well as the retail and hotel space—went unchallenged. When officials of the LMDC were asked by reporters about this, they tended to reply with comments such as "it's their land," as if the Port Authority's ownership of the Ground Zero site on September 11 were the only thing that mattered, even in the face of the extraordinary events that had occurred. The only person who had the power to challenge the Port Authority's control of the land—and, by extension, Larry Silverstein's—was Governor Pataki, who, as early as September 12, 2001, could have insisted that the authority negotiate a fair price to turn it over to the public or could have initiated a process to condemn the land or Silverstein's lease.

Pataki did none of these things and chose, at least in the first half of 2002, to allow the myriad of governmental, quasi-governmental, and private parties to continue to squabble over almost every aspect of the rebuilding process. It often seemed that Pataki, who was in the midst of a reelection campaign, did not want any resolution of the planning dilemma before election day. Why, after all, should the governor risk offending people who did not like a particular plan? It was far easier to leave all options open, at least for the moment. Pataki talked about bringing consensus and public input to the process, but he seemed often to be working to assure that the process would be slow, convoluted, and more than a little bit opaque.

. . .

Still, the LMDC had to move forward, even if it was to be at a deliberate pace. What Whitehead had called the listening period could not last forever, even if you believed—as many citizens and planners did—that decisions of this magnitude should not be made quickly. The agency put together a "blueprint" for the redevelopment of Lower Manhattan, which it released on April 9. It turned out to be a summary of general principles and guidelines, most of them familiar to anyone who had attended Listening to the City at the South Street Seaport or read the report issued by New York New Visions. Indeed, Alexander Garvin, who had wanted to give New York New Visions a larger role in the planning process, had gone so far as to incorporate some of its recommendations almost literally into the LMDC's document. The guidelines included a recommendation for extensive improvements to the Lower Manhattan transportation infrastructure, including an intermodal transit hub that would tie together the PATH trains to New Jersey and the New York City subway lines; the creation of a park encompassing some form of memorial to the victims of the terrorist attack; and the establishment of a museum devoted to the story of the September 11 attacks. The guidelines also endorsed the notion of providing space for major cultural facilities at Ground Zero and the reconstruction of some of the streets of the original downtown street grid.

There was nothing new to the guidelines and little that anyone could argue with unless they held to the increasingly tenuous position that nothing other than a memorial should occupy Ground Zero. (And that was literally impossible anyway, since the MTA had been moving ahead with repairs to the 1 and 9 subway lines that had run directly underneath the trade center, and the Port Authority was working on plans to get the PATH trains that had run through the heart of Ground Zero moving again, too. Even if nothing were ever built aboveground, the site was still going to have transit lines running beneath it, which somewhat compromised the notion of keeping the sixteen acres as entirely pure, sacred ground.)

The new guidelines taken together with the Port Authority's program seemed to add up to a prescription for trouble, since it all but guaranteed a dense, overpacked sixteen acres. The streets that were being returned to the site would themselves take up a huge amount of space before the buildings were even considered. A few weeks after the guidelines were issued, fifteen architectural firms replied to the revised request for proposals that the Port Authority had sent out. Among them were Kohn Pedersen Fox, a rival of Skidmore, Owings & Merrill that was known chiefly for its skyscraper designs; Robert A. M. Stern Architects, a firm known mainly for its traditional designs that was run by the dean of the Yale School of Architecture, who was, in effect, Alex Garvin's boss in his teaching career; a consortium of three prominent New York firms, Hardy Holzman Pfeiffer Associates, Gruzen Samton, and Fox & Fowle; Ehrenkrantz Eckstut & Kuhn, whose best-known designer, Stanton Eckstut, was a former partner and now uneasy rival of Alexander Cooper; Beyer Blinder Belle, a firm known mainly for its restorations of major landmarks like Ellis Island and Grand Central Terminal; and probably the most unusual response of all, a pairing of the internationally known Rem Koolhaas with Davis Brody Bond, a New York firm that mainly produces housing and academic and institutional buildings. Koolhaas was the only architect here who might be considered to have a cutting-edge reputation, which made it appear in the spring of 2002 that there was very little likelihood that Ground Zero would be planned by anyone who seemed even remotely connected to the latest developments in architecture. Most of the firms were either known for fairly conservative design or, more troubling still, not known for design quality at all. Both Skidmore, Owings & Merrill and Cooper, Robertson & Partners, which was working with John Zuccotti and Brookfield Properties on their privately commissioned plan, declined to participate. The two firms decided that, despite how much they knew about the site, for the moment at least they were better off staying on Silverstein's and Brookfield's payrolls.

But the real question was whether any any architect, however creative, could produce anything worthwhile out of the Port Authority's overstuffed program. Was it all going to fit? Garvin insisted that it could, based largely on some initial studies done by Peterson/Littenberg, a small architecture and urban-design firm he had hired as consultants to the LMDC soon after he began work at the agency. Steven Peterson and Barbara Littenberg had taught for a time with Garvin at Yale, and they shared his combination of pragmatism and idealism about New York, as well as a bias toward what might be called traditional urbanism. They preferred the city of streets, old-fashioned blocks, and public squares to the modernist city of vast open spaces and superblocks, in other words. Peterson and Littenberg, who had been working out of a small office on the Upper East Side, quickly rented a couple of rooms on the ground floor of an elegant old office building that had been converted to apartments just south of Ground Zero and set up a new office where they began to study ways to translate the Port Authority's demands into what they would consider a viable urban design.

Peterson and Littenberg's office served as a kind of think tank for Garvin, a laboratory in which he and his staff could test various possible layouts for the site. For Garvin, Peterson and Littenberg could also serve as a counterweight to the Port Authority, since the agency clearly expected to have the upper hand in the design process and to control whatever architect was selected as the prime designer for the site. The LMDC and the Port Authority wanted the chosen architect to prepare six different design alternatives, which the agencies wanted to release to the public early in the summer. It would be a rush job, done under the double pressures of time and intense public scrutiny, so it was not surprising that Garvin found it helpful to have Peterson/Littenberg do some studies of their own—work against which he could measure whatever the official architect was producing.

The LMDC and the Port Authority jointly reviewed the submissions from architects at the end of May, and a committee made up of representatives from both agencies voted on them. The winner, Beyer Blinder Belle, had been Garvin's own choice. He was to come to regret it and later claimed that he had favored Beyer Blinder Belle largely because it had allied with a large engineering firm, Parsons Brinckerhoff, that was known for its transportation work. Given how important an improved transportation infrastructure was to the overall downtown plan, Garvin felt that Parsons would provide a good counterbalance to the bureaucracy of the Port Authority's in-house engineers and would ensure that some degree of imagination was brought to the realm of transportation design. He was not thinking much about architecture, Garvin said, because he did not envision the project as including architecture—at least not yet.

CHAPTER 7

Boldness and Vision

The Public Demands More

THE PUBLIC RESPONSE TO THE hiring of Beyer Blinder Belle was mixed at best. After months of "listening" by the LMDC as well as a lot of high-minded talk from all the participants about their noble ambitions for the reconstruction of Ground Zero, it seemed odd that the commission would go to a midlevel firm known mainly for its restoration projects. This was, after all, the most sought-after architectural assignment in the world. Where were the leading architects of our time, and why weren't they being considered? Never mind that few of them had shown any formal interest in the project or that the job, right now, was technically only to study some options. Hiring Beyer Blinder Belle would prove to be a significant miscalculation, for reasons that had to do as much with the public perception of the role architecture could play in solving the Ground Zero problem as with the firm's own shortcomings. Architecture had become an increasingly conspicuous presence in the broader culture over the past several years, and there was no shortage of powerful creative voices in the field. Projects such as Frank Gehry's Guggenheim Museum in Bilbao, Spain, had led people to expect that contemporary architecture would have a powerful emotional component. Buildings now loomed large on the cultural radar screen, so to speak, and people were more inclined than ever to discuss architecture in terms of art, not real estate. Indeed, before the events of September 11 pushed it aside, the building project most talked about in Lower Manhattan was a proposal by Gehry for a huge new Guggenheim Museum to be built on the East River, just a few blocks from the World Trade Center. New designs had recently been completed in Manhattan by Tod Williams and Billie Tsien, Raimund Abraham, Rem Koolhaas, Aldo Rossi, Bernard Tschumi, and Christian de Portzamparc, all of whom had international reputations. Renzo Piano had a couple of commissions, including a skyscraper for *The New York Times,* and a pair of Manhattan apartment towers designed by Richard Meier was already under construction. It seemed like a time of architectural renaissance in a city that had long discouraged adventuresome, cutting-edge design in favor of the commercial. By choosing Beyer Blinder Belle, the LMDC and the Port Authority seemed to be going against the trend.

There was another reason the decision to hire Beyer Blinder Belle was to be unsatisfying, and it had little to do with the avant-garde architectural culture. Alex Garvin and the Port Authority failed to realize that what the firm produced would inevitably be viewed by the public as if it were a real architectural design, not just a feasibility study. For months, people had found it easier to discuss their visions for Ground Zero in terms of images of actual buildings. It may have been premature to talk about real buildings, but people did not care; they were impatient, and in any case laypersons are often more interested in literal images than in abstract concepts. They wanted to see pictures of what a new Ground Zero might look like. Max Protetch's show attracted such crowds and publicity a few months earlier because it contained real designs, however far-fetched and impractical they may have been. When CNN, which covered the reconstruction process extensively, invited people to submit their own designs to a special website, it was deluged with sketches. Most of them were earnest and unbuildable fantasies that made little sense, but they satisfied an emotional need not only in their creators but also in the people who viewed them. And since people craved real designs, they were going to evaluate anything they were shown as if it were an actual piece of architecture and judge it accordingly.

The period allotted for Beyer Blinder Belle to prepare its initial studies for Ground Zero was brief, but there was no shortage of conflict during it. Governor Pataki had told Lou Tomson, Joe Seymour, and the others in charge of the rebuilding process that he wanted to present plans to the public by July 4, and that gave the architects only a few weeks to devise something. Actually, the architects had to produce several somethings, since the LMDC and the Port Authority had decided that they wanted to unveil six designs in July. The plan was to invite public comment on the six and to narrow the list down to three options in September and then to a final version by the end of the year.

As Beyer Blinder Belle began its work, Steven Peterson and Barbara Littenberg continued to produce studies of their own for ways in which the Port Authority's demanding program could be squeezed into the sixteen acres of Ground Zero. They came up with eight different schemes, each of which used a different urban-design element as the starting point for a memorial. One plan was based primarily on a pair of public squares, another on a large, sculptural object, another on a below-grade memorial, and another on the notion of buildings forming a tight enclosure to create an urban, outdoor "room." In another plan, the memorial and all of Ground Zero fused into a single "memorial precinct." Another was based on the notion of a memorial as a major public building with a public roof garden, and another on the idea of a memorial boulevard.

While Peterson and Littenberg worked, Skidmore, Owings & Merrill continued to produce a design for Larry Silverstein, and Cooper, Robertson & Partners went on working for Brookfield. Late in June, after Beyer Blinder Belle had been working for about a month, officials from the LMDC and the Port Authority met in joint session to review the architects' progress. Jack Beyer, the partner in charge of the project, showed Roland Betts and other members of the committee six different schemes his firm had come up with to show how the program could fit onto the site. Steven Peterson and Barbara Littenberg were asked to show their work as well, and they showed four of the schemes they had devised. At an earlier session, Cooper Robertson and Skidmore had presented their schemes. The committee, believing it had an obligation to show the public a range of options, decided that it would present to the public three of Beyer Blinder Belle's designs and three of Peterson and Littenberg's as the six Ground Zero alternatives.

Beyer was upset—he had thought that his firm had been hired to be the sole architect for these designs—and he returned a few days later with more alternatives. The result, at first, was the opposite of what Beyer had intended: a decision to present two rather than three of Beyer Blinder Belle's options, two of Peterson and Littenberg's, and the Skidmore, Owings & Merrill and Cooper Robertson designs as the fifth and sixth alternatives. With a public announcement planned for July 16 (the governor's target date of July 4 had been relaxed a bit), time was tight. Beyer went to Joe Seymour and pleaded his case. Seymour agreed to let Beyer's firm be the only official presenter, and Lou Tomson—who had always prided himself on his ability to work closely with Seymour, an old colleague in George Pataki's circle—agreed. It would, if nothing else, make for a simpler and clearer presentation to the public. Skidmore, Owings & Merrill's and Cooper Robertson's plans were taken off the agenda, but then a strange thing happened: the Beyer Blinder Belle schemes were revised to include versions that were based on the designs by Skidmore, Owings & Merrill, Cooper Robertson, and Peterson/Littenberg. All of the designs presented, however, would be described officially as the work of Beyer Blinder Belle.

Garvin realized that he was quickly losing control of the process to Jack Beyer, whose own schemes, Garvin believed, were the least interesting of the lot. But in a sense, what was really going on was that Beyer had become closer to the Port Authority, and the authority was squeezing the LMDC, its supposed partner. As Garvin worried about the Port Authority's program, Jack Beyer seemed not only comfortable with it but enthusiastic about it, and he and Joe Seymour were eagerly working together. As the program for July 16 came together, Garvin was to play no role—he was not even on the platform—and Lou Tomson and John Whitehead were scheduled to make introductory remarks. The body of the presentation was to be devoted to statements by Joe Seymour and other Port Authority officials and a review of all six plans by Jack Beyer, who was the only person who would talk about the actual designs.

Beyer had some private doubts about the Port Authority's insistence on building ten million square feet of office space, but he had been given strict orders by the authority not to make them public. The day before the press conference, Beyer was called to a session with the Port Authority to review his presentation for the event. Officials fired mock questions at him, as if at a practice session for a presidential debate. What if you are asked what you think of the program? a Port Authority official asked. Beyer replied that while he might consider it too big, he could still work with it. That seemed like a reasonable response, but it did not impress his Port Authority coaches. The program is fixed, they said to him, and the only thing you can say about it is that it is not up for discussion.

A few days before July 16, Governor Pataki and Mayor Bloomberg were both given previews of the six Beyer Blinder Belle plans. Pataki, who was not particularly attuned to design issues at that point, gave them the go-ahead. Pataki had a tendency, particularly in the early months of the planning process, to make a lot of high-minded statements about Ground Zero as "hallowed ground," but his subordinates tended to talk in terms like "obligations to leaseholders," which suggested that the governor was more than willing to consider Ground Zero primarily a real-estate opportunity for the Port Authority. The mayor was less supportive when he had his advance look. He asked why the plans all seemed so similar. Where is the no-build alternative? Isn't that one of the possible options? Bloomberg asked. And where is an option with housing? he asked, bringing up a subject that stuck in the Port Authority's craw. Bloomberg had expected that the Port Authority and the LMDC would show the public six completely different options for the site, not six similar schemes, and he was not pleased. Although no one was supposed to say a word about the plans before the official unveiling, Bloomberg spilled the beans in a casual news conference three days before the event. He said he had seen the designs, and he described them coolly as "a starting point." The mayor encouraged people to write to the LMDC to comment on the plans as soon as they saw them.

The news conference to show the plans was held in the rotunda of Federal Hall, the venerable classical building at the intersection of Wall and Broad streets. It was under such tight security that the press was crowded under the entry colonnade facing Wall Street for the better part of an hour, as screeners slowly put all of the attendees through metal detectors. Inside the rotunda, there were folding chairs and six large panels with renderings. One was called Memorial Plaza; the next, Memorial Square, followed by Memorial Triangle, Memorial Garden, Memorial Park, and, finally, Memorial Promenade. They were all collections of office towers arrayed around some open space, and the renderings suggested that the designs were almost as interchangeable as their titles.

John Whitehead spoke first. "Today we are presenting to you six conceptual plans for the redevelopment of the World Trade Center site and adjacent areas," he said. "When the terrorists attacked the World Trade Center site on September 11 they thought that if they knocked our buildings down they would damage our spirit. It turned out that the result of September 11 was exactly the opposite. We will rebuild—it is not a question of whether, but of how," Whitehead said.

"Each of these plans is feasible and buildable," he said. "Each represents a package of proposed ideas. They can be mixed and matched. Nothing is etched in stone. The best ideas will survive," Whitehead concluded. And then, after a word of praise to Roland Betts for overseeing the joint LMDC–Port Authority planning committee, he introduced Lou Tomson, who praised the openness of the design process. "What we create will be consistent with and testament to the principles which came under attack on September 11—democracy," Tomson said.

Joe Seymour followed. He referred to the designs as a step in "the process of rebuilding the World Trade Center," which was nothing if not a revealing slip, and then went on to describe the plans as "conceptual land-use plans, different ways of arranging blocks on the site," a description that, while literally correct, would be ignored by almost everyone in the days to follow. Jack Beyer then presented the plans, one by one, making no mention of the fact that Memorial Plaza, the first, was based largely on the work of Cooper

Robertson; that Memorial Garden, the fourth, was a version of the plan devised by Skidmore, Owings & Merrill, and that Memorial Park and Memorial Promenade, the fifth and sixth, were derived from schemes that were Peterson/Littenberg's.

On the other hand, the differences between the plans were much less important than their similarities. Was it of much significance that Beyer Blinder Belle had planned a triangular memorial space in one plan and a parallelogram-shaped one in another? Or that the Cooper Robertson plan had an eight-acre memorial plaza that went all the way up to Vesey Street at the north end, while the Skidmore, Owings & Merrill plan had only a four-acre memorial area that stopped at Fulton Street on the north and included museums built into its southern end? All of the plans included restoring streets; all of them proposed covering West Street; all of them included a transit center toward the eastern end; all of them included office towers along the eastern side and some or all of the north side of the sixteen acres; and all of them proposed some kind of very tall skyline element, which most of the architects located toward the northeastern corner of the site.

The Peterson and Littenberg plans were actually the most inventive, largely because Peterson and Littenberg decided not to leave the footprints of the original twin towers empty, as the other four schemes did. They included plenty of memorial space, but they were able to arrange things in a much more creative way. Memorial Park contained a six-acre park on a deck over West Street that also covered a portion of the footprints, while other sections of the footprints would have had streets and buildable real-estate parcels on them. Memorial Promenade contained a large oval park on a deck over West Street, which would be connected to a new, tree-lined boulevard, with a central pedestrian mall that would lead from Ground Zero to the southern tip of Manhattan. It would have had a direct view of the Statue of Liberty and would thus have tied the site, both spatially and iconically, to the most important symbol of freedom in New York. But this plan, too, would have required building on the footprints. The trade-off, however, was that the Peterson and Littenberg plans, by using somewhat more of the land, were less dense overall than the other four.

At the end of his presentation, Beyer took questions. He followed the orders that the Port Authority had given him. A reporter asked him if the requirement to put more than ten million square feet on the site constricted the planning effort. "We do not consider this to be a constraint," Beyer said. "Planners and architects have clients, clients have programs. We are proud of these plans and feel that they satisfy the client's program in a variety of ways." It was a response that, if nothing else, showed Beyer's loyalty to the Port Authority.

Another questioner asked about preserving the footprints of the twin towers. "Our job is to consider all the possibilities for the site," Tomson replied. "We all recognize that the footprints are very important to the families," Whitehead said. "Three or four [of the plans] do preserve the footprints—this is something we still have to decide."

Whitehead then decided to make another statement about the whole question of the Port Authority's program. "To those of you who question commercial buildings on the site and how firmly we are tied to them, we recognize that the owner and leaseholder have certain rights," he said. "We believe that these plans all represent respecting these private property rights and creating a beautiful center for New York. The belief is that it is possible. This is a very, very large site. I do not believe that these towers will be a solid block of warring buildings—they will be beautiful architecturally." He paused for a moment and went on. "If it is not possible to meet these requirements, these criteria," Whitehead said, "then we will change our plans."

The Port Authority could tell Jack Beyer what to say, but it could hardly muzzle John Whitehead in the same way, and Whitehead's last remark became the lead in the next morning's story about the plans in *The New York Times*. "On the day that six proposals for the redevelopment of the World Trade Center site were unveiled, the chairman of the Lower Manhattan Development Corporation said yesterday that the public could consider a seventh possibility, a new design without some of the requirements for office and retail space that shaped the initial proposals," Edward Wyatt, the paper's reporter, wrote.

Whitehead had deftly distanced himself from what, in the coming days, was to be increasingly viewed as a disaster. Nobody thought much of the plans—nobody but Jack Beyer and the Port Authority, that is—and Garvin was particularly upset as he watched Peterson and Littenberg's work, which he thought represented a significant attempt to weave Ground Zero into the overall fabric of Lower Manhattan and develop creative alternatives while still respecting the Port Authority's program, be subsumed within the heavy-handed efforts of Beyer Blinder Belle. Nearly everyone in the architecture community responded negatively to the six plans, particularly to the ones originated by Beyer Blinder Belle, and even Peterson and Littenberg's more inventive efforts were far from popular, in part because they, and Garvin, miscalculated the extent to which the public would feel comfortable with allowing any new building on the footprints of the twin towers. Garvin's vote in May had been a key reason Beyer Blinder Belle had been hired, but the firm had, in his view, made a bad situation—the Port Authority's program—much worse. He saw only one hope for the planning process, which was that the public become so vocal in its dislike of the six plans that the Port Authority and the LMDC would have no choice but to scrap them. It was an irony that Garvin not only had to dissociate himself from the work he had commissioned but would have to put his faith in the fickle public to save the day.

The public came through, in a way that Garvin had not been prepared to expect. On the Saturday following the Tuesday unveiling of the six plans, the Civic Alliance held its second Listening to the City event, much bigger and more ambitious than the first. Instead of a catering hall in the South Street Seaport, the venue was the Jacob Javits Convention Center on the west side, the largest assembly room in the city. Instead of room for a few hundred civic do-gooders to squeeze in, there would be space for more than four thousand. Because the scale was so much larger than the first session in February, Robert Yaro enlisted the support of the LMDC and the Port Authority as cosponsors. It was a risky decision, since while it gave the event a more official tone—this time, the people who had put out the plans were helping to sponsor the public evaluation of them—there was a danger that the Civic Alliance would be perceived as having given up its independence. Still, there was probably little chance that the Port Authority and the LMDC could control the outcome, since AmericaSpeaks and Carolyn Lukensmeyer had been enlisted again, along with their instant polling technology, to take the pulse of the crowd.

There were also concerns that a Saturday in July was not the wisest time to hold a public meeting in New York City. Summer weekends were traditionally the time when New Yorkers who can get away are happy to leave Manhattan to the tourists. Those who have country houses go to them, and those who don't are likely to take day trips to the beach or the mountains, especially if the weather is hot and sunny.

But Listening to the City upset the equilibrium of the weekend. It is hard to know how many of the four thousand–plus people might otherwise have been away, but the fact is that thousands of New Yorkers considered the future of Ground Zero more important than an afternoon at the beach, and they were indoors at the Javits Center, many of them for most of the day, at round tables of ten, this time hundreds and hundreds of them. The speakers were in the center of the enormous room, and most people saw their images on eight huge television screens that had been hung over the low, square central platform. By the end of the day, the public had made it clear that it found the six plans to be banal, lacking in vision, excessively devoted to commercial concerns, and inadequate as settings for the kind of memorial they had hoped to see. The message of the day was not that people did not yet feel ready to see something happening at Ground Zero—ten months had passed, and most people were increasingly eager to see signs of progress—but that they thought things had started off in the wrong direction.

The event began with words of welcome from most of the officials, including Lou Tomson, who urged people to see the exhibition of the plans at Federal Hall, where they had remained on view, as if seeing Beyer Blinder Belle's renderings would somehow make the plans more palatable. The most striking opening presentation, however, came from Frank Lombardi, an executive of the Port Authority, who, after saying that the authority's "top priority is to build a fitting memorial," then launched into a ringing defense of his agency's program for the site.

"The consultants were instructed to recognize the legal right of the leaseholders, Silverstein and Westfield," Lombardi said. "Some have expressed the concern that the office buildings may overshadow other uses of the site. But the site is not a blank slate. It would be easier for the planners if it were."

Of course, the site could have been a blank slate had public officials decided that turning it into one was their most important obligation to the public after September 11—that was the very point made by people who were objecting to the Port Authority's program. Had Governor Pataki decided that the Port Authority's demands were not acceptable, history would have been entirely different.

Lombardi continued. "It is a good thing to replace the offices that were there, and the jobs that they represented," he said. And then he asked the crowd, "Is it possible to balance all the needs, all the things we would like this site to be?" He did not answer.

Alex Garvin spoke next. He said not a word about his own disappointment with the six early plans but encouraged the members of the crowd to speak their minds. "All of you are testimony that those criminals failed—democracy is alive today," he said. And he praised the aspects of the plans he felt most comfortable with, such as the attempt in many of them to integrate Ground Zero with the rest of Lower Manhattan. "You will not see architecture," Garvin warned the audience. "We are not talking about architecture today—we are talking about site plans and principles."

Jack Beyer had hoped that either he or his partner John Belle could speak and explain the rationale behind their plans. But the firm was told there was no room for it in the program. Instead, Robert Davidson, the Port Authority's chief in-house architect, spoke and outlined several urban design issues, including ways in which West Street might be altered, such as turned into a tunnel or covered by a deck, and about the transit hub that had been proposed. Then participants at each round table were asked to talk among themselves for an hour or so, evaluating the new plans and the underlying urban-design questions.

"This is amazing," Garvin said, as he walked around the room, observing the groups. "Five thousand people arguing passionately about urban design is an extraordinary event in history. This fills me with hope."

Garvin may have been optimistic about the numbers—the total registration was closer to four thousand—but he was correct about the nature of the event, which turned out to be unusually attentive to serious design issues. After the discussion hour, Carolyn Lukensmeyer took over the platform, and while she had not lost the amiable but slightly patronizing tone she had displayed at the first Listening to the City event—her first words were, "Okay, folks, did you have a great discussion about the advice you want to give to the LMDC?"—she then oversaw a fairly sophisticated electronic poll, using questions that had been put together by Yaro and the Civic Alliance and approved by the LMDC and the Port Authority.

The first question asked how important attendees believed it was to restore a major skyline element to Ground Zero, either in the form of a skyscraper or just a symbolic tower. An overwhelming number—57 percent—answered that it was very important, 14 percent said it was important, and 12 percent said it was somewhat important, a positive total of 83 percent. Only 13 percent said it was unimportant to them.

The next question asked about the restoration of the street grid, which had become something of a litmus test of attitudes toward city planning. Indeed, the movement to restore some or all of the removed streets to the site seemed in a way to represent the ultimate triumph of Jane Jacobs over Robert Moses, and the attendees at Listening to the City were clearly part of that movement. Thirty-five percent of them said it was very important to restore part or all of the street grid to Ground Zero, another 21 percent said it was important, and 19 percent found it somewhat important, for a total of 75 percent. Only 20 percent thought it was unimportant.

On the subject of connecting the site to the rest of Lower Manhattan, the group was even more clear in its views. Seventy-one percent thought it was very important, another 17 percent said it was important, and only 6 percent found it unimportant. The electronic poll also asked people whether they preferred to see one large open space at Ground Zero or several different-sized open spaces. That question did not have such broad implications, since, unlike the idea of putting back the streets, the type of open space was not as clear an indicator of general views about urban design, although it was probably fair to say that a single large open space seemed more in accord with the design of the old twin towers and multiple smaller spaces seemed more Jane Jacobs–esque. Fifty-three percent of the registrants preferred to see a variety of open spaces of different sizes, while 34 percent preferred one large open space.

The most revealing part of the poll came when Lukensmeyer asked the participants to rate all six of the Ground Zero memorial designs as settings for a memorial: excellent, good, adequate, or "poor or unacceptable." The phrase "memorial setting" was a clever one, since it took as a given the notion that the sixteen acres would contain a mix of uses and also that it would not resemble a conventional development. The question also gave the attendees a chance to evaluate the general appropriateness of each plan without literally ranking the plans, and it emphasized what for most people, not just the families of the victims, was the most important aspect of any potential master plan.

The stunning result was that the memorial setting of every single plan was voted poor or unacceptable. Sixty-two percent of the attendees rejected Jack Beyer's Memorial Triangle as unacceptable, and the Memorial Park by Peterson and Littenberg was dismissed by the same number. Only 41 percent found the Memorial Promenade unacceptable, which seemed almost like a ringing endorsement, especially since that design was considered excellent by 23 percent, the highest positive ranking of any of the schemes. The Memorial Triangle, by contrast, was voted excellent by a mere 6 percent. Memorial Gardens, the Skidmore, Owings & Merrill design, was ranked as excellent by only 5 percent of those attending, and as poor by 52 percent. Memorial Square, the other Beyer Blinder Belle scheme, was considered poor by 50 percent of the attendees and excellent by 11 percent. Memorial Plaza, the Cooper Robertson–originated design, was voted poor by 35 percent of the participants and excellent by 15 percent.

The specifics of the numbers were much less important than the overall point, however, which was that most people did not much like any of the designs. Lukensmeyer followed the poll on the memorial settings by asking each table to take three minutes to come up with some thematic ideas "about what is lacking in the memorial settings." As at the first Listening to the City event in February, the facilitator at each table had a laptop computer set up to communicate directly with the central platform, and a few minutes later Lukensmeyer read the main themes that had been e-mailed to her. They included a request to preserve the footprints of the original twin towers; to depress and cover West Street; to create an extended promenade from Ground Zero to the Battery; to restore the street grid; to create cultural uses; to make interesting buildings on the skyline; to include more nonoffice uses; to make the plans less dense.

Lukensmeyer recited them, one by one. Then she came to one that was less a request than a plea. "The schemes are not ambitious enough, and the buildings are too short," she said. The audience broke out into loud applause. "Nothing here is truly monumental—it feels like Albany," Lukensmeyer continued, to further applause and laughter throughout the room.

"Now let's not be too hard on the planners here," she scolded. "These are just concept plans."

She turned with what seemed like relief to her next task, which was to poll the attendees on which design themes were most important. Preserving the footprints of the towers carried the day, garnering the votes of just over 35 percent of the participants; second was creating a visually interesting skyline, at about 22 percent. Asked to evaluate the problems with the existing plans, nearly 40 percent voted that the most serious issue was that the schemes were not ambitious enough, and another 23.5 percent said that the need for more nonoffice uses was the most urgent problem.

That question listed only those themes that were within the context of the Port Authority's program, and it avoided anything that implied radical change. Next, Lukensmeyer asked the attendees to vote on some of the other themes that had been e-mailed to her from the tables, which she described as "outside the Port Authority's program." The first was "be bold in design, more innovative, hold a design competition." Thirty-nine percent voted in favor of that. The second was a plea for greater diversification of use on the site, including more social uses such as schools, libraries, and recreational centers, and 23 percent supported that. A request for more safety and security interested only 7 percent of the attendees, but the fourth theme, "cancel the leases, start fresh, seek other ways to solve the leaseholder's requests," was approved by 31 percent of the attendees—and once again caused the room to break out into applause.

By then, nobody, including Jack Beyer and John Belle, who were watching the proceedings with dismay, or the representatives of the Port Authority, could miss the point. The public was dismissing the plans as lacking in vision and believed that the planners had applied conventional thinking, not to mention a conventional set of real-estate values, to a situation that called for conceptual boldness. Later questions underscored the extent to which the participants believed that affordable housing in Lower Manhattan was a redevelopment priority, along with more cultural facilities and green space. Just about the only time the LMDC got a nod of approval was in one of the final polling questions, when attendees were asked if they thought the pace of the design process at Ground Zero was too fast or too slow. Only 13 percent wanted it to go faster, and 28 percent thought it should go slower, but 50 percent said it was fine the way it was. John Whitehead breathed a sigh of relief as he stood at the side of the room and watched the number 50 flash on the huge hanging screens—it was the only majority vote the LMDC had gotten all day.

Lou Tomson was asked to make some concluding comments from the LMDC, and it was clear from his tone that he was shaken by the outpouring of negative feelings about the plans. "I said I was excited this morning, and I'm still excited," he said, but his voice sounded less excited than angry. "We've learned a lot about the planning process. Your desire for boldness, to diversify uses, that we seek ways to diversify the leasehold relationship. We've heard 'Be more ambitious, include more nonoffice uses.' We have to go back and figure out how to turn the comments we've heard into amendments to what we are doing. I just love hearing from everybody—it just helps us so much," Tomson concluded, in a tone he may have been hoping would sound pleased but actually sounded quite grudging.

He was followed by Daniel Doctoroff, representing Mayor Bloomberg. Doctoroff took a very different tone. He was clearly thrilled, and he seemed to want nothing so much as to congratulate the attendees for doing what he and the mayor did not have the power to do themselves, which was to reject the Port Authority's plans. "In the 1860s, a town-hall meeting in New York brought people together and changed the course of history," Doctoroff said, referring to Abraham Lincoln's famous speech at Cooper Union that ignited his campaign for the presidency. He continued, his voice reaching the cadence of a campaign speech. "It strikes me that what occurred today has been profound—five thousand people came to speak their minds," Doctoroff said. "We heard you say that the long-term interest of our city must first and foremost be our guide as we move forward. We've heard you say that we could not and we should not accept mediocrity. What we build must inspire. We must heal our wounded spirits by somehow healing our skyline and honoring our heroes. If I had to summarize, I'd say don't settle, do something great. It has to capture our dreams. Today, we took one more step toward making that a reality."

Doctoroff clearly had a hard time containing his enthusiasm, Tomson a hard time hiding his unhappiness. Both men understood that something had changed, and that the gathering at the Javits Center had had an effect that the earlier Listening to the City event had not come close to. It was easy to be somewhat cynical about the notion of thousands of people trying to communicate about urban design at a public meeting—Michael Sorkin, walking around the room, said it reminded him of a Stalinist congress—but the fact is that the event did not really have much of a party line, except a kind of general belief in earnestness and vision and the apparent view of most of the participants that the Port Authority and the LMDC were sorely lacking in those qualities. There certainly was no attempt made to propose alternate designs, and when a man at one of the round tables muttered, "Thank goodness the Acropolis wasn't built by committee," he may have thought he was dismissing the whole event, but in fact he was supporting it, since the organizers were careful not to try to turn the participants into amateur architects, believing that there were enough amateur designs for Ground Zero floating around already. The goal of the day had been to see what the public liked and what it disliked about the six plans that had been made public, and the answer was clear.

For most of the Robert Moses era—which is to say for most of the middle decades of the twentieth century, into the seventies—the notion of public participation in planning seemed synonymous with the idea of protest. People became involved to stop projects, not to get them started. They stopped the Lower Manhattan Expressway, which was one of Jane Jacobs's great triumphs over Robert Moses in the 1960s and a harbinger of new planning attitudes to come. They stopped Westway, the highway that was to have been built on landfill in the Hudson River. They stopped a bridge that would have gone across the Long Island Sound from Rye to Oyster Bay, which was the last major project Moses promoted, and one of his final defeats. They stopped a tower that would have gone on top of Grand Central Terminal, leading to a lawsuit that went all the way to the Supreme Court and established the constitutionality of landmarks-preservation laws. And they stopped an enormous café that would have taken over the southeast corner of Central Park. In those years, the idea of thinking big all too often meant thinking bad—boldness meant an unwelcome intervention. The bold projects that did get built in those years seemed to confirm this. Whether it was the General Motors Building or Madison Square Garden or the towers on the Avenue of the Americas—or, of course, the World Trade Center—people tended to associate large-scale projects with things that threatened their streets, their neighborhoods, or their entire city. And so they programmed themselves to say no.

At Listening to the City, they programmed themselves to say yes, to ask for more vision, not less. That was the great significance of that day, not just that it made clear that the constituency for the six plans did not extend much beyond Beyer Blinder Belle and the Port Authority and that the alliance between the authority and that architecture firm had become a political liability. Far more important, the day showed that people had become willing once again to ask for boldness in the public realm. It may have taken the extraordinary circumstances of September 11, or it may have been part of a broader evolution, a swing of the pendulum away from the instinctive dislike of daring, visionary projects that had marked New York for so long. Or it may have been some of both. In any event, attitudes were different when it came to planning Ground Zero. People were demanding a level of vision and imagination in the public realm that they had not called for in New York for more than a generation.

CHAPTER 8

The Innovative Design Study

IT WAS IMPOSSIBLE TO IGNORE the results of the Listening to the City event at the Javits Center on that hot Saturday in July, and the Lower Manhattan Development Corporation did not try to. The mess was especially awkward for Governor Pataki, who faced re-election in November and did not want to be associated with a failed planning effort. Yet Pataki was no more inclined at the end of July than he had been at any other time since September 11 to break ranks with the Port Authority or with his close aides such as Lou Tomson, who had given the planning process its pragmatic thrust. His response was to encourage the impression of a change in direction but at the same time to avoid making any significant decisions. Those who wanted a practical, business-oriented plan would think that Pataki was moving as fast as he could to satisfy their wishes, and those who wanted a commemorative, ceremonial plan would feel the same way, or so Pataki appears to have hoped.

For his part, Alex Garvin saw the July fiasco as an opportunity to shift the direction of the planning process, and Roland Betts saw it similarly. Making such a shift would not be easy, especially for Garvin, who had to dissociate himself from a problem that many people believed was at least partly of his own making. Betts could shift gears more easily, and he had always wanted to assume more control. The public's rejection of the first phase of work gave Betts an opportunity to be more assertive. No one knew what the long-term implications of the public demand for something bolder and more imaginative would be, but for the short term it certainly meant that the pragmatic alliance of the LMDC and the Port Authority, driven largely by the close relationship of Lou Tomson and Joe Seymour and their mutual desire to express loyalty to Pataki, could not be permitted to appear to be controlling the process. Betts, as the most visionary member of the LMDC's board, now had a justification to assume a much more visible role.

Betts has had an unusual career. Trained as a lawyer, he has taught school in Harlem; founded a company, Silver Screen Productions, that financed films in the 1980s; owned the Texas Rangers baseball team; and built the Chelsea Piers athletic complex on the Hudson River. His passion for architecture is genuine. When he owned the Texas Rangers (and his classmate George Bush was the team's operating head), Betts organized an architectural competition to find a design for a new baseball stadium. He ended up giving the job to David Schwarz, a Washington, D.C.–based architect who had never designed a baseball park before. Schwarz's Ballpark in Arlington is handsome, if rather retro, and a bit self-conscious in its references to places like Ebbets Field and Wrigley Field, not to mention Camden Yards. But it is the sort of project that emerges only from an organization with a strong design sensibility. Similarly, Betts's Chelsea Piers, which was designed by the firm of Butler Rogers Baskett, suggested a level of design ambition beyond that of the normal gym or hockey rink. And it showed that Betts and his longtime partner, Tom Bernstein, could fight their way through the painful process of public projects in New York and emerge with only minimal compromise.

Betts was eager to prove that design could save the Ground Zero planning process. He suggested that an architectural competition would bring some new ideas into the mix and take the curse off the six Beyer Blinder Belle plans. And with the Port Authority's insistence on building ten million square feet of office space now widely discredited, a design competition run by the LMDC might offer up some strong alternatives that could capture the public's imagination without directly attacking the Port Authority, Betts believed. "It would help with putting pressure on them to reduce square footage," Betts said later.

His initial notion was that if an architectural competition produced a spectacular design that captured the public's imagination but could not accommodate the full amount of commercial space demanded by the Port Authority, the authority would have no choice but to accept it. As things turned out, however, the Port Authority, which at first expressed disdain for the idea of an architectural competition—the authority "hated the idea, they were hoping that all the architects would go off and do stupid things," Betts said—agreed that something had to be done after Listening to the City and ended up giving tacit, if hardly enthusiastic, approval. Probably Betts's most important accomplishment in the weeks following Listening to the City was to convince the Port Authority to accept the notion of a range of office space rather than an absolute number and to agree that some of it might be provided on adjacent sites that the LMDC could acquire rather than shoehorned into the sixteen acres of Ground Zero. (The most likely adjacent site was just south of Ground Zero, across Liberty Street, where the former American headquarters of Deutsche Bank stood. A banal black box, the little-admired building had suffered significant damage on September 11, and it remained empty, covered in black netting that looked like a shroud, while the bank and its insurers fought over whether it was salvageable or not. Finally, in February 2004, they settled on terms to demolish the tower, and the LMDC was able to announce plans to take over the land.)

Betts, Joe Seymour, and Lou Tomson met at the Port Authority's offices on Park Avenue South on September 20 to discuss Betts's plan to allow a range of office space. After a long negotiating session, Betts wrote down the revised program on a sheet of paper and asked Seymour, Tomson, and the others present to initial it. The agreement felt like a breakthrough to the participants, and Betts remained so proud of orchestrating it that he would show a copy of the initialed sheet to visitors to his office months later. In the end it made relatively little difference. The bottom end of the range of office space in the revised program was six and a half million square feet, and the top was ten million; the revised program also called for between six hundred thousand and one million square feet of retail space, and an equal range of hotel space. If all of this was spread out into adjacent sites, the result would lower density at Ground Zero somewhat, but not dramatically. And it would not change anything about the type of uses that would go there, of course. But Betts had begun to overcome the rigidity that had constrained the process up to that point.

It fell to Garvin to handle the problem of organizing the new design effort. His first step was to go back to the New York New Visions group, which he asked to suggest names of distinguished architects who might serve on an advisory panel to help him and Betts evaluate the qualifications of architects who were interested in developing new designs for Ground Zero. At that point, no one was actually calling the process an architectural competition. The official name of the effort was the Innovative Design Study, and it was different from most architectural competitions for reasons that went beyond its name. The LMDC was using it to cast its net wide into the architectural world, but it was not promising to build the winning design. It was not actually even agreeing to choose a winning design. The chosen participants would not even be asked to produce a complete design for Ground Zero anyway. What they were going to be told to come up with was more of a master plan, an overall layout for the sixteen acres that would provide a kind of general guideline for development and a location for a memorial. It was possible, Garvin said, that elements of various different schemes might be chosen and integrated into a final plan. The request for qualifications that the LMDC issued on August 19 went so far as to state, in boldface type: "This is NOT a design competition, and will not result in the selection of a final plan. It is intended to generate creative and varied concepts to help plan the future of the site."

The Request for Qualifications stated that "approximately five respondents representing a range of urban and architectural design philosophies will be asked to participate in a four-week planning and design study. The results of this study will be presented to the LMDC and to the public to promote a free-flowing exchange of ideas." The fee paid to each participant would be forty thousand dollars. Responses were due on September 16, and the plan was for Betts, Garvin, and Billie Tsien to make the final selection of participants after the advisory panel consisting of Toshiko Mori, chairman of the architecture department at Harvard; Terence Riley, head of the architecture and design department of the Museum of Modern Art; and the landscape architect Michael Van Valkenburgh, among others, reviewed all the submissions and narrowed them down to a manageable number.

As first conceived, the whole thing had a mix-and-match quality, like an old-fashioned Chinese-restaurant menu: take one idea from Architect A, choose another from Architect B. Its real purposes were twofold. First, it would suggest to the world that the LMDC was not a stifling bureaucracy caught in the web of banal commercial design and might actually be open to hearing what major figures in architecture had to say about Ground Zero. Second, it would slow the process down just enough so that no conclusions could be reached before the gubernatorial election in November.

Still, it was possible to view this phase with some optimism, since there was not yet a revised version of the formal program for the site, and for a brief moment it looked as if the LMDC might be open to some radical rethinking of Ground Zero. Instead of a program, the initial document offered only a set of general guidelines, such as the suggestion that participants provide "a tall symbol or structure that would be recognized around the world," that they avoid building on the footprints of the original towers, that they restore portions of the street grid, that they look into the provision of residential construction on the site, that they connect the Ground Zero site with Battery Park City via a grand promenade similar to that envisioned in Peterson and Littenberg's plan, and that they provide a central transit center, cultural facilities, and public open spaces of different sizes. The plan also had to allow for commercial and retail space, the statement said, and the Port Authority would inform participants once the project got going as to the necessary amount.

Reflecting Absence *by Michael Arad and Peter Walker*

AP PHOTO/RICHARD DRE

The Winter Garden at the World Financial Center on December 18, 2002, the day seven design teams presented their visions of how to rebuild

JAMES ESTRIN/*THE NEW YORK TIMES*

Redevelopment leaders John Whitehead and Louis Tomson at a press conference in September 2002

John Whitehead and mayor-elect Michael Bloomberg in November 2002

AP PHOTO/RICHARD DREW

MICHAEL APPLETON/CORB

Daniel Libeskind presents his design at the Winter Garden

FRED R. CONRAD/*THE NEW YORK TIMES*

Sir Norman Foster presents his design at the Winter Garden

The THINK team's proposed design, World Cultural Center

AP PHOTO/RICHARD DREW

Architects Bill Morrish (left), Rafael Viñoly (second from left), and Frederic Schwartz (right) of the THINK group listen to Alexander Garvin

The Listening to the City event at the Jacob Javits Convention Center in July 2002, attended by more than five thousand people

REPRODUCED BY PERMISSION OF LMDC

GETTY IMAGE

The site of the former World Trade Center, as it looked in the spring of 2002

GETTY IMAGI

And on that minor phrase, everything turned. It was during the review period that Betts got Joe Seymour and the Port Authority to agree to the possibility of shifting a bit of the commercial space to an adjacent site, therefore lessening the density at Ground Zero slightly, but this had the effect of pulling the Port Authority back into the process and of creating a final program for the Innovative Design Study that turned out, in the end, not to be very different from the original program at all. By the time a final program document was issued for the participants on October 11, it had hardened in a way that made it clear that any optimism had been unfounded. "Residential development is permitted only in the project area south of Liberty Street," the new document proclaimed, which meant that there would be no housing permitted on the Ground Zero site at all. The Port Authority's agreed square-footage totals for hotel and retail space became absolute requirements for the new group of designers, and the same went for the commercial office space. If anything less than ten million square feet was provided on the site, the difference had to be allowed for on sites just outside the project area.

So the Innovative Design Study was not really a call for new ideas so much as it was an invitation to better-known architects to produce something more compelling than Beyer Blinder Belle and the others had been able to do with essentially the same program. This time there were firm restrictions on building on the footprints of the original twin towers, and there were more precise requirements about some of the ideas that had been floating around since the Beyer Blinder Belle phase, such as a major transit hub. Garvin had given the program a more sophisticated urban-design gloss than earlier versions had had. But no one could deny that this program was fundamentally the same as the one that had been rejected so roundly at Listening to the City just a few weeks before.

If the participants in the study—which people were with increasing frequency referring to as a competition—were discouraged by the enormity, not to mention the familiarity, of the program, they did not complain. One of the architects chosen was Skidmore, Owings & Merrill, which had been allowed to participate on the grounds that it agree to suspend all of its work for Larry Silverstein other than on 7 World Trade Center for the duration of the study.

Another was Norman Foster, the British lord who had designed some of the largest and most important skyscrapers of the last decade; another was a team of prominent New Yorkers with a strong modernist slant, Richard Meier, Charles Gwathmey, Peter Eisenman, and Steven Holl; another was an unusual consortium working under the architect Rafael Viñoly that included Frederic Schwartz, a former employee of Robert Venturi and Denise Scott Brown who had been practicing on his own for several years, and the Japanese architect Shigeru Ban.

Much of Viñoly's group, which became known as the THINK team, as well as the Meier group, had their roots in a project devised over the summer by Herbert Muschamp, the architecture critic of *The New York Times*. Muschamp, who tends to view modernism through the kind of romantic haze that is usually reserved for Tuscan villas and Greek temples, believed that the problem at Ground Zero was the result of bureaucrats and politicians not paying enough attention to architects. Avant-garde aesthetics should be leading the public debate, he felt. He decided to step out of the usual critic's role, and with the *Times*'s approval, he turned himself into an impresario. Several weeks before the LMDC's Innovative Design Study started—indeed, before the full extent of the problems with the Beyer Blinder Belle plans was even known—Muschamp convened a group of his favorite architects and ordered them each to come up with a building for the Ground Zero site, with himself as the master planner. The Muschamp plan was worked on over the summer and presented in a special issue of *The New York Times Magazine* in September 2002, its publication timed to coincide with the first anniversary of September 11.

"Now is the time for New York to express its ambition through architecture and reclaim its place as a visionary city," the magazine proclaimed. What followed was a World's Fair of cutting-edge architecture: a "cultural building" by Steven Holl, a school by Richard Meier, a somewhat Gehry-esque office building by Peter Eisenman, an office tower that grew wider at the top by Rem Koolhaas, and various kinds of housing blocks by Charles Gwathmey, Enrique Norten, and several other architects. None of it fit together into any kind of coherent plan, but almost all of it was visually dazzling. If there was any larger concept, it was Frederic Schwartz's notion that West Street not only should be turned into a tunnel (something that others had suggested before) but should become the site for almost all of the new construction. Muschamp jumped on Schwartz's idea, since it seemed like a way to eat one's cake and have it, too. He wrote that all of the LMDC's space needs could fit over West Street, fulfilling the Port Authority's program, while the space of Ground Zero itself could be devoted to a memorial, held for future development, or both.

Muschamp's favored architects spread out their wares along West Street, which in his vision was less a meaningful urban street than a cavalcade of experimental architecture, its showpieces lined up in a row, striving for attention. His text suggested that he believed that the primary purpose of architecture was to challenge the status quo, and he appeared quite embittered at what he considered New York's reluctance to embrace his ideas. "Our architecture no longer reflects this cosmopolitan spirit," Muschamp complained, as if he were scolding his readers for not liking his favorite architects as much as he did. "In fact, our buildings have turned it upside down—into a rage for dreariness and provinciality, an intolerance for the progressive ideas that have regenerated many cityscapes overseas."

Muschamp's attempt to inject himself into the design process did not find favor with many of his fellow critics, including those who, like Michael Sorkin, believed themselves to be every bit as open to progressive ideas as Muschamp. Sorkin, writing in *Architectural Record,* called for "an open process, a genuine competition, in which public bodies devoted themselves to promoting the widest—and wildest—styles of inclusion, not this endless, mad favoritism," which is what, to Sorkin, Muschamp's project represented. Several other architecture critics agreed that the Muschamp effort came off more as a commemoration of architectural celebrity than as a useful presentation of anything that could truly be called a new idea. Martin Filler, writing in *The New Republic,* later called it a "high-style beauty pageant" and said that Muschamp "by acting as a patron as well as a commentator placed himself in the indefensible and untenable position of both judge and jury." The one exception to the rejection of Muschamp by his peers was Joseph Giovannini, the architecture critic of *New York* magazine, who generally shares Muschamp's leanings toward a certain genre of celebrity architect. He offered the *Times* critic the highest form of flattery by imitating the project with a series of Ground Zero architectural commissions of his own. Although Giovannini's effort, which included proposals by Zaha Hadid, Peter Eisenman, Thom Mayne, William Pedersen, and Carlos Zapata, attracted less attention than Muschamp's, it actually possessed a stronger design ethos. Each architect who submitted a scheme for *New York* magazine was required to produce a coherent vision for the entire sixteen-acre site. Giovannini's published feature still looked like a cavalcade of celebrities, but at least it was offering several complete alternatives rather than suggesting that the idea of an all-star lineup was itself the idea of how to rebuild Ground Zero.

During the design process, Muschamp's team of architects had not functioned smoothly. Many of the participants were uncomfortable taking design orders from a critic, and some of them talked about wanting to leave the project, but they remained for the same reason that they participated in the first place: they did not want to offend the critic of the city's most powerful newspaper. In the end, Muschamp's jeremiad had little effect. His uncritical adoration of avant-garde form was confusing and off-putting to many readers, and the most important message his project contained—the need to pay more attention to aesthetics—while unquestionably correct, was a few weeks too late. By the time the magazine appeared, the LMDC had already switched strategies and issued its call to architects around the world to participate in its new design study. Muschamp published his complaint that the design process was not including serious architects several weeks after the LMDC had already invited every architect in the world to participate in it. And while the architecture community had certainly known that Muschamp's project was being pulled together behind closed doors during the summer, this knowledge in itself was hardly enough to have shifted the direction of the official planning process.

Not that the official process was the work of the angels. It had been crippled by laboring under the enormous weight of the Port

Authority's program, so the best that could be hoped to come of it would be a more attractive answer to the wrong question. But then again, the same could be said of Muschamp's project. Neither the LMDC nor *The New York Times* was truly visionary, for the simple reason that neither started with a fresh program. While the *Times* project did contain housing, it also envisioned fulfilling all of the Port Authority's demands for commercial space, and it ended up being less a fresh set of ideas than a set of new and fashionable wrappings for ideas that had been around all the while.

In the end, it was a romantic exercise, as much, in its way, as a little-noticed scheme for Ground Zero commissioned by another publication, *City Journal,* several months before. At the end of 2001, *City Journal,* which is published by the conservative Manhattan Institute, went in the opposite direction from that which Muschamp was to choose and asked a firm of classical architects, Franck Lohsen McCrery of Washington, to propose a new design for Ground Zero. The architects came up with a grandiose, formal plaza, a few streets, and some handsome office towers that looked like renderings of an idealized city of the 1930s. It was rigidly symmetrical and somewhat stultifying.

For all that Muschamp's later exercise seemed so different from Franck Lohsen McCrery's, however, the two emerged from the same confused notion of how to give architecture more prominence in the rebuilding process. In both cases, aesthetic ideas came first: a particular aesthetic vision was paramount, and it was to be imposed on the site before other decisions were made. Whatever society might truly want or need for the site was expected to fit into it. Both Muschamp and the classicists seemed to believe that they possessed an aesthetic vision that was precisely what society needed but had simply failed to ask for, and that by producing their design they were leading the world to its true desires.

It's true that the classical design was presented with grandiose pomp, as if it expressed a kind of inevitable, time-honored authority, while Muschamp cloaked his plan in an air of irreverence, taking the view that architecture's purpose was not to celebrate authority but to challenge it. But both attitudes were more than a little caught in the past. Not only does classicism no longer symbolize authority in the way it once did, modernism, for its part, no longer represents the kind of automatic challenge to authority that it once did, either. For all their differences, both the classicists and Muschamp shared a nostalgic view of the past as a time when a traditional, bourgeois culture could be shaken up by the avant-garde. The fact that the classicists wanted to protect that culture and Muschamp wanted to disrupt it is irrelevant; both the classicists and Muschamp believed in an outdated cultural construct that held sway only in the nineteenth century and the first two thirds of the twentieth.

Precisely what architecture could do at Ground Zero, and what it could not, was the subject of a symposium called Monument and Memory, sponsored by the art-history department of Columbia University at the end of September. There had been plenty of public programs about the architectural issues at Ground Zero over the last year, but this one was different, since it came just a few days after the LMDC had designated the seven teams that would work on the new master plan, and the featured speaker was one of them, Daniel Libeskind, who was especially known for architecture that attempted to address the issue of memory. And the respondents were equally notable: Leon Wieseltier, the critic and literary editor of *The New Republic,* and Sherwin Nuland, the surgeon who had written extensively on death. The event was held on a Friday evening at the New-York Historical Society, and the auditorium was full.

"I have been trying to redefine the relationship between architecture and memory," Libeskind said. "To describe memory onto a building as the postmodernists tried to do is only a banality. Architecture is a communicative art, it tells a story. But so many buildings tell a story of a solipsistic kind. They are autistic, they tell a story only of their own making. But I believe architecture should tell stories about other things, that go beyond themselves."

Libeskind filled his talk with sentences such as "space is a spiritual entity, a soul, like a person" and "the personal soul is the great matrix of the community," and he went on to present several of his projects, including an entry into a competition for housing near a former SS headquarters in Germany. He insisted that the housing include some kind of marking of the site's past, "and not only did I not win the competition, I was disqualified," he said. "I thought it is not possible for an architect to do that, to put eight thousand units here and obliterate what happened there," Libeskind continued. "How to deal with such a piece of land, where evil took place? You communicate to the public the vastness of catastrophe but also make a new ecology, a new topography, a contribution to a better life."

Libeskind's comments were his first public statement in New York to suggest that he would approach the Ground Zero problem not primarily in terms of a memorial or in terms of commercial construction, but as a question of establishing a balance between the two. His essential message, however, was his assertion of the potential of architecture to convey the kind of powerful emotions that literature is expected to express and his belief that architects have an obligation to build as a part of the healing process. "You can never be an architect unless you're an optimist," Libeskind said.

Wieseltier was not impressed. "Cleverness is an inadequate response to suffering," he said, and then, taking issue not only with Libeskind but with Muschamp's project in *The New York Times Magazine,* he added, "Lower Manhattan must not be transformed into a theme park of advanced architectural taste."

Architecture, Wieseltier believed, was part of the problem, not part of the solution. "Among the many illusions that surely crashed to the ground with the towers was the belief in architecture," he said. "The spiritual challenge of Ground Zero is plainly greater than the architectural challenge—all I need at Ground Zero is a void and a flag. Emptiness is the spiritual equivalent of silence. A void is a retort to the din."

Jewish tradition, Wieseltier said, uses words and rituals, not buildings, as monuments. "It chose culture over stone. We have the option of stone, but I wonder if we have the option of culture."

Nuland in effect endorsed Wieseltier's view and called for a meditative garden instead of any structures at Ground Zero, "a place where we can free ourselves from the hurly-burly of our daily lives, a garden of thought and retreat in the midst of the towering city where our souls may recover from the busyness of living."

Libeskind responded to Wieseltier. "I do not accept your critique of architecture as a necessary evil," he said. "The poets have been overestimated in their power." Everything is material, Libeskind said. "Language is not the home. We are not at home in language. We are at home at home." Even the Jews did not rely on words alone, he said; they built synagogues and cemeteries. "I would invite every intellectual to be an architect," Libeskind said. "It is always about making something—you have faith in the future."

Nuland, trying to support Wieseltier, said, "I am offended by the thought that there will be a piece of architecture on that spot, because ultimately architecture is about the architect, not about the people who died. What name would you have people think about? Libeskind? Gehry?"

Later, a questioner asked Nuland if he understood that everything, including the tranquil garden he envisioned, had to be designed and that the issue was not the presence or the absence of a designer but the skill with which any designer could integrate aesthetics and human needs. Nuland seemed not to grasp this idea, at which point Libeskind told him, "You have an idea of architecture that comes straight from Ayn Rand." In fact, both Nuland and Wieseltier, oddly, seemed intent on viewing architecture as incompatible with human spiritual needs—Nuland saw it as nothing more than an expression of ego, and Wieseltier saw it as materialistic. Nuland's misunderstanding brought much of the discussion into focus, however, since it made clear that if people as sophisticated as he and Wieseltier were so put off by the current state of architectural culture that they could see no social value in architecture at all, what could less educated people be thinking? Libeskind had tried to present architecture as capable of telling stories and presenting ideas that relate to human life, of using space and form and light to instill particular emotional responses. Hovering over his argument were not only powerful and popular contemporary buildings like Frank Gehry's Guggenheim Museum in Bilbao, but great works of the past like Chartres Cathedral, which have always been testament to the ability of architecture to create profound emotional responses and to inspire as well as to provide solace. Wieseltier and Nuland seemed to be trying to tell Libeskind that there was no such thing, that architecture was inevitably self-referential, and that it had no purpose except to celebrate the architect's ego. Although Wieseltier denounced Muschamp's project (and Libeskind tried to separate himself from it as well), Wieseltier seemed to be saying that Muschamp had actually gotten it just right, and that his "theme park of advanced architectural taste" actually depicted the reality of architecture and how little it could do to alleviate human suffering.

Roland Betts, Billie Tsien, and Alex Garvin had originally planned to select five teams to participate in the design study, but after giving the first four slots to THINK, United Architects, the Meier team, and the Skidmore, Owings & Merrill team, they could not agree on the fifth. Betts wanted Norman Foster, and Garvin wanted Libeskind. When neither would yield, Tsien, observing that Betts had no strenuous objection to Libeskind and Garvin had no strong objection to Foster, suggested that the easiest thing was to designate them both. And so the project expanded to six teams, and shortly thereafter grew again, when Peterson and Littenberg convinced the LMDC that its consulting work on the earlier phases of the process, which had been given little recognition by Beyer Blinder Belle, entitled it to a position in the competition, too. Beyer Blinder Belle itself had no such privilege; its name had become too much of a liability, the architectural equivalent of box-office poison. ("We were the first line of soldiers over the trenches, and you know what happens to them in wartime," John Belle said later. "We were too bloodied.")

Garvin called the seven teams of architects with the news that they had been selected and asked them to come to an all-day briefing session at Ground Zero on October 11. (Betts later referred to it as "Ground Zero school.") The architects met with John Whitehead and Lou Tomson, and they toured the site. Only one of them asked to descend into the pit of Ground Zero, to walk around the excavations and the cleanup process: Daniel Libeskind. Libeskind was one of only two participants who had chosen to submit a plan on his own rather than as part of a large team. Since the other solo entrant was Norman Foster, who commanded the machinery of an enormous corporate architectural practice in London that was accustomed to churning out skyscrapers and airports, Libeskind's small atelier seemed, in the context of the Ground Zero process, to be even more modest than it was.

Garvin spoke to the participants about the urban-design guidelines he had drawn up and about the program. He tried to avoid making it seem as if the Port Authority and Silverstein's commercial program was too restrictive a factor, and he talked as much as he could about his own vision for the site, putting it in deliberately humanistic, not technical, terms. Garvin talked not about the physical form of the site but about four different kinds of people he envisioned the rebuilt Ground Zero serving. "The first is a person who lives there, south of Liberty Street, in a converted office building, works in Tribeca, and walks through the site to work and sees a poster advertising a cultural event right there that he decides to attend," Garvin told the group.

> The second person is a business traveler, who comes to Lower Manhattan via a new train connection from the airport to attend a conference in a new conference center at Ground Zero and checks into a new hotel. He takes a free bus on Fulton Street to the South Street Seaport, sees a small restaurant, has lunch, then goes to his conference, and from there to an opera in the new opera house on the site. The third person is a tourist, who arrives on a bus, stays at a less expensive hotel in the neighborhood, walks through the memorial area and down the promenade that replaces West Street to Battery Park, where he takes a ferry to Ellis Island, then comes back to visit the new museum on the site, then ends his day with a visit to a jazz club that has just opened on Fulton Street. And finally there is the fourth person, a commuter, who arrives across the river at a ferry station, walks to his office by crossing the restored Ground Zero, has lunch in a new restaurant on Fulton Street, then enters the new transit hub to take the number 4 train to a meeting in Midtown.

"I've never met a planner like you," Daniel Libeskind told Garvin at the end of his presentation. Garvin, who had wanted

Libeskind in the group from the beginning, was pleased. He had given up on the notion of making any significant change in the Port Authority's program, but he was hoping to at least create the impression that Ground Zero was being designed as much for the pleasure of its ultimate users as for the profits of the Port Authority and Larry Silverstein. He hoped that by focusing his presentation on his imaginary characters, he could get the architects to think in terms of designing for them as much as for the Port Authority and Silverstein.

"I can't deliver the Port Authority—nobody can," he later said. But if he could get the architects to produce architecturally ambitious plans that the Port Authority would be willing to accept, Garvin felt, he would have accomplished his task. In any event, things were progressing about as fast as Governor Pataki was going to allow them to.

The LMDC kept the architects on a fairly short leash. As they worked through the autumn, they were required to meet with Garvin and his deputy, Andrew Winters, every two weeks to review their progress. Expenses were paid for the out-of-towners to make frequent trips to and from New York, but the only fee the firms got—forty thousand dollars—was barely enough to carry most of them through the first phase of their work, let alone to cover all of the overhead costs that completing the study would actually entail. The architects were not permitted to speak to the press about their work, and Garvin, Winters, and representatives of the Port Authority critiqued it continually as it was being developed. Later, one of the losing entrants in the competition said, "I've been working for twenty years as an architect, and I've never had anyone treat me like that. They totally controlled the process, they wanted us to show them stuff every two weeks—and on the other hand they wanted us to work for free, and dream."

A couple of weeks after Ground Zero school, Garvin went to Las Vegas to speak at a panel at the Urban Land Institute's fall convention on the subject of planning at the trade-center site. The public at that point still saw the process as mired in the confusion that had followed the release of the Beyer Blinder Belle plans, and the stresses among the Port Authority, the LMDC, and the public, not to mention the state and city governments, the architectural community, and the various civic organizations, all loomed large. The various players seemed to be crashing into one another like bumper cars at an amusement park, and no one had any idea at that point whether the design study was going to produce anything of value—and if it did, whether it could get built.

In the unlikely setting of the Venetian Hotel on the Las Vegas Strip, the members of the panel, which included Marilyn Jordan Taylor of Skidmore, Owings & Merrill; Joseph Rose, former chairman of the New York City Planning Commission; and Steven Spinola of the Real Estate Board of New York, talked on and on about the intricacies of the process and about the discouraging results so far. It was a largely political discussion, and it could not have been more different from the conversation between Libeskind, Wieseltier, and Nuland at the New-York Historical Society just a few weeks before. As he listened to his colleagues on the panel gripe about the complexities of the process and compare it to the market-driven nature of conventional real-estate development, Garvin suddenly had a new idea of how to explain and justify what, to many of them, seemed less a rational process than an inexplicable circus.

"More than two hundred years ago there were conflicts and difficulties and competing groups, too," he said, "and they struggled and struggled, and finally they came up with what we now know as the American Constitution. The process of dealing with this piece of land is difficult, but I am beginning to think it may be just like the writing of the Constitution, really—lots of competing views that will clash, and out of it we will eventually have some kind of resolution. It looks messy when it is happening, but out of it comes something coherent and democratic. That is how democracy works, and I am confident that we will figure out how democracy will prevail in the same way here, too."

CHAPTER 9

Making Things Better

The City Responds to the Designs

DEPENDING UPON WHOM YOU talked to, the Lower Manhattan Development Corporation's Innovative Design Study was either an impressive turnaround after a grim start or a brilliant ruse designed to fool the public into thinking that things had changed when they were really pretty much the same. Actually, it was a little bit of both. There is no question that by the time the autumn of 2002 arrived, power in the design process had shifted somewhat toward people who were strong advocates of the role of architecture and design—Roland Betts and Billie Tsien on the LMDC board, Alexander Garvin and his staff inside the agency—the very people who had been somewhat marginalized in the planning process just a couple of months earlier, when Jack Beyer and the Port Authority were calling most of the shots.

But the power that Betts and Garvin had assumed was based on their understanding that the Port Authority was as much in control as ever, even if it was now willing to play a less conspicuous public role. The starting point of the entire planning process, after all, was still the Port Authority's program for the site, and the concessions Roland Betts convinced the authority to make regarding square footage did not change that at all. The purpose of the design study was simply to give architects who were more creative than Beyer a shot at fulfilling the Port Authority's program. Garvin and Betts were not being cynical—they truly believed that this phase offered up the possibility of making things better, and they had long ago accepted the notion that a truly visionary plan for Ground Zero stood no chance of surviving the political process. They saw their role as trying to squeeze as much design quality as they could out of that process, not of bypassing it altogether. But that stance meant that any truly different ideas, such as using Ground Zero for housing or for some kind of new public institution, or turning the site over to existing New York City organizations, would not be welcome. There was no room for an architect like Michael Sorkin, for example, because he had already made it clear that he had no intention of accepting the program.

As the design study moved ahead, there was only one real possibility for significant change in the planning process. It lay in the desire of Dan Doctoroff to play a more active role in the process himself, as well as to give his patron, Mayor Bloomberg, and the city government a larger stake than they had had up to that point. Doctoroff had begun to explore a way in which to dispose of the Port Authority far more decisively than anyone had imagined back in July. In August, he let word leak out about an idea he had been toying with that would take Ground Zero away from the Port Authority altogether and put the land in the hands of the city.

Doctoroff knew that the city had been involved in long and difficult negotiations with the Port Authority over the leases for John F. Kennedy and LaGuardia airports in Queens, both of which are owned by the city and operated by the Port Authority. The Giuliani administration had objected to the low rent the Port Authority was paying the city—roughly $3 million per year—under the current leases, which expire in 2015. Rudolph Giuliani had threatened to take control of the airports away from the Port Authority and set up an airport authority of the city's own so that more of the airports' profits could return to the city coffers. It is difficult to know whether Giuliani could ever have made good on his threat—he would likely have had to take on the governors of both New York and New Jersey—but his insistence that the Port Authority was diverting profits from the airports to areas outside of New York City made a compelling argument, and the Port Authority, unwilling to face even the remote possibility of losing the airports, had already begun to renegotiate the current leases.

Doctoroff figured that he could solve two problems at once if the city traded the land under the airports for the land of Ground Zero. The Port Authority would have the two airports, free and clear, and the city, for its part, would have ownership and complete control over what seemed, at that moment, to be the most important piece of land in the five boroughs. It would not be an easy trade, since both parties would have to agree not only on the comparative values of Ground Zero and the airports but on the value of any future amount of income the airports would bring and on whatever back payments the Port Authority might be willing to make to compensate the city for the unfair airport lease. And if the city, upon taking control of Ground Zero, were to condemn Larry Silverstein's lease so as to wrest the land away from commercial interests and devote a significant amount of the site to civic purposes, that would reduce its economic value, however wise it might be as public policy. How do you value a swap when it is worth $120 million per year in rent to the Port Authority but might bring in little or no money if the city owned it and used it for a different purpose? Do you value Central Park as a priceless urban amenity or by adding up what its 843 acres might bring if they were put on the open market?

For all the difficulty such questions posed, Doctoroff still found the idea appealing, even exciting, and over the course of late summer so did most of the other participants. No one rejected it outright, even if no one else jumped on the land-swap bandwagon with Doctoroff's enthusiasm; most public officials described the idea in cautious, wait-and-see terms. Even Charles Gargano, who as vice chairman of the Port Authority ran the risk of losing much of his power over the planning process if the swap took place, referred to it as "a serious first step toward resolving long-standing issues involving New York airports and the Port Authority leases." A spokesman for Governor Pataki said the governor "was willing to listen" to the proposal but had not been briefed fully on it.

The most enthusiastic initial comment came from Robert Yaro. He called the land swap "a brilliant idea" and said, "It is in the regional interest, and it would fix a big problem for both agencies by clearing up the very confusing lines of authority downtown and out at the airports."

Yaro had not been a fan of the Port Authority's position from the beginning, and he had wondered, sometimes privately, sometimes publicly, why the Port Authority had not been bought out of the planning process at the very beginning—why Pataki, who was the one person who could have clarified the lines of authority, had chosen instead to sustain the confusion.

Pataki was certainly not going to let the land-swap idea move to the forefront immediately. First, he had no desire to give a certain advantage to Doctoroff and Bloomberg by allowing them to appear to be setting the agenda in the planning process; for all that Pataki and Bloomberg avoided major public clashes on matters regarding planning at Ground Zero, the fact of the matter was that the mayor and the governor, and even more their staffs, were highly competitive. Their public position of cooperation downtown was the result of a carefully crafted, delicate détente, which an intense, determined negotiation over the land swap would upset completely.

More to the point, pursuing the land swap quickly would also violate Pataki's unspoken policy of postponing all major policy decisions about Ground Zero until after the election. Giving up control of the most intensely watched piece of urban real estate in the world was not something that a governor, especially a governor known for the caution of his positions, wished to do in the weeks preceding an election. Ground Zero was not a political liability for Pataki, so there was no political benefit to him in making the land swap quickly. And to the extent that rebuilding the World Trade Center site could continue to hold a degree of potential benefit for Pataki, he had no great incentive to agree to the land swap once the election was behind him, either. The proposal remained on the table for several months, and there were numerous negotiation sessions between the city and the Port Authority, but none of them had any compelling urgency. Ultimately the idea died, a victim partly of the difficulty of reaching a fair valuation of pieces of land that could not be easily compared but more of Pataki's failure to signal that it would be useful to him to have it happen.

There is no way to be certain what would have happened at Ground Zero if the land swap had occurred. But it is hard not to believe that Bloomberg and Doctoroff would have pursued a radically different course from Pataki's. If the city replaced the Port Authority as the landlord at Ground Zero, that in itself would not have eliminated Larry Silverstein's lease or the obligations connected to it, since existing leases are assumed by new owners as a matter of course when real estate is transferred. But Doctoroff's very goal was to assert a more civic identity for the land than Pataki had chosen to impose. There was little political incentive for the city to embark on the complicated process of takeover if it were ultimately to mean nothing more than the name of a different entity at the top of Silverstein's lease. The whole idea was for the city's ownership to have a visible effect, which would probably have led to the city government attempting to renegotiate Silverstein's lease or eliminating it entirely by condemning it and then starting the planning process all over again.

But with the land swap absolutely certain not to happen quickly, Doctoroff pursued another course of action to give the city more leverage during the fall of 2002. He recognized that the power of the state and the Port Authority, however absolute it might be within the sixteen acres of Ground Zero, was essentially nonexistent just outside those acres. Both the public and planners had frequently expressed the belief that the World Trade Center site should not be planned in isolation, that any plans had to consider the area in relation to the rest of Lower Manhattan. That view had been reaffirmed during the Listening to the City event, and it had been a part of public policy ever since the planning process had begun a year earlier, when the LMDC had been given the authority to study the entire area south of Houston Street. With that in mind, Alex Garvin had commissioned several studies of urban-design issues outside Ground Zero, but unlike the plans within the site, nothing the LMDC wanted to do on the neighboring blocks could happen without the city's cooperation.

Doctoroff decided that if the state was going to assert its will on its sixteen acres, the city could do the same for the rest of Lower Manhattan. He concluded that the best strategy for the mayor was to remind everyone that if the city did not directly control Ground Zero, it had plenty of authority over everything around it and had some very clear ideas about it, too. Doctoroff decided that the time had come for the mayor to present a vision for all of Lower Manhattan, and he envisioned it as a major statement of urban design that might stand in contrast to the uncertainty being played out at Ground Zero.

Over the course of the fall, Doctoroff and his staff put together a series of ideas for the mayor to present. Bloomberg scheduled the speech for December 12, six days before the LMDC's elaborate presentation by the seven teams of architects in the Winter Garden. While the mayor ran the risk of appearing to be upstaging the big event, he could just as easily justify the timing by saying he was simply setting the context for the Ground Zero presentations.

Bloomberg began his speech, delivered at a breakfast meeting of the Association for a Better New York, a business group, in the landmark ballroom of the Regent Wall Street Hotel, by acknowledging the LMDC and the upcoming proposals, which, the mayor said, "will be very different from the six site plans that were presented last summer." Then Bloomberg went on: "But no matter how magnificent the best design for the sixteen acres of the World Trade Center site proves to be, it must be complemented by an equally bold vision for all of Lower Manhattan—a new beginning for Lower Manhattan—that meets the needs of all of New York City and of the entire region."

Bloomberg began, subtly but firmly, to distance himself and the city from responsibility for the LMDC's plans. "We cannot afford to assume that what goes on the sixteen acres will itself guarantee a bright future for Lower Manhattan," he said, and then, in a remarkable jab at the original World Trade Center, he continued:

> We've done that before. When the World Trade Center was first built, it was hailed as a cure-all for everything that plagued downtown. True, it came, over time, to embody the

> spirit of Lower Manhattan. It was commercially bustling—and an international icon. That's why the terrorists destroyed it. But, if we are honest with ourselves, we will recognize that the impact on our city was not all positive. The twin towers' voracious appetite for tenants weakened the entire downtown market. The underground mall, while popular, detracted from the vitality of the streets that surrounded it by siphoning pedestrians away from aboveground streets. The World Trade Center did not, as its objective was [to do], increase employment below Canal Street. In the 1970s, 22 percent of all Manhattan jobs were downtown. By 2000, that had declined to just over 19 percent.

Bloomberg went on: "Of course, it wasn't just the World Trade Center that contributed to this decline. We have underinvested in Lower Manhattan for decades. It's been seventy years since we built a new transit line downtown. There is far less open space here than in other places around the city. There aren't enough schools, either. The time has come to put an end to that, to restore Lower Manhattan to its rightful place as a global center of innovation, and make it a downtown for the twenty-first century," the mayor said. His plan, he went on to explain, was to make public-sector investments in key areas that would "trigger a response by the private market that will create the kind of Lower Manhattan we want."

"The public sector's role is to catalyze this transformation by making bold investments with the same sense of purpose and urgency that allowed us to clean up the World Trade Center site months ahead of schedule and hundreds of millions of dollars under budget," Bloomberg said. The mayor went on to detail the specific public-sector investments he wanted to make, which he listed in three separate categories: developing infrastructure to better connect Lower Manhattan to other places, including the airports; building new residential neighborhoods downtown; and creating appealing public places and cultural facilities that would draw both tourists and residents. He ended his speech by referring to doubters who questioned the wisdom of building Central Park in the 1850s. "If you study New York history, you realize that it is often at the moments when New York has faced its greatest challenges that we've had our biggest achievements. Central Park was created on the heels of a financial panic. The subways were built at the turn of the century as [the] overcrowding [of] downtown reached life-threatening proportions. During the Great Depression, New York set the national standard by putting its people to work building parks and highways," Bloomberg said. As an example of the kind of public space he envisioned, Bloomberg showed a series of possibilities for a new park along the East River, across Lower Manhattan from Ground Zero. The highly conceptual project, designed by the firms of Diller & Scofidio and the Rockwell Group, included a new, permanent home for the Cirque du Soleil, a floating forest and lawn, a skating rink, an aquarium, and a hotel.

Bloomberg's ambitious "vision" for Lower Manhattan bore a close resemblance not only to Doctoroff's views but to the priorities of the planner who, behind the scenes, had done the most to shape Doctoroff's thinking. Indeed, the speech could be considered as much a summary of Alex Garvin's hopes for Lower Manhattan as the mayor's. Garvin had been pushing for increased connections between Ground Zero and the rest of Lower Manhattan, and he had come to believe that better airport access was potentially the trump card that would allow Lower Manhattan to compete more successfully with Midtown for office tenants. He had also argued for more attention to housing, public space, and cultural facilities downtown, and he had been among the most ardent opponents of Westfield's attempt to insert a suburban-style mall into the plans. All of these ideas were prominent in Bloomberg's speech, sometimes in language that closely resembled Garvin's own—and sometimes with drawings prepared by Steven Peterson and Barbara Littenberg, who had been drafted as consultants to the city. And the mayor, unlike most other politicians, had not been shy in reminding people that the original World Trade Center had failed to turn around the downtown economy, as David and Nelson Rockefeller had expected it to do—a point that had been too often overlooked in the rush to sanctify the twin towers as skyscraper martyrs. Bloomberg's willingness to confront the problematic history of the towers, rather than to hide behind rhetoric as Pataki had done, was a striking aspect of his speech, and one that seemed to tie the talk even more to Garvin.

But the ultimate sign of Garvin's hand in the mayor's speech was the way Bloomberg explained the goal of his downtown program. He aimed to use public spending on major infrastructure and public projects as a means of encouraging private-sector investment, which all but echoed Garvin's definition in *The American City* of urban planning as "public action that will produce a sustained and widespread private market reaction." Garvin had concluded that "only when a project also has beneficial impact on the surrounding community can it be considered successful planning"—which, translated into the terms of the mayor's speech, became his argument that however good the plan for the sixteen acres of Ground Zero turned out to be, something more would be needed if Lower Manhattan were to be transformed into the vibrant part of the city that everyone wanted it to become.

The mayor's speech—by any measure the most sophisticated statement on urban design and planning delivered by any mayor of New York since John Lindsay—was well received, but it did little if anything to shift the focus of the public dialogue. After a few days of respectful press reports, attention went back to the LMDC and the imminent release of the results of the design study, which had come to take on the allure of a horse race. Beside the excitement of a competition, the mayor's speech was merely an earnest policy statement. By then, there was no longer any pretense that the study was simply an informal presentation of ideas from which Garvin, Betts, and the others could pick and choose. The seven teams of architects had all produced real architecture, not just site plans, and the LMDC, increasingly alert to the publicity possibilities in a whole series of dazzling images of future Ground Zeros, did nothing to discourage the perception that this had been the intention. If the dreariness and banality of the original six plans had gotten the LMDC and the Port Authority into such trouble over the summer, at least that mistake would not be repeated. And the fact that the architects, or at least quite a number of them, were famous did not hurt, either: the celebrity quotient could only make the situation more enticing. And the sexier and more exciting both the buildings and their designers were, the more the public would be likely to be distracted from the underlying fact about all of the new plans, which was that they were based on the Port Authority's commercial program.

The evolution of the design study into a full-fledged competition among celebrity architects was less a conscious strategy, planned from the beginning, than a set of circumstances that the LMDC and the Port Authority found themselves in as the level of buzz continued to rise. But however much the LMDC may have backed into it, it ended up playing the competition for all it was worth. The press conference in the Winter Garden on December 18, which began with Daniel Libeskind describing in highly wrought, emotional language his arrival as an immigrant in New York harbor, and ended with Roger Duffy relating in a monotone his plan to use Ground Zero to evolve a new model for urban density, may have been the most widely covered architectural event in history. The *New York Post* put its favorite design, Norman Foster's "kissing towers," on the front page, and immediately launched a poll to ask readers to indicate their preferred designs. So did the local NY1 News and CNN. The designs and their creators were all over the newspapers and the television news, and when the LMDC posted the schemes on its website, the site was so overwhelmed with hits that it was briefly shut down.

The editorial page of *The New York Times,* which had been less than enthusiastic about the planning process up to that point, was ecstatic. "Yesterday morning at the Winter Garden in Lower Manhattan, New York City received a gift of a kind it has almost never received before," an editorial proclaimed. "Some of the world's greatest architects presented plans for the reconstruction of the World Trade Center site, plans of a truly visionary scale. What the city witnessed yesterday was a seminar in architectural thinking, a master class in making sense of space, function, civic commitment, and public emotion. . . . The government's obligation is to protect the scale and ambition of these plans against what are almost certain to be challenges from commercial and political interests."

Even Herbert Muschamp, who tried to claim credit for inspiring the competition by stating that it was a response to his gathering of celebrity architects in *The New York Times Magazine,* gave grudging approval. "The architects have risen to the occasion," he wrote. "So should we," he concluded, giving his readers, once again, an order to listen to him. Muschamp liked every one of the projects except Peterson and Littenberg's, in which he saw not intelligent urban design but only the traditional planning and design that he hated. He was exceptionally positive about Daniel Libeskind: "If you are looking for the marvelous, here's where you will find it. Daniel Libeskind's project attains a perfect balance between aggression and desire. It will provoke many viewers to exclaim that yes, this design is actually better than what was there before."

Other newspapers were more skeptical. *The New York Sun,* a small, conservative daily, produced a long editorial with the portentous title "Capitalism and the Architects," which said that "the process has been hijacked by architects. Only an architect, after all, would be so disconnected from reality as to propose to build—as four of the seven teams of architects have—the world's tallest building at the World Trade Center site. . . . While the Lower Manhattan Development Corporation commissioned the plans, it doesn't have the money or the authority to actually build any of the buildings. . . . [A]mid all the excitement about fantasy architecture, it is worth asking the question: who is to build these buildings, and with whose money?" *The Sun* answered its own question by acknowledging that if the insurance money Larry Silverstein was due to receive was to be the source of funds for building at Ground Zero, then "it would make sense for him, and not the LMDC, to design the buildings, in consultation with whatever architect he chooses."

A columnist in *The Wall Street Journal,* Daniel Henninger, was less concerned about capitalism than simple realism. "Let's get something straight: There is no chance that any of these outsized buildings will ever be realized, and these architects surely know it," he wrote. "But anyone with an ounce of interest in reviving the dead zone known as Lower Manhattan should send every one of these architects a kiss. In just a few hours they brought more energy, excitement, and yes, their word, 'vision,' to a project that had begun to look irretrievably adrift." And then Henninger went on to praise Barbara Littenberg as "the only person who made complete sense and the only woman who spoke; consider Jane Jacobs and Ada Louise Huxtable and you begin to think women have some advantage in understanding urban life. Barbara Littenberg certainly understands downtown Manhattan."

The enthusiasm of *The New York Times*'s editorial page was not shared by many of its readers, if the letters the paper published two days after the Winter Garden press conference were any indication. "The designs suggest visionary yet disturbing directions about what forms should occupy this sacred ground," wrote Mark Francis, a professor of landscape architecture at the University of California, Davis. "Looking beyond the poetic statements of the designers, buildings loom large. I wonder what would result if this most important of design exercises was first approached by asking how to create the most important and memorable public open space in the city, if not the world. More human and perhaps more hopeful ideas may emerge than seen here. Great architecture could then follow as it has in other parts of the city."

"The proposals for ground zero are, as you say, proud and bold," Abe Fabrizio, from Long Beach, California, wrote. "Unfortunately, they are also, without exception, extremely ugly."

"I am horrified to think that one of these firms may actually get the job," wrote George Abruzzese of Bohemia, New York. "Most of the designs look as if they should be stage sets for a circus, where double-jointed athletics and illusions are appropriate." And a woman from Niskayuna, New York, Barbara Mark Mauro, wrote that she hoped the unveiling of the new designs "will create a stampede back to the earlier, 'boring' proposals. These new proposals are overly male, aggressive and insensitive, and moved me to tears of exasperation."

Only two letter writers singled out specific schemes to praise, and the choices were telling. Rita L. McKee, a woman from New Haven, liked the latticework towers proposed by Rafael Viñoly's THINK team, partly because they reminded her of the original twin towers. Annlinn Grossman, from Silver Spring, Maryland, wrote that she found Daniel Libeskind's proposal, with its centerpiece of an exposed excavation revealing the original slurry wall as well as its tall tower, "the embodiment of all the newly designed and built site should be. . . . [H]is plan literally and figuratively takes us from the depths to the heights; it answers workaday and memorial needs in a manner that is at once grave, celebratory, and seamless."

CHAPTER 10

Architecture as Democracy

Building a Consensus

MOST OF THE PUBLIC HEARings the Lower Manhattan Development Corporation held in 2002 were dreary, conventional affairs that did little to encourage genuine dialogue about the future of Lower Manhattan. Compared to an event like Listening to the City, which made use of electronic polling technology, the LMDC's public hearings felt tired and rote, old-fashioned events that tended to attract the sorts of citizens who were more interested in three minutes on a soapbox than in engaging in real discussion. The LMDC had been more effective in opening the planning process to the public through its website, which offered images about all of the proposed schemes for Ground Zero, and through the exhibition of models and renderings of each scheme that it mounted in the Winter Garden. Since the unveiling of the plans a week before Christmas, all nine of the schemes had been on view, each elaborately presented behind glass in a storefrontlike enclosure. While the presentation in display windows created an awkward sense of distance from the models, at least the exhibition was open from early morning to late evening every day of the week, and visitors were invited to leave comments on postcards. Over the course of December and January, roughly one hundred thousand people visited the Winter Garden, and twelve thousand of them left comments. It was an enormous number, and yet it was dwarfed by the number of hits the LMDC's website received during the same period: more than six million. The website was designed to encourage the submission of electronic comments, complete with a selection box for people to identify themselves as rescue workers on September 11, survivors of September 11, former or current residents of Lower Manhattan, residents of other parts of New York City, residents of the tristate area outside of New York City, residents of other parts of the United States, residents of other countries, real-estate owners in Lower Manhattan, students in Lower Manhattan, or as members of six other categories.

Given all of that, it seemed odd that when the agency held one of its old-style public hearings about the plans at Pace University a few blocks from Ground Zero on January 13, 2003, the issue that dominated the discussion did not seem to be the plans themselves but the extent to which the planning process was, or was not, democratic. John Whitehead introduced the event with his usual dignity, and Kevin Rampe, Lou Tomson's deputy, followed with an impassioned but highly defensive discussion of the planning process. We want to hear the diversity of viewpoints of residents of Manhattan and Staten Island, Rampe said, and he claimed that every step of the process had been shaped by public input. He seemed so determined to make the case that the agency had put the public in charge of determining the future of Ground Zero that it was possible to think that he believed there was no virtue to having leaders with ideas of their own. The entire thrust of Rampe's remarks, like the ones Tomson had made at other events, was directed toward the notion that the agency put listening to the public ahead of all other obligations.

The format of this hearing was slightly different than earlier ones. In the hopes of enlivening the proceedings, the LMDC had invited John Schumo, a reporter from NY1 News, to act as a kind of master of ceremonies, and the event was simulcast to smaller, local public hearings in the other boroughs. Schumo stepped onstage and showed that he had gotten with the program. "Whenever someone asks me who is truly in charge of the process, I say it's you, the citizens," he said. He then introduced Alex Garvin, who explained the basic outlines of the design study and was to have presented a detailed review of the nine new proposals. But the elaborate, computer-driven video system failed. So Garvin left the stage, and Schumo moved quickly to open the floor to public comments.

Jonathan Hakala, a proponent of rebuilding the original towers, spoke first, and called Garvin and Stanton Eckstut, the Port Authority's planning consultant, "two men meeting in a back room deciding the future of Ground Zero." He received wide applause. He was followed a few minutes later by another proponent of rebuilding the old towers, Andrew Olas, who said, "The vision of the terrorists, I am sad and disgusted to say, has prevailed—our center of commerce remains in ruins, the future of our downtown has been hijacked, those in charge of rebuilding have unconditionally surrendered. The destruction of the World Trade Center has been taken as a signal to have an urban-renewal orgy. Stop wasting our time and tax money—the only consideration for this site should be twin towers as tall or taller." Olas, too, was applauded. The audience showed no such enthusiasm for a woman who followed him, Margaret Hughes, who called for low-income housing on the site, or for the architect Hugh Hardy, whose thoughtful remarks urging the audience to look at the design exercise as "a competition of ideas, not of designers" seemed barely to have been heard. The audience was more interested either in cheering on proponents for rebuilding the towers as they were or in hearing people like a later speaker, Paul Epstein, who complained that there was too little public participation in the process. "We need a slower, more dialogic process," he said.

Actually, the problem was not a lack of public participation in the process, since there was nothing if not plenty of dialogue. The problem was that the officials never showed any real interest in the public's views on the all-important issue of what uses the site should contain. It was made clear from the beginning that the program was the Port Authority's, not the public's, to decide. The public was given opportunity to comment not on how the site might be used but only on how the uses that the Port Authority and the LMDC wanted might be configured on the site. For all the LMDC's constant self-congratulation about how public the planning process was, what might be considered the most important part of it was none of the public's business.

Still, the middle of January was an intensely busy time in the planning process: as in the golden age of Broadway, when there was an opening every night, there seemed to be a public event about Ground Zero every night. The evening after the public hearing on the plans, there was a second hearing about the mission statement and program for a memorial, also sponsored by the LMDC, which had been hoping to launch an international competition to find a memorial design once the master plan for the site was determined. Later in the month, on a particularly frigid night, the auditorium of the City University Graduate Center was nearly filled for what may have been the most bizarre, if endearing, event of all: a presentation about a design the great Catalan architect Antonio Gaudí had created in 1905 for a skyscraper hotel for New York City. Gaudí's design, which never got past a sketch entitled "Project for a Grand Hotel in New York," would have been the tallest building in the world in 1905, a vast, bulky, torpedolike structure that seems to combine the naturalistic forms of his built work with an almost *Jetsons*-like futurism. It was actually to have been a cluster of towers hugging an enormous central tower, which was to have been topped by an observatory in the form of a star. The project was not only taller than the Eiffel Tower, the highest structure in the world at that time, but considerably bulkier at its base than the Empire State Building was to be. Gaudí's hotel was commissioned by some entrepreneurs who have gone unidentified in history, and it is unlikely that the plan was ever serious or even buildable in 1905. But it was proposed for a locale in Lower Manhattan that eventually became a part of the World Trade Center site, and this extraordinary historical coincidence encouraged several scholars with an interest in Gaudí's work to suggest that the Gaudí building be constructed now, as an alternative to the new plans being put forth at Ground Zero. "With modern technology it would be possible to finish the work on a reasonable deadline," one of the speakers said. "Even though Gaudí was Catholic, he had an enormous respect for Islamic culture. [His architecture was in part] inspired by Islamic mosques," he continued, as if to suggest that constructing a hundred-year-old, never-completed design by a brilliant and long-dead architect from Barcelona were the perfect means to satisfy both the pan-religious impulses that many people felt should be expressed at Ground Zero and the widespread desire for a new symbol on the skyline.

In fact, the Gaudí design was no more than a historical curiosity, a minor footnote to a career that otherwise had no connection either to New York or to skyscrapers. And far from paying honor to Gaudí, turning his sketches over to contemporary architects and engineers so that his vision could be turned into a buildable structure would in fact have disrespected his work, since thousands of decisions would have to have been made that inevitably would have changed Gaudí's concept. Gaudí made many of his design decisions as his buildings were rising, and there is no way to know how he would have completed this one. The hotel would not have been a true Gaudí building at all; it would have been a series of guesses about what Gaudí might have done, a conjecture based on a sketch—the future of Ground Zero turned into a conceit.

In comparison to the Gaudí event, the two-day forum about the LMDC plans sponsored by the Architectural League of New York, the Museum of Modern Art, and the New York chapter of the American Institute of Architects seemed like the height of realism. On the first evening, which was held in the Great Hall of Cooper Union, the architects presented their plans in detail, without discussion from the audience. Even without questions, the event lasted for more than six hours. On the second evening, which was held at Town Hall, the concert hall in Midtown Manhattan, fourteen architects from the seven teams sat on the stage at a long table that had been covered by a maroon cloth, and they were prepared to answer questions. There were thirteen men and one woman, Barbara Littenberg. They looked something like presidential candidates in a debate, being quizzed by the press, although in this case the inquisitors were Rosalie Genevro, president of the Architectural League; Terence Riley, head of the department of architecture and design at the Museum of Modern Art; and Anthony Vidler, head of the architecture program at Cooper Union.

Rosalie Genevro had the first question, which she directed to Greg Lynn of United Architects, the group strongly oriented toward design influenced by computer technologies. She asked Lynn about the enormous size of the United Architects design, a kind of mega-structure skyscraper. "The size was to respond to the gravity of the situation, and the symbolic was already there," Lynn said. "There is no way not to make a new vertical building the biggest and tallest. We want to bring pride back to the site."

"It is a mistake to think of the ground plane as the only repository for public space—it also belongs in the sky," said Kevin Kennon, one of Lynn's partners.

Vidler asked the THINK group to talk about the third of its schemes and the purpose of its plan, which contained a pair of structures that echoed the size and shape of the original twin towers. In the THINK plan the towers would not have been solid buildings but open frameworks, versions of the Eiffel Tower in the shape of Yamasaki's boxes. The architects wanted to set smaller structures containing cultural and public functions into the huge open trusswork. THINK had also left undifferentiated areas around for private development. Rafael Viñoly answered Vidler by saying that the goal of the plan was to ensure that the site would be dominated by a commemorative, public structure, not by commercial concerns. "We wanted to make real public space and not have it as part of some developer's amenity package," he said.

Vidler asked Richard Meier's team to explain what relevance their design, which they called a "new skyscraper typology," had to other situations. Skyscraper development usually does not come from purely symbolic origins, Vidler said. Peter Eisenman responded in an odd way, calling the strange, gridlike tower the group had designed "nonphallocentric."

Riley asked Libeskind to talk about the urban-design aspects of his plan. "Is a personal vision of a city precluded by the anonymity that a city's structures require? I think no," Libeskind said. He then talked of how there was a sense of anonymity behind "Stalin's

Moscow or Speer's Berlin, but behind them stood individuals who were criminals." The audience applauded, for the first time. Then Genevro asked Norman Foster to explain why he proposed a tower in open space—"the old modernist idea rather than a [street-oriented] twenty-four-hour city."

"The issues raised by this site are unique and special to this location," Foster said. "If it really works, it will offer lessons to the world at large."

And so it went on, with most of the architects answering questions obliquely, if at all. As they had at the Winter Garden presentations a month before, their speaking styles were as different as their architectural ones, and sometimes more revealing. Libeskind in particular used most questions as an excuse to deliver short sermons and tried hard to set his architecture within a moral context, hoping that the audience would be sufficiently moved by his remarks to associate his architecture with a sense of goodness and appropriateness. "Too many people think of September 11 as a simple event," he said. "It is complex and an urgent memory. The world shifted that day—it was an attack that is not really over—it stood against the foundations of what we are about. On the one hand, devastation and destruction and murder. On the other hand, revelation of what continues to support free people." Libeskind's comments, of course, could have been used by any of the architects to justify anything they had come up with—there was nothing inherent in his remarks to connect directly to his own plans for Ground Zero. But none of the other architects could speak so convincingly to a lay audience, and Libeskind's eloquence and passion had an impact at Town Hall, as they had at the Winter Garden.

If Libeskind came off as an eloquent, if somewhat sentimental, preacher, Foster was highly focused and seemed to be speaking to the LMDC and the Port Authority more than to the architecture buffs in the audience. Meier, Eisenman, and Gwathmey never quite managed to generate a sense of momentum, which was precisely the problem they had faced a month earlier. Their scheme was perplexing, their defense of it by turns opaque and vague. Viñoly and Frederic Schwartz of THINK were hardly paragons of clarity themselves at Town Hall, although they seemed more conciliatory than Meier and his partners. The United Architects group was far stronger, at least in terms of their ability to communicate. Peterson and Littenberg were also articulate, but as traditional-leaning architects and urbanists they were so clearly the odd people out in the group that it was difficult to get beyond that. And finally, confirming the way in which the architects replicated the tone they had set at the Winter Garden, the Skidmore, Owings & Merrill group seemed somewhat lost.

The most interesting question of the evening came from Rosalie Genevro, who asked all of the architects what they might have done differently if they had been given a less defined program. Richard Meier ignored the opportunity and said only that it was not the architect's job to determine the program of a building, that it was the client's business, period. Norman Foster, too, defended the program. "The more specific the brief that an architect is given, the easier the task," he said. "It is unprecedented the way this project has entered the public debate and extended so widely beyond the site and the city," he added, as if he worried that the LMDC had not been sufficiently flattered by his earlier remark. It was not surprising that the architects were hesitant to criticize the program, since they had agreed to work with it when they began their participation in the competition, and in any case attacking the client is rarely the route to success. Still, since an implicit theme of the Town Hall event, not to mention the entire design exercise, was to elevate the role of architects in the planning process, there was a contradiction in the architects' complacent view about the program. On the one hand, they believed that determining the program for Ground Zero was not their job, but on the other hand they wanted to be consulted at the beginning of the process and to have their ideas prevail. The underlying contradiction that was evident in the conception of Herbert Muschamp's project had not disappeared.

Jesse Reiser, a member of the United Architects team, hinted at the problem when he said, in response to Genevro's question, "Our project is a microcosm for our desire for a wider urban vision," although he did not say much about what that vision might be. His partner Greg Lynn seemed to be willing to acknowledge that Genevro had a point, even though he did not answer her question directly, either. "The piece we found most missing was the sense of what kind of vision, and not just the numbers for this project," he said. "It will take public leadership and vision."

Rafael Viñoly took on the question more forthrightly. "I think if there's anything interesting in what we've produced, it is that we have overcome the program," he said.

The most significant remark of the evening, however, was made by Kevin Kennon, in response to a question from Vidler about what a rational planning process for the site might consist of. "Implicit in the question is that the process is irrational—a pre-9/11 view would say that the process is an irrational mess and that we need a new Robert Moses," Kennon said. "But a post-9/11 view is that the public has finally taken control and we are watching the transformation"—so of course it is confused, Kennon argued. "It will continue to be messy and perhaps incoherent to those who think how we used to do things. Let's keep it as messy as we can as we try to understand the memory of 9/11."

In their closing remarks, most of the architects remained true to form. "Behind every good building is a good client," Foster said, a statement that seemed intended for the ears of the executives of the LMDC and the Port Authority. "One should think of the civic importance of what has happened here—the world's eye is on this," said Libeskind. "We came here because we believed we could make a difference—architects have taken a leadership role for the first time in recent memory, but it takes a political will," Meier said. "I am stunned by the silence of the developer community—their obligation is to support the vision we have committed to," Gwathmey said, in a deft swipe not only at Larry Silverstein but at the relative indifference of most of the city's real estate industry to the planning process at Ground Zero.

And then Barbara Littenberg, who had cut through the jargon and the rhetoric several times before, did so again, with a remark that broke away from the self-referential architectural culture that most of her colleagues seemed trapped in. We have to remember, Littenberg said, that "fifty percent of the people in polls still want to rebuild the towers. People are waiting for the architectural messiah, but the problem is also with democracy. It is very hard to have a plebiscite about what to build. I'm not sure that a perfect vision would lead everybody to stand up and cheer and line up behind it."

If Littenberg and Steven Peterson were architecturally out of sync with the rest of the group, they were even more on their own as far as their view of the overall process was concerned. Littenberg was the only architect with the courage to confront the paradox that the very notion of planning as a form of participatory democracy represented. Everyone—the other architects, the developers, the family members, the local residents, the civic groups, and most of all the public officials engaged in the planning process—had hailed the idea of an open, democratic process time and time again. When their remarks were challenged, it was usually to complain, as some of the speakers at the LMDC's public hearing had done, that the process had not been open enough, that the people in charge had given lip service to the notion of a public, democratic planning process but were really making decisions in a back room, as they had always done—Robert Moses hiding behind a mask of Jane Jacobs.

But Littenberg's criticism was different. She was saying that even if the process were truly public and fully open, as it purported to be, it might not, in the end, provide the best result. She understood that planning is not pure democracy, and it is certainly not a referendum. It is one thing to have an open planning process in which the public's views are solicited, and it is quite another to put complex planning decisions up to the highest vote. When Littenberg said "I'm not sure that a perfect vision would lead everybody to stand up and cheer and line up behind it," she was acknowledging that the best ideas, and the best designs, were not likely to be the most popular. Public taste rarely operates at the highest levels of sophistication. And great design requires a degree of leadership, not only from architects but from clients. The Grands Projets that so transformed Paris in the 1980s were partly the result of the vision of great architects, of course, but they were even more the result of the vision of François Mitterrand, the socialist prime minister who built like an emperor. If Mitterrand had put I. M. Pei's pyramid at the Louvre or the Opéra Bastille up to a popular vote, it is highly unlikely that they ever would have been built. Mitterrand dreamed of transforming Paris with a series of great structures that would represent the most advanced architectural ideas of the time, and he knew that the only way this would happen would be if the state commissioned them. Mitterrand pushed forward, with only casual nods to public opinion.

It does not take a great deal of knowledge of contemporary history, or of contemporary architecture, to know that George Pataki was no Mitterrand: he possessed neither Mitterrand's inherent passion for great architectural statements nor his inclination to impose his will over an uncertain electorate. Pataki seemed quite indifferent to the paradox of democracy and architecture. He remained committed to the notion that it was possible to create a design for Ground Zero that would be both widely popular and architecturally significant. He appeared to have convinced himself that if the greatest vision was put before the public, the electorate would embrace it.

The architects, for their part, seemed to be hoping that if the public was sufficiently awed by their work, that would allow them to transcend the whole problem. Like the LMDC, they were counting on the "wow factor" to bring the public in and to make the democratic process compatible with sophisticated design.

By January 2003, Pataki had been reelected by a wide margin. Before the election, he had enforced his wishes about Ground Zero largely from behind the scenes, forcibly but often indiscernibly so far as the public was concerned. But now, he was emboldened to begin to play a much more visible role in the process.

All through the month of January, as thousands of people were filing through the Winter Garden to view the models, the LMDC and the Port Authority were working to dissect each proposal and evaluate its practicality. Roland Betts felt that the only way to convince the Port Authority to endorse the winner and to accept the fairly radical plans that were afoot was to prove that they could meet the Port Authority's largely pragmatic goals for the site. Alex Garvin and Stanton Eckstut, the urban designer whom the Port Authority had hired as an outside consultant, were asked to rate the plans according to several criteria, such as how well they handled traffic, how easily they could be integrated into the rest of Lower Manhattan, how well they met the LMDC's criteria of a plan that could be constructed in phases, what kind of public open space they provided, and how appropriate a background setting they provided for a memorial. Engineers, traffic experts, and financial consultants were hired to study all of the plans in detail and rank them in twelve categories on a five-point scale. The plans that were ranked as "ideal" got two green dots. A single green dot meant "excellent"; a yellow dot "acceptable." One red dot was a sign of concern, and a pair of red dots indicated complete failure in a particular category.

Not much was said about who was getting the most green dots, but it was apparent that the scheme produced by Richard Meier, Charles Gwathmey, Peter Eisenman, and Steven Holl had plenty of red ones. The architects and Garvin had not had a smooth working relationship, and Garvin found their plan both aesthetically disappointing and functionally impractical. In some ways, the entire experience of the competition was a difficult one for the quartet, whose members were in many ways the city's preeminent modern designers and who felt they were being treated more as if they were young interlopers. The group had friction with others, too: when Frank Gehry provoked a small controversy by stating in an interview in *The New York Times* that he had chosen not to participate in the LMDC competition because he found the forty-thousand-dollar fee so small as to be demeaning, Eisenman complained that Gehry was insufficiently philanthropic and civic minded, and soon Gehry and the architects who had long been close colleagues found themselves in a public feud.

Skidmore, Owings & Merrill was having an even harder time of it. Garvin was extremely unhappy with the firm's proposal, which had been developed with several younger architects and artists under Roger Duffy's direction and which called for nine towers of equal height, more or less filling the site, even bridging the footprints of the original towers. After telling the firm in the fall that if it wanted to participate in the competition it would have to suspend all of its work for Larry Silverstein other than 7 World Trade Center, the LMDC said after Christmas that it would prefer that the firm continue to work actively for Silverstein and that David Childs, who was in charge of the work for Silverstein, separate himself from any connection with the Skidmore entry. Childs had all but done so on his own weeks earlier, when he had realized that things were not going well. Late in January, however, the LMDC changed its mind again and told Skidmore that it felt it was in the firm's best interest to withdraw entirely from the competition. Duffy agreed, not wanting to put the firm's relationship with the LMDC or with Larry Silverstein in jeopardy, and wrote a letter indicating that the firm would resign from the team that had prepared the entry and leave it to the group of younger architects and artists that Skidmore had assembled. The LMDC, strangely, said that was unacceptable and insisted that the entire team resign and that the Skidmore entry be withdrawn from consideration.

Childs, for his part, was furious. "The decision would have been moot, since we were not going to win, so why disqualify the entire team?" he said. Since the Skidmore entry had no chance of winning, it seemed an odd gesture to insist on punishing the firm for its ongoing relationship with Larry Silverstein when that relationship had already been redefined at the LMDC's request. It was hardly a secret. The other team that was doing poorly in Garvin and Eckstut's rankings, the joint venture of Richard Meier, Charles Gwathmey, Peter Eisenman, and Steven Holl, had not been asked to resign or do much of anything other than suffer through a plethora of red and yellow dots in its evaluation forms. The Skidmore, Owings & Merrill entry had not been much of a success, either architecturally or collegially, since the team had been plagued by disagreements and tensions. Although Childs was too diplomatic to say so, he had clearly felt for some time that his most important role at Ground Zero, and his firm's, would be defined by whatever work he did directly for Larry Silverstein, not by anything that Skidmore might do in the LMDC's competition. Indeed, there were moments when Skidmore's very participation seemed to have an air of noblesse oblige, as if the firm were humoring itself by participating in a competitive exercise with less exalted firms. Still, Childs liked playing both sides of the street, as both a high-design firm in the competition and as a real-estate developer's architect. But Skidmore's disqualification seemed intended only to remind the powerful firm that its position as Larry Silverstein's architect did not put it in control of the planning process, however much it may have thought that it was.

In fact, Larry Silverstein was not much of a fan of any of the plans the LMDC and the Port Authority were considering. Silverstein had bided his time, content to have the LMDC go about its business while he went about his own, so long as nothing the LMDC did got in his way. As the competition was nearing its end, however, Silverstein met with Roland Betts, who asked him what he thought of the schemes. Silverstein said that was the first time any of the officials involved in the planning process had bothered to ask him what he thought, and he realized that the LMDC's efforts might well saddle him with a plan that he did not much like. He decided to write a letter to the LMDC formalizing his objections to the plans that were under consideration and suggesting that the very idea of the competition infringed upon his rights as the leaseholder and presumed developer of the Ground Zero site. "None of the plans as currently configured presents a viable and safe vision for the redevelopment of the World Trade Center site," Silverstein wrote. And while he conceded that he was "fully cognizant of the intense public interest in, and symbolism of, the World Trade Center site," Silverstein claimed that his lease with the Port Authority "provides that our group has the right to select the architect responsible for preparing rebuilding plans. . . . As you know, we have engaged Skidmore, Owings & Merrill to work with us on a site plan." Silverstein then said he would be "fully amenable" to having Skidmore work with any architects selected by the Port Authority and LMDC—although it was hard to miss his implication that any architect chosen would, in his view, be subservient to his own.

Silverstein's lieutenant in charge of Ground Zero, Geoffrey Wharton, had resigned some weeks before, frustrated at Silverstein's continually adversarial relationship with the planning agencies. Wharton had argued from the start of the process that Silverstein should be more cooperative and accommodating. He was an experienced real-estate entrepreneur—before Silverstein hired him to oversee improvements to the World Trade Center, Wharton had been the executive in charge of upgrading Rockefeller

Center for the development firm Tishman Speyer—but his own experience on September 11, when he escaped death only because he had to depart early from a breakfast meeting at Windows on the World, had left him shaken. He firmly believed that Ground Zero could not be treated as a conventional real-estate project that could be squeezed for maximum profits. For better or for worse, Ground Zero had become a public trust, Wharton thought, and he opposed the aggressive stance Silverstein took with the insurance companies, telling his boss he would win much more public support if he adopted a more statesmanlike role rather than appearing to view Ground Zero solely in terms of money. Wharton believed that Silverstein could reach a settlement with the insurance companies that would not only avoid the expense and stress of a trial, but would be better, in the end, for his public image. Wharton had good relations with many of the architects (he even owned a country house in Westchester County that had been designed by Richard Meier), and he might have been able to convince Silverstein not to send his letter rejecting all of the LMDC's plans. But with his departure, Silverstein was like a secretary of defense who was being advised only by hawks. Wharton had been his dove, and he was gone.

CHAPTER 11

Libeskind and THINK

Design Gets Personal

WITH SKIDMORE, OWINGS & Merrill's entry into the Ground Zero design competition out of the running, and with the New York all-star team of Meier, Gwathmey, Eisenman, and Holl having ranked poorly, there were five possible winning teams left: Foster and Partners, United Architects, Studio Daniel Libeskind, Peterson and Littenberg, and the consortium known as THINK. THINK had originally presented three different designs, but as the process unfolded both the architects and the LMDC focused primarily on the most striking of the three, which the group called the World Cultural Center. It called for enormous latticework towers that echoed the profile of the original twin towers in open gridwork, into which smaller structures containing cultural facilities would be inserted at various levels. Although the scheme did not violate the program, it took an unusual stance toward it, since it relegated all of the commercial office space, both literally and figuratively, to the sidelines. Rafael Viñoly and Frederic Schwartz, the main designers, did not even attempt to design office buildings; they simply left the eastern and northern sections of the site free for commercial development. The only thing they cared about designing, it seemed, was the commemorative structure, which overwhelmed all else. It not only occupied the footprints, it occupied the sky, and the architects wanted it to be seen not only as a memorial but as a symbol of the public realm. The message was that civic and public uses overrode private uses. The issue of office space, which had so dominated the dialogue about the program, was neutralized by THINK's gesture. It was no small achievement to have been able to tease such moral high ground, so to speak, out of the LMDC and the Port Authority's excessively commercial program. By leaving the commercial aspects undesigned, Viñoly and his colleagues effectively gave a certain amount of control back to the Port Authority, which was clever. The THINK design, more than any of the others, at once deferred to the agency's claims over the site and asserted the primacy of civic space.

Lord Foster was clever in a different way. He designed an exquisite, powerful building that seduced both sophisticated connoisseurs—Foster has created some of the most important, and refined, skyscrapers of the last generation all over the world—and people who wanted nothing more than to see the twin towers rebuilt. His double tower, which he referred to in his presentation as "kissing towers," may have been the most powerful skyscraper image created during the entire competition. You could read it as a daring new form that embraced the latest structural technologies, or you could read it as an intentional evocation of the original World Trade Center. In fact, it was both. Foster's project was exceedingly popular, and that, coupled with reports that Foster and Larry Silverstein had gotten along well when Silverstein visited Foster's office overlooking the Thames in the fall (before Silverstein had decided to distance himself from all of the work in the competition), led to expectations that Foster would progress further in the design effort.

Unfortunately for Foster, the LMDC evaluators did not look as kindly on his scheme as a lot of the public did. His project mainly consisted of the enormous, 98-story, 1,764-foot-tall double tower and not much else save for a memorial proposed for the footprints of the original towers. Foster had designed something that was less a true master plan than a single building. It could not be built in phases, at least not easily, and it did little to integrate the site into the city. In fact, it all but re-created the World Trade Center superblock. For all of that, his huge building contained six million square feet of office space, not the ten million that the Port Authority was asking for, which was another reason that Foster's plan, despite its popularity, did not rank exceptionally high in the LMDC's evaluations.

Neither did United Architects' work, despite the level of excitement that surrounded that project, too. The megaskyscraper proposed by the team was only slightly easier to create in increments than Foster's design. It was potentially a bedazzling form on the skyline, but it was also gargantuan and, in the end, probably too visionary to be buildable in what was, in the end, a much more pragmatic process than those architects had wanted to believe it was.

If United Architects and Norman Foster produced more architecture than urbanism, and thus lost some points in the evaluation process, Peterson and Littenberg had the opposite problem. They created a design of beautiful, if traditional, urbanism, an intelligent plan that wove Ground Zero graciously into the surrounding cityscape. But there was no architecture to speak of, or at least no innovative architecture, and Peterson and Littenberg's precept that New York is a city dominated by its grid and its streets, while true, does not necessarily lead to the conclusion that a layout of traditional city blocks and inviting open spaces and boulevards is the best solution for Ground Zero. For a competition that was officially called the Innovative Design Study, Peterson and Littenberg seemed to be hesitant to embrace the new, certainly in terms of architecture. They understood a great deal about the city but less about the nature of the competition, which may have been intended initially to encourage a range of ideas but was coming increasingly to function mainly as a showcase of images. United Architects, Foster, Viñoly, even the Meier team understood this and produced powerful and memorable, if often impractical, images. Peterson and Littenberg seemed not to have grasped this notion at all. They played by the rules, or at least the original ones, which presented the competition more as an exercise in urban planning than as a vehicle for architectural expression. But even as the pair worked, the nature of the design exercise was changing around them, and in the weeks after the Winter Garden extravaganza the whole thing had become more of an architectural beauty contest than a laboratory of ideas. Peterson and Littenberg were left with a scheme that, for all its quality, was unable to stir the emotions of the public. Still, its virtues as a work of urban design and its practicality and flexibility ranked it third in the LMDC evaluations of the schemes, which made it the runner-up to the two finalists.

It was Libeskind who balanced the various forces at play the most effectively. He came up with a pair of highly memorable images. Retaining the "bathtub," the concrete enclosure that surrounded the foundations of the original trade center, as a sunken area around the footprints of the original towers and keeping a portion of the original concrete slurry wall exposed was the first. The second was his plan for a tall tower that would be one part office building, one part commemorative tower. Libeskind planned an office tower to rise roughly sixty stories, with a spire extending up to perhaps twice that height, with the final height of the overall structure precisely 1,776 feet. It was typical of Libeskind's fondness for sentimental, almost kitschy gestures—he called one of his open spaces on the site the Wedge of Light and claimed that the sun would shine there from 8:46 A.M. to 10:28 A.M. every September 11, the period representing the span between the impact of the first airplane and the collapse of the second tower. Another area was called the Park of Heroes. Yet Libeskind's actual designs were not kitschy at all but crisp, sharp, crystalline forms. He gave a general outline to several other office buildings, a transportation center, and cultural buildings, and he laid out enough streets to suggest that, while he may not have embraced Peterson and Littenberg's traditional urbanism, he was not one of those modernists who were indifferent to the city grid, either. And Libeskind, more than any of the other competitors, had managed to create a design that seemed to integrate expressions of commemoration and expressions of renewal throughout. The sunken bathtub area was the heart of Libeskind's commemorative expression, but the tower was presented as a portion of it as well, and so were the public spaces.

When the LMDC held a news conference at its headquarters at 1 Liberty Plaza on February 4 to announce the two finalists in the design competition—a role that fell to Roland Betts—it was not surprising, then, that Libeskind and the THINK team were the names chosen. Foster was surprised and angry to have been left out;

Meier's group was not surprised by then but was no happier than Foster. United Architects and Peterson/Littenberg fared somewhat better than Foster and Meier, in part because neither firm had truly expected to win, and yet both saw their stature elevated by their participation in the competition. The young members of United Architects had been known primarily in academic circles, but now they were international names. So were Peterson and Littenberg now, and that would have to make a difference in all of their careers.

The news conference followed by a couple of days the loss of the space shuttle *Columbia,* and its start was delayed so as not to conflict with the live telecast of a speech President Bush was giving at a memorial service for the astronauts in Houston. The press sat in the LMDC briefing room while the public officials and the architects waited in separate conference rooms. Finally, John Whitehead stepped to the podium, accompanied by Lou Tomson, Joe Seymour, Daniel Doctoroff, Diana Taylor (who was representing Governor Pataki), Alex Garvin, Stanton Eckstut, and Roland Betts. "These plans have the audacity and the faith to suspend bridges in midair and to make meaning of the void," Whitehead said. "Rarely has design so captured the public imagination. Rarely has architecture so eloquently demonstrated our spirit." He was followed by Tomson and Seymour, both of whom recited what had become their mantra, a celebration of what they believed to be the democratic nature of the planning process. "We have had over fifty public meetings, and our website has had over eight million hits," Tomson said. "We have not only supported this dialogue, we have acted upon it." The planning of Ground Zero had been "the most open, inclusive, and responsive public process in the history of this city and region," Seymour said.

Doctoroff followed Seymour and took his hand as he walked toward the lectern. "We've just shaken hands on the agreement about the land swap," he said. "That's a joke." But Doctoroff retained his upbeat air throughout—this was, after all, only seven weeks after Bloomberg's vision speech, and since one of the categories the competitors were rated on was the extent to which their plans were compatible with the mayor's vision for Lower Manhattan, Doctoroff was feeling positive about his and the city's ability to influence things at Ground Zero.

When Betts took the podium, he combined praise for the process with praise for the architects themselves, who "served this city, served their country, and served their profession with extraordinary distinction," Betts said. "What we are doing today is advancing two extraordinary designs and their teams," he continued. "What we are not doing is saying that either plan is set in stone. This problem is a puzzle of enormous complexity, and the next three weeks will be a period of modification and review. But rest assured that the goal is not to compromise the plans but to make them better."

Garvin followed and described the process by which the nine plans had been evaluated, and he praised both finalists for the extent to which they were integrated into the larger cityscape, which was clearly a priority for him. "It is no accident that both of these have Fulton Street and Greenwich Street going through the site, in response to the mayor's vision," Garvin said. And then he concluded, "These plans must be adjusted to reality—we understand it, and so do the designers."

The architects were introduced. Viñoly seemed overwhelmed. "This is an honor for all of us—it is something I never expected to be blessed with," he said. And then Schwartz spoke, with words that seemed almost a conscious attempt to outdo Daniel Libeskind in the memorial game. "It is a day like any other day—a day that two thousand eight hundred and twenty people cannot spend with us," Schwartz said. "Every day we remember this and think of the loss, so we can envision something great for the future."

Libeskind himself was somewhat less mawkish. "It is a great privilege to be here," he said. "This project has to combine the essence of the tragedy and show the world that life is good, that there is optimism, not only for New York but for the world. Most people think cities are made out of concrete and glass and steel—but cities are made of citizens."

The news conference at the LMDC headquarters was probably the last time Viñoly, Schwartz, and Libeskind would appear together in a dignified setting. The new phase of the competition—and when it was down to two finalists, the last fig leaf of pretense that this was only a "design exercise" was gone—turned nasty and bitter. It became an architectural catfight. Libeskind at one point called Viñoly's towers "skeletons in the sky" and said that the title of the THINK project, the World Cultural Center, made it sound like a Stalinist building. Viñoly called Libeskind's design, with its exposed slurry wall, "the Wailing Wall."

Both firms hired public-relations representatives. Libeskind for a time was represented by Howard Rubenstein, a well-connected operative who handled much of New York's real-estate industry, and soon he seemed to be everywhere—on television, in every magazine and newspaper that usually pays attention to architecture, and in plenty that do not. Viñoly kept a slightly lower profile, but not much. He and Libeskind both appeared on *The Oprah Winfrey Show* and the *Today* show, as well as on *Charlie Rose*. Long before the competition, each architect had crafted a physical image that played well on television: Libeskind dressed in black, with heavy, black-rimmed French eyeglasses and American cowboy boots, while the silver-haired Viñoly kept multiple pairs of eyeglasses on strings around his neck and atop his head. Viñoly's large office in Lower Manhattan, in an old industrial building, had been one of the headquarters for planning sessions of Muschamp's architecture group the previous summer, and Viñoly's ties to the city's cultural community were close. Both architects targeted civic and community groups, meeting frequently with every constituency that might possibly have some influence over public opinion, from organizations of relatives of people killed on September 11 to downtown residents' groups to the boards of the city's venerable civic organizations.

Even though Libeskind's career had its roots in academia, Viñoly had the advantage of support from much of the city's cultural and intellectual community, which considered him to be one of its own and launched a major lobbying effort on his behalf. Viñoly's architectural practice seemed more like a conventional business than Libeskind's atelier, and it certainly had a far larger oeuvre of completed academic and institutional buildings, but Viñoly had always positioned himself as a member of New York's cultural elite, not as a corporate architect. He lives on Fifth Avenue and has a summer home in the Hamptons, but his largest commissions are for institutions, not corporations, and his sleek, white basement office is about as uncorporate as an architect's space can be: it is large and sprawling, and amid the drawings and the books is a grand piano, which Viñoly, a talented pianist, plays when he chooses to take a break from work. (Among Viñoly's recent projects is the Kimmel Center in Philadelphia, the new home of the Philadelphia Orchestra.) The style of his office encapsulates Viñoly's unusual position in the architectural community of New York—it has neither the casual, chaotic sprawl of many younger architects' offices, nor the established formality of many older firms, and the energy level is high. The city's academic architectural community, which considered Libeskind excessively ambitious, favored Viñoly.

Viñoly was also very much the preferred candidate of Herbert Muschamp, who not only wrote almost worshipfully about his proposal but denounced the Libeskind plan in almost vicious terms. Two months earlier, Muschamp had written that Libeskind's plan was "marvelous." Now, in a total about-face, he described it as "an astonishingly tasteless idea" and "emotionally manipulative." Viñoly's plan, on the other hand, was described as "a soaring affirmation of American values." Earlier, Muschamp had seemed happy to write positively about Libeskind as one of the group of avant-garde architects he was known to favor, but that was before Libeskind ended up in a one-on-one battle against an architect whom Muschamp was personally close to and about whom he had always written in a tone approaching veneration. It was hard to know whether Muschamp was so blinded by his passion for the Viñoly plan that he failed to understand that he had entirely reversed himself, or whether he believed that denouncing Libeskind would in some way help Viñoly's cause. Either way, he seemed to have all but put aside his role as a critic who could responsibly evaluate the entire process. Muschamp also wrote admiringly of Frederic Schwartz, Viñoly's main partner in THINK, whose ideas for building along West Street had formed the basis for Muschamp's own *New York Times Magazine* plan. Libeskind's chief assistant in his office in Berlin was so upset by Muschamp's unrelenting advocacy of THINK and his sudden reversal of his previous position that he sent out a mass e-mail that urged the recipients, who included numerous other journalists, to write in protest to *The New York Times* and ask that Muschamp be replaced. The e-mail was signed by Nina Libeskind, the architect's wife and business partner, but far from helping Libeskind's cause it backfired, suggesting that the Libeskind camp had begun to feel rather desperate. The embarrassed Libeskinds ordered the assistant to e-mail an abject retraction that stated that his first message had not been authorized by either the architect or his wife.

Muschamp's closest fellow traveler in the press, at least in terms of the absoluteness of his anti-Libeskind position, was not another architecture critic but Steve Cuozzo, a real-estate reporter for the *New York Post* who had begun writing architecture commentaries since the advent of the Ground Zero planning process. Cuozzo's reasoning was not the same as Muschamp's—he had been complaining throughout the process that it was moving too slowly and that it was not oriented sufficiently to the demands of business, issues Muschamp did not much care about—but the two writers were joined in their insistence that the Libeskind plan exemplified everything that was wrong at Ground Zero and represented not the high aspirations of public officials but their total abdication of responsibility. "What ever happened to the office space?" Cuozzo wrote. He objected to Libeskind's sunken centerpiece and found his entire project too focused on negative imagery. Cuozzo seemed only to want something upbeat, and his shrillness made him a kind of redneck Muschamp.

Things got stranger and more heated. The day the final decision was to be made, *The Wall Street Journal* reported that questions had been raised about the early work of Viñoly, a native of Uruguay who began his career in Argentina and in 1978 had designed sports facilities for the World Cup matches in Buenos Aires, which were sponsored by Argentina's brutal military junta. Viñoly immigrated to the United States the following year, in part, he said in a memoir, because he could not stay in a "state of denial" about the repressive generals. He omitted mention of his own work for the junta. Still, he did choose to leave the country rather than to continue to work for the corrupt junta, and the criticism seemed not unlike past attempts to discredit German architects who worked briefly for the Nazis in the 1930s before fleeing Germany.

The real oddity, however, was the timing. It was clearly not an accident that a suggestion that Viñoly was hiding a questionable past should appear at the end of February, just as the competition was nearing its conclusion. Someone with an interest in derailing the THINK proposal had, it would seem, convinced the paper that the story was worth pursuing. The headline, "Ground Zero Finalist's Past Draws Questions," seemed forced, especially since Viñoly's past had not, in fact, drawn questions, until someone convinced *The Wall Street Journal* that it had.

While the public-relations war played out in public, both Viñoly and Libeskind were busy revising their schemes. Roland Betts, Alex Garvin, and the other officials involved in the planning process had given both teams specific instructions as to how to revise their plans to bring them more in conformity with what the LMDC and the Port Authority considered practical needs. Libeskind's plan to leave the bathtub area excavated to a depth of seventy feet interfered with the Port Authority's wish to have a parking area for buses and other service functions below, and the engineers who evaluated the scheme pointed out that the concrete slurry wall was not likely to stand without additional support, which had once been provided by the horizontal thrust of basement floors below the World Trade Center towers. Roland Betts suggested that both problems could be solved by dividing the bathtub horizontally, putting a new floor about halfway up, which would create new, usable space underneath and also provide structural support for the wall. Libeskind agreed. Libeskind also agreed to Garvin's request to revise the configuration of some of his buildings at street level to allow for a better, more street-oriented arrangement of shops, and he also changed the shapes of the floor plates of his towers to make them somewhat less eccentric and presumably more easily rented to commercial tenants. He removed an elevated, curving walkway that had swooped over West Street, which would have been expensive and impractical, and he changed the spire of his 1,776-foot-tall tower to remove the woefully impractical gardens he had envisioned as filling the top, replacing them with a much more useful broadcast antenna.

The problems with the THINK scheme were more complex, in

a way, even though Viñoly had not outlined the commercial space in much detail. The twin latticework towers, besides being quite expensive, were not easily buildable as the architects had outlined them, and the foundations of one of them would have come down right through the tracks of the PATH commuter trains to New Jersey. There were also significant concerns about some of the imagery Viñoly and his partners had included, especially a swooping museum structure they had wanted to place near the top, bridging the two structures. To many observers, it looked eerily like an abstract version of a jet plane crashing into the towers, and it was made clear to the architects that even if this resemblance was inadvertent, it had to be eliminated as the plan was revised. But the entire structural system was also changed and made more efficient; the resulting towers were smaller, lighter, thinner, and shorter than the ones that had first been proposed. It was more elegant than the initial scheme, more a true latticework, and much less like a heavy space frame. The original version, with its notion of small, irregularly shaped buildings as sculptural elements inside a larger framework, bore some resemblance to the work of the 1960s Japanese architectural group known as the Metabolists, as well as to the work of Archigram, radical architects who worked in London. But as the design evolved, it seemed to depend less on those precedents and to be more original. By the time the revised plan was complete, the cultural facilities had been pushed toward the bottom, which meant that a lot of the framework, which in the original version had been filled up with elevators and conduits carrying mechanical equipment to the upper sections, could become almost entirely an open trellis. In addition to redesigning their twin towers, THINK added more streets and more retail space and figured out what the height and bulk of the surrounding office buildings should be, although they still did not specify any more complete architectural designs for them, as Libeskind had done.

By the last week of February, both schemes had changed significantly, and Garvin was pleased with both of them. "They have made real progress, and we have two really good choices," he said. "I was truly astonished at what Viñoly has done—he has made all the changes we asked for, and Libeskind has, too. He placed the slurry wall under glass, [he's] gotten the buses below the bathtub the way the Port Authority wanted. His gardens are gone, and the top of his tower is now a television antenna—it will be an icon."

Both architects made two-hour presentations to the senior staff of the LMDC and Port Authority, Libeskind speaking by phone from Berlin, where he had gone to tend to other jobs in his office. Rumors were flying that the Libeskind plan was close to being selected, in part because Pataki and Bloomberg were said to have favored it, although they had not yet had detailed briefings of the schemes, which were scheduled to take place just before the final decision was to be made. Alex Garvin had not fully made up his own mind yet. He liked both plans, and he believed that each plan had its advantages. If the THINK master plan were selected, the site would take on a public function immediately, and Garvin liked the symbolism of elevating the public realm in that way, sending the message that commercial concerns were secondary. The Libeskind master plan, Garvin thought, was ultimately a better piece of urban design, but it also depended more on quality architecture, and could private developers like Silverstein or anyone who might succeed him in future years be trusted to carry out the vision on a high enough level? Garvin wasn't entirely sure, but he had begun to lean toward Libeskind.

Roland Betts, on the other hand, had made up his mind. He liked the Libeskind plan, but he admired the THINK scheme more. He worried that the sunken area around the footprints that Libeskind had made a centerpiece of his plan would be a depressing symbol, and he wanted to feel that he was helping to put a great landmark on the site, the sort of extraordinary structure that would attract people from all over the world. He talked in terms of wanting a postcard image, of wanting to see something created on the site that was so compelling that tourists would feel they had no choice but to tell taxi drivers to take them there. The sunken bathtub, Betts felt, was not that sort of symbol, but Viñoly's twin latticework towers could be.

Whether because of the force of his personality or the depth of his convictions—or perhaps both—Betts was taken seriously by his colleagues, many of whom had come to similar conclusions on their own. They recognized that while Libeskind's plan also had a tower, it was a very different kind of tower, largely commercial even though it had a spire that was purely symbolic, and it would have to be built as a commercial venture. It might take a long time to line up the financing, and Larry Silverstein or another private developer could dictate certain things about the design. Viñoly's latticework towers, on the other hand, were to be an entirely public project, and while a lot of money would have to be found to get them built, at least the LMDC could be in complete control. The major statement of the plan was its commemorative aspect, not its commercial aspect, and Betts thought that was the right statement for the LMDC to be making. The joint committee of the LMDC and the Port Authority that was charged with making a decision about the master plan met to review the plans on February 25, and while a formal vote was not scheduled until the next day, after Pataki and Bloomberg had weighed in, the committee was ready to endorse Viñoly and Schwartz's THINK plan.

After the meeting, Betts, Garvin, and Dan Doctoroff were discussing a meeting with Pataki and Bloomberg that was scheduled for the next afternoon at the LMDC office. It was more than a courtesy visit, since technically the two officials had the final say in the decision. Garvin asked whether it really made sense for him to be presenting the plans, and Betts asked him why the architects weren't showing the plans to the governor and the mayor themselves. Garvin agreed that they should. They asked Lou Tomson for his assent, and then they called the architects and asked them to clear their schedules and come the following day at noon.

That day, before the officials arrived, they had a surprise: the front page of *The New York Times* reported that the committee had agreed on THINK and that the decision was all but final. "Several committee members believe that the mayor and governor should pay heed to their preference," Edward Wyatt, the reporter covering Ground Zero, wrote. "We don't expect anyone to overrule us," Wyatt reported a committee member saying.

The architects had seen the story, and Nina Libeskind decided it was right. "We may head back to Berlin tonight," she said, as she prepared to accompany her husband to the LMDC meeting. "I know when it's over. If Roland Betts firmly believes in those towers, then he should get them."

Nina and Daniel Libeskind did not, in fact, leave for the airport that night. Pataki and Bloomberg both spent much of the afternoon at the LMDC offices, sitting through extended presentations by the architects. Viñoly delivered a lecture about his plan, and Libeskind offered one of his more gemütlich ramblings, mixing comments about himself, New York, patriotism, and architecture, which Pataki seemed to find engaging. More important, as the meeting went on it became increasingly obvious that the governor seemed to have a visceral discomfort with Viñoly's latticework towers, which to him seemed not the striking symbol of renewal that they were to Roland Betts but only a ghostly reminder of the lost World Trade Center. Some of the people present in the meeting thought that Pataki seemed to agree with the sentiments Libeskind himself had expressed during the public-relations wars, when he called the THINK scheme a pair of skeletons. He found them off-putting, an evocation of a dead building rather than an inspiration for a fresh beginning.

When the architects had gone, the public officials lingered to discuss their reactions. "I take it you are all in favor of Viñoly," Pataki said, referring to the story in the *Times*. Garvin shook his head. Pataki looked at Garvin and said, "You're not going to build these skeletons." Bloomberg, who had been relatively silent, said that they reminded him of the famous gas tanks along the Long Island Expressway in Elmhurst. Still, Bloomberg did not seem to object to the THINK plan as strongly as Pataki did. Bloomberg was more interested in larger questions of downtown renewal, and he had generally been content to leave a lot of the Ground Zero symbolism to the governor. He seemed to be willing to live with either plan. Pataki left for another meeting, and Bloomberg turned to Garvin and asked him what he thought. "I prefer the Libeskind plan," Garvin told him. "I will have to talk to the governor," Bloomberg said.

The selection committee's meeting was set for four o'clock, and shortly before that Bloomberg, who had conferred with Pataki by cell phone, reported the decision: Pataki was certain that he wanted Libeskind, and Bloomberg preferred to go along with him. The committee could not take on the governor, and so Libeskind it was. Many of the committee members were not unhappy—Joe Seymour of the Port Authority, for example, had been edging toward the Libeskind plan as the deliberations went on, and many of the others had felt that they could live comfortably with either scheme. Roland Betts, however, was enraged—he felt he had laid his prestige on the line to convince his colleagues to support the Viñoly plan, and the governor had pulled the rug out from under him. It was not that Betts was strongly opposed to the Libeskind plan. He agreed that it had certain strengths, and he had been happy seeing it as a finalist. But he wondered if part of the reason that the officials preferred the Libeskind plan was that they viewed it as more malleable and saw that it did not require as huge a public investment. Betts, as much as the architects, had dreamed of making possible a daring and radical piece of public architecture, and he thought that with the Viñoly plan he had almost managed to do it—and then, he felt, his vision was stymied by the kind of conventional thinking that had made the whole process of planning Ground Zero such a frustrating business in the first place.

The Libeskinds did not board a plane back home to Berlin. At 5:30 in the afternoon, they got a call from Whitehead, who had leaned toward Viñoly's plan because he believed that the latticework towers would be a powerful magnet for tourism. Whitehead told them that the governor wanted to announce the next morning that Daniel Libeskind had been chosen as the master planner for the World Trade Center site and asked them to attend a press conference in the Winter Garden, the very place where Libeskind had first presented his plan ten weeks before. It fell to Garvin to call Viñoly, which he did at six o'clock, when he told him that despite the story in that morning's newspaper, he had not been selected.

Pataki's willingness to enforce his own view seemed to suggest a new determination on the part of the governor to play a more conspicuous role. That was certainly the case the next morning at the Winter Garden, where Pataki seemed to be running the show. "We reached out to the best architects of the world, and this has been the most incredible process that I have ever managed to witness," he said, and then he praised Alex Garvin, John Whitehead, and Roland Betts by name Pataki referred to Libeskind's master plan as "emotional" and praised it as a means of restoring life to the city, creating a setting for a memorial, establishing cultural institutions, and setting out "an inspiring spire that will stretch 1,776 feet as a symbol of our love for this great city and our confidence in its future." None of the other speakers was quite as effusive—Joe Seymour said the plan "is both visionary and practical" and, in what may have been the most realistic comment of the day, said "our work is just beginning." John Whitehead called Libeskind's plan "the most compelling vision" and said that it had "resonated with the public—it succeeds both where it rises into the sky and where it descends into the ground."

There was a somewhat outdated elaborate model of Libeskind's scheme, which did not show all of the revisions, and plenty of renderings, but there was no sign at all of the other finalist. The THINK scheme might as well have never existed. Viñoly, Schwartz, and the other members of their team were not present, and there were no pictures or models of the runner-up. Whitehead was the only official who so much as acknowledged the THINK team's plan, which he said "seemed to defy gravity with its optimism."

Libeskind spoke, and he was more impassioned than ever. "It is really about the heart," he said. "Surely buildings are built of concrete and steel and glass, but it is about the heart. I really did come on a ship called the SS *Constitution,* with my parents, as an immigrant. My parents were lovers of America. It is about paying homage to the great heroes and also about seeing the city move forward. I wanted to make a site for the greatest memorial the world has ever seen." He described his design in some detail, and then he concluded, "It speaks to the heart and soul of this great city, this great nation, and the world." He received a standing ovation, and the press conference was over. Larry Silverstein, who knew he would have to figure out a way of working with the LMDC and appreciated the prominence Libeskind's plan gave to a commercial tower, watched the proceedings from a front-row seat. "They picked the right one," he said.

CHAPTER 12

The Marriage of Politics and Building

THE FALLOUT FROM THE Libeskind announcement was mostly positive. *The New York Times* editorialized in praise of his plan, and Joyce Purnick, a columnist for the metropolitan section, wrote that she felt that the architect had the drive necessary to surmount the inevitable political, financial, and engineering obstacles that he would confront. Herbert Muschamp was silent. There were rumblings from the THINK camp that Pataki had been influenced by a large campaign contributor who was known to have personal ties to Libeskind, but those who had been in the Lower Manhattan Development Corporation conference room when Pataki looked at the plans sensed that the governor's negative reaction to the latticework towers was so instinctive that it could not have been conjured up just to please a supporter. For a while, Libeskind was the toast of New York, and he reveled in his celebrity.

Even Larry Silverstein seemed to want to get on the bandwagon. "Larry says the plan presented today is extraordinary, and he's completely supporting the plan," a Silverstein spokesman said after the announcement, a comment the *Daily News* naïvely interpreted as meaning Silverstein was prepared to build and pay for the 1,776-foot-tall skyscraper. In fact, it was a case of Silverstein wanting to be sure he remained in the spotlight. As the winter of 2003 gave way to spring, staying close to Libeskind seemed like the best way to do that. Silverstein even made plans to travel to Berlin in late March to visit the Jewish Museum, which he had never seen, and tour Berlin with the Libeskinds. The trip was canceled when the Iraq war began—Silverstein was uncomfortable traveling out of the country, although Libeskind went anyway—and even though Libeskind lost the chance to bond with the real-estate developer on what was, in effect, his home turf, their relationship at that point seemed more than cordial.

Lou Tomson retired as president of the LMDC after the choice of Libeskind was announced, and Pataki named Tomson's deputy, Kevin Rampe, as interim president. Rampe, a young lawyer, was as much a Pataki loyalist as Tomson had been but much less of an old-style political operative. Where Tomson seemed to operate on the principle that loyalty to the governor was all that mattered—and as a consequence found himself in conflict not only with people like Alex Garvin but even with John Whitehead from time to time—Rampe saw himself as a conciliator. He was more interested in getting good press than in squeezing out his enemies, and he promoted the agency's experienced public-relations chief, Matthew Higgins, to the role of chief operating officer. Rampe also wanted to win over the architectural community, and he genuinely liked Libeskind. Like Silverstein, Rampe also realized that he could take advantage of the Libeskind aura. He did all that he could to appear to be Libeskind's greatest promoter. Shortly after Rampe was appointed, he introduced the architect to an overflow crowd at a breakfast meeting of the Association for a Better New York in the ballroom of the Plaza hotel. "I present to you the architect formerly known as Daniel Libeskind—now he has become such a New York icon that he is known by only one name, Dan-*yell*," Rampe said, using the European pronunciation that Libeskind and his wife favor. "Unfortunately as we know rents are a little bit higher in New York than Berlin, so Daniel is launching a new line of eyewear and boots." And then, to huge applause, a beaming Rampe brought Libeskind, clad in his black collarless shirt, black suit, cowboy boots, and heavy, square-rimmed black glasses, to the podium.

Libeskind responded with enthusiasm equal to Rampe's and then some. "It's really the people who make the cities, their hearts and souls, not just the inert material," he said, offering up what was increasingly coming to seem like his stump speech. "New York is the capital of the world—it has to be optimistic, a cultural answer to the shadows that fall on the world. I want to assert the true beauty of New York, which is in the streets of New York. It is not only the skyline of New York, it is the streets, and streets are made of people." Libeskind went on, his voice rising to a fevered pitch. His goal, he said, was "to invite the public to share in this great moment of history" and to make "a very important place for the spirit, a composition which glows with its own beauty. The answer to these tragic events is to reassert life, the victory of joy." And then he reminded the audience about his arrival in New York harbor as a thirteen-year-old immigrant in 1960 and showed a slide with the new tower he envisioned in the background and the Statue of Liberty in the foreground. His new skyscraper, Libeskind said, "answered the call of the Statue of Liberty."

It was a virtuoso performance. Libeskind is probably more at ease in public than any architect since Philip Johnson. But for some time there has been an odd lack of connection between Libeskind's speeches and his work, as if he had decided that the best way to sell avant-garde architecture was to be so gemütlich that no one could be put off by him. Libeskind designed buildings that featured sharp angles, glass ceilings, and slanted walls, and then he described them as if they were the inevitable result of his patriotic and optimistic instincts and as down-home as Colonial Williamsburg. It is as if John Cage had decided that the best way to get the public to accept his music was to present himself as if he were Irving Berlin.

For an architect who loves to talk, Libeskind says very little about his buildings that could be considered analytical. He tends to present his work almost as if it were someone else's that he had just seen for the first time and found dazzling. His projects have simple names: a new building for the Denver Art Museum, his biggest project in the United States until he won the Ground Zero competition, is called the Eye and the Wing; the new Danish Jewish Museum in Copenhagen is the Mitzvah; an entry in a competition for an addition to the Corcoran Gallery in Washington, which Libeskind eventually lost to Frank Gehry, was the Kaleidoscope. And at Ground Zero, he used not only the overall title of Memory Foundations but gave the open spaces names like the Wedge of Light and the Park of Heroes.

Libeskind did not start out wanting to be an architect. He was born in 1946 in Poland, the child of Holocaust survivors, and he showed an early gift for music; his father bought him an accordion because he thought it would attract too much attention if a piano were seen being delivered to the home of working-class Jews. The Libeskinds moved to Israel in 1957, where eleven-year-old Daniel won a music competition after which Isaac Stern, one of the judges, urged him to switch to the piano, which he did. When the family moved to New York in 1960, they settled in the Amalgamated Houses, the workers' co-op in the Bronx. Libeskind continued to play the piano, but his fondness for performing waned as he became more interested in abstract, intellectual thought. For a while he pursued mathematics, read Hegel and Spinoza, and somehow moved gradually toward art and architecture. But even then, there was little hint that he would devote so much effort to winning a wide public for his architecture. He started out doing the opposite and being almost deliberately obscure. He studied at Cooper Union, whose architecture program was a center of theoretical exploration where attention to practical matters was openly discouraged. He worked briefly for Richard Meier, whose office he left after only a few days because he disliked the way architects in the office replicated Meier's characteristic white buildings over and over again, and he decided his future lay more in academia. In 1978, when he was thirty-two, he was offered a job as head of the architecture department at the Cranbrook Academy of Art in Bloomfield Hills, Michigan. His work at the time was heavily theoretical, virtually unbuildable, and frequently incomprehensible. "Chamberworks: Architectural Meditations on the Themes of Heraclitus," for instance, a project that he produced a couple of years before he left Cranbrook in 1985, is intended to explore the connection between music and architecture. It consists of twenty-eight drawings, many of them reminiscent of the work of Kasimir Malevich and Wassily Kandinsky, but with an energetic panache that is very much Libeskind's own. The drawings are breathtaking, but the connection between architecture and music remains obscure. "Architecture is neither on the inside nor the outside," Libeskind wrote in the accompanying text. "It is not a given nor a physical fact. It has no history and it does not follow fate."

Libeskind got a big break in 1987, when a project he designed for a competition for housing in West Berlin won first prize, and a bigger break when, the following year, Philip Johnson put it on display in his *Deconstructivist Architecture* exhibition at the Museum of Modern Art. The project was never built, but getting into the MoMA show anointed Libeskind. The housing consisted of space in a structure that looked like a huge bar elevated at an angle, so that at one end it was ten stories above the street and supported on a series of angled legs. Libeskind intended it to be a comment on the Berlin Wall, as if a piece of the wall were flying into the sky, and on the relationship between order and disorder in the city. "This space of nonequilibrium—from which freedom eternally departs and toward which it moves without homecoming—constitutes a place in which architecture comes upon itself as beginning at the end," he wrote. His language could not have been more different from the speeches he was to give in New York.

It was his wife, Nina, who set in motion the change from obscure avant-gardist to determined populist. In 1989, when Libeskind had won the competition for the Jewish Museum in Berlin, the couple and their three children were en route to Los Angeles, where Libeskind had just accepted a position as a senior scholar at the Getty Center. The Jewish Museum was the first of Libeskind's designs that stood a real chance of getting built, but Nina knew that there was significant opposition to it in Berlin and that her husband's design, which was only slightly more conventional than his housing project, could be torn to pieces or abandoned altogether while he sat reading books at the Getty. "Libeskind," she said to him, "if you want to build this, we have to be in Berlin." The Libeskinds reversed course and set up shop in Berlin, where they stayed for fourteen years.

It was the first time in his career that Libeskind had to run a real architectural office that was equipped to build buildings, not just to think about them. Nina organized it, and at that point she became her husband's managing partner. "When Nina entered the office, I had to explain everything to her," Libeskind said. "She said, 'I just see a bunch of lines, explain it to me.' At first, I was very angry. I said she knew no architecture, this wouldn't work. Then I started to think that if she was so intelligent and didn't understand it, I had to draw it and explain it in a way that she would understand. That Nina did not understand architecture was a great advantage. She was not initiated into the secret language—but the public wasn't, either."

What Nina Libeskind did understand was process. Trained as a labor arbitrator, she was exceptionally well organized, and she devoted her considerable management skills to helping her husband design and build. The Libeskinds made a formidable, if unusual, team. He designed experimental, often difficult, buildings, while she negotiated contracts, ran the office, and ran political interference. She knew that Libeskind's angular, crystalline forms often provoked dissent, and she was patient. While her husband spoke engagingly at public meetings, she worked behind the scenes, whether in London, where Libeskind's addition to the Victoria and Albert Museum remained unbuilt, the victim of funding problems as well as aesthetic objections; or Denver, where Libeskind was preparing for the 2003 groundbreaking on his new art-museum building; or Toronto, where he was working on final designs for his addition to the Royal Ontario Museum. They all took years, Nina understood, and she had no illusions that the process of getting her husband's buildings built would ever be simple or easy.

When the Jewish Museum opened, in 1999, it was one of the most talked-about pieces of architecture in the world, not only because of its unusual zigzagging shape and narrow windows, which looked like slashes across the bright zinc facade, or its interior, which contained, among other elements, a tall, empty concrete shaft called the Holocaust Tower and a long, inaccessible void that cut through the length of the building and was crossed by catwalks. It was distinctive also because for the first two years after it opened, the museum had nothing on its walls; it was an exhibition of itself. Libeskind had not been commissioned to design a Holocaust memorial, but he had produced a de facto one, and in his new, help-everyone-understand mode, he made each architectural gesture a metaphor. He called the central void, for example, "the embodiment of absence," a reminder of the emptiness that the slaughter of millions of Jews had left in German society and culture. The building has its share of architectural conceits, but it also has a pure force that transcends Libeskind's gimmicks. The disquieting spaces are dignified and powerful, and when you stand in them you do not feel manipulated by a metaphor. You feel that you are in a work of architecture that is brooding and, at its best, profound. Still, the building is hardly a complete success as museums go, despite the enormous crowds it continues to attract. Once it was filled with historical artifacts, the intense, angular spaces became highly distracting. Libeskind is capable of making extraordinary forms that affect the emotions as few works of contemporary architecture can, but practical matters must often be contorted to fit, which is why it is not surprising that the Jewish Museum worked better when it could be seen as pure form and space inspiring emotion, not as a housing for historical and artistic objects. The Berlin Jewish Museum is still Daniel Libeskind's most famous work, and it shows both his strengths as an architect and his limitations.

The honeymoon at Ground Zero lasted a few weeks for Libeskind, and its high point, other than the breakfast at the Plaza, may have been an event that Libeskind himself missed. He was in Berlin, preparing for the move of his office to New York, when Governor Pataki addressed the Association for a Better New York at a lunch meeting in mid-April at the new Ritz-Carlton hotel at Battery Park City, just a few blocks south of Ground Zero. In a talk that seemed intended to continue his effort to be more obviously in charge of the planning process and to counter the view that only Mayor Bloomberg and the city had a vision for Lower Manhattan, Pataki was clearly eager to claim some of the high ground of planning for himself and for the state government. He spoke first about the need to revitalize all of downtown, just as Bloomberg had done a few months earlier. "Lower Manhattan's best days are yet to come," he said. "The Libeskind plan will be the catalyst, but the challenges extend far beyond the sixteen-acre site. Today I am asking the LMDC to move forward on $50 million in short-term projects to enhance the quality of life in Lower Manhattan." Some of the things Pataki outlined were admirable, but relatively minor, urban-design amenities, such as enhancements to public open space, new granite sidewalks, and contributions to Lower Manhattan schools and institutions that could be put in place quickly. Pataki also reasserted his commitment to more long-term goals such as major transit improvements for Lower Manhattan and solving the problem of West Street. By the time the work was finished, Pataki said, West Street would rival "the Champs-Elysées—or, should I say, surpass it."

But the real news of the day was Pataki's announcement that he intended to push forward quickly on the design of the major tower Libeskind had proposed, which Pataki had dubbed the Freedom Tower. In 2006, "New Yorkers will reclaim their skyline," Pataki said, promising that by the end of that year the city would "top off a new icon, Daniel Libeskind's 1,776-foot Freedom Tower. I am pleased to announce the first tenant in that new tower, the governor of New York State. We will lead by example, and I invite the business community to follow suit."

Pataki did not discuss the fact that he might not still be governor in 2008, which was the earliest possible completion date for the building, and no one was rude enough to ruin the lunch by suggesting that a future governor might not feel quite so strongly about putting state offices into a tall tower at Ground Zero. Pataki delivered his speech in front of a six-foot-tall banner that displayed Libeskind's rendering of the Freedom Tower. Since the tower design seemed already to have gotten Silverstein's endorsement—Silverstein was present at the lunch as well and had accepted warm praise that Pataki offered from the podium—there seemed no reason to believe that Libeskind's design was not firmly on the way to getting built.

The governor now had a strong reason for wanting the project to move quickly. With the Republican National Convention set to come to New York in the summer of 2004, Pataki wanted to show his fellow Republicans how much progress he was making at Ground Zero. They were likely to be at least as impressed by a monumental building for business as they would be by anything else planned for the site. If Pataki could get the world's tallest skyscraper started by the time of the convention, it could symbolize to President Bush and the rest of the party his ability to get things done and to turn tragedy into triumph. But for that to happen, the enticing picture that hung behind Pataki would have to be turned into a real, buildable design in just a few months. At that point, it had not been developed much beyond an initial concept, and you cannot build a skyscraper based on a few sketches. Libeskind had never built a skyscraper at all, let alone the world's tallest, but Pataki seemed to be putting his faith in him to do it. At that point, the Freedom Tower became not only Daniel Libeskind's vision but Pataki's own.

It did not take long for the reality of politics and building in New York to set in. Indeed, the first sign of trouble came in between Libeskind's breakfast address to the Association for a Better New York and Pataki's luncheon talk to the group eight days later, when it became clear that Alex Garvin, one of the most ardent proponents of Libeskind's master plan within the LMDC, had been doing better at protecting Libeskind than covering himself. His role as a member of the New York City Planning Commission, not to mention his close ties to Daniel Doctoroff and to Mayor Bloomberg himself, had always created some tension within the LMDC, a state agency. Some members of the governor's entourage seemed to think of Garvin less as a professional planner than as an agent for the city who was operating under the cover of the state government. Garvin resigned in mid-April to return to his teaching, writing, and consulting career. Kevin Rampe appointed Garvin's handpicked deputy, Andrew Winters, to succeed him, which meant that the LMDC did not intend to use Garvin's departure as an excuse to reverse any of the design directions he had set. But if the Libeskind plan was to be threatened by Silverstein, the Port Authority, or anyone else, Garvin would no longer be there to defend it. Winters, while bright, hardworking, and knowledgeable, did not have Garvin's stature within the architectural community, and neither, of course, did Rampe, however eager he seemed to support Libeskind in the political arena. Roland Betts had recovered from his dismay at Pataki's dismissal of the Viñoly plan and had become a loyal supporter of the Libeskind scheme, but even with Betts's prestige now behind the plan, it was still not surprising that one of the civic groups active in the planning process, Rebuild Downtown Our Town, announced that Garvin's resignation "leaves a dangerous vacuum in the process of rebuilding downtown."

"Now that Alex Garvin is gone from the LMDC, who will stand up for solid planning, based on the needs of the people, not just the Port Authority and the developers?" the group asked in a press release. R.DOT had been increasingly critical of the planning process for some time. Shortly after Libeskind was selected, the group had complained about the fact that the Libeskind plan contained ten million square feet of commercial space. "What's happened to the democratic process that's supposed to be at the bedrock of replanning Lower Manhattan? It's been hijacked by the Lower Manhattan Development Corporation, the Port Authority, the governor, and it looks like the mayor had something to do with it, too," said Beverly Willis, cochair of the group. Willis noted that the Libeskind master plan called for the same amount of commercial space as the original six proposals by Beyer Blinder Belle, despite the fact that the presence of so much commercial space "was the major reason the public rejected" those plans, Willis said.

"There should be a huge public outcry about this shift back into gigantism," said Susan S. Szenasy, Willis's cochair. "While we continue to admire Mr. Libeskind's architecture and his excellent listening skills in public forums, which make him the ideal architect for the job, we feel that the LMDC/PA are cynically exploiting his heartfelt patriotism, his love of New York City, New Yorkers, and his adopted country, America. And that is really distressing for those of us who still believe in the American system of government."

Szenasy's comments may have sounded a bit shrill, but they

were not entirely off the mark. Robert Yaro and the Civic Alliance had said similar things, and not always more diplomatically, either. ("It's like putting lipstick on a hog," Yaro had said of the attempt to get better design for the same discredited program at Ground Zero.) The public outcry over the original plans in the summer of 2002 had been directed toward two separate shortcomings—their perceived banality from an aesthetic standpoint and the Port Authority's program. The LMDC competition addressed the first problem but not the second, and it continued to seem to many people that Libeskind had simply conferred an avant-garde veneer on an immense business development.

Libeskind was also continuing to have trouble with his usual journalistic critics like the *New York Post* and Herbert Muschamp. The tabloid turned up the heat by publishing an editorial titled "Control Freak," which called Libeskind "self-promoting" and "bizarre" and said he should have no influence at all in deciding what should be built at Ground Zero. But the most awkward criticism of Libeskind's plans came from Eli Attia, the architect who had designed the Millenium Hilton, a glass-sheathed slab just to the east of the Ground Zero site. Attia published a study suggesting that Libeskind's Wedge of Light, the plaza at Fulton Street, was based on a fraudulent principle. Libeskind had claimed that every September 11 the sun would shine on the plaza between 8:46 and 10:28 A.M. But, Attia pointed out, this would be impossible, since the Millenium Hilton was in the way. *The New York Times* printed a story publicizing Attia's charges, and Libeskind was caught in a difficult bind. Instead of admitting that his original concept was not achievable, he said he had not meant that the plaza would be in direct sunlight for the entire time, even though he had claimed it would be. Libeskind said he had meant that the sun would shine directly on the plaza at precisely 8:46 A.M. and at precisely 10:28 A.M., not the time in between. Then he rambled on about Stonehenge and the sun as a ball of fire and said he believed his design "is about radiating light, reflecting light, the atmosphere of light. It's not about tricks of light but about how light behaves when you look at the sun in three-dimensional form." For the first time, he sounded as though he did not know what he was talking about.

Things were also getting more complicated for Libeskind with the Port Authority, whose officials began to talk about the need to have an expert in transit architecture design the new central station that was called for in Libeskind's master plan. By late spring, it was clear that Libeskind would not end up with more than a consulting role in the station. By keeping Libeskind on the sidelines, however, the Port Authority was not trying to marginalize architecture. In fact, the agency, which had been such a reluctant participant in the LMDC competition and a few months earlier had seemed like the least progressive public agency in the entire planning process, had actually made a significant leap. Joe Seymour had observed the extent to which architectural patronage had improved the image of his boss, Governor Pataki, as well as the LMDC itself, and he decided that there was no reason the Port Authority could not itself sponsor a small architectural competition for the transit hub, the one part of the project that it controlled completely. True to its traditions, the authority conducted its process with minimal publicity. But one of the architects who was invited to submit a proposal was Rafael Viñoly, Ground Zero's most famous also-ran. Another was Santiago Calatrava, the gifted Spanish architect and engineer whose spectacular and lyrical bridges, train stations, airports, and museums had graced numerous European cities and who had recently purchased a town house on Park Avenue and announced his intention to move his family and his office part-time to New York. Calatrava had completed only one significant project in the United States so far, an addition to the Milwaukee Art Museum that opened in the fall of 2001, but he was a figure of such international renown that any commission he was given was bound to attract attention, and the decision to hire him would even impart a certain amount of luster to the client.

Anthony Carrachiola, the Port Authority's powerful director of capital projects, had been a fan of Calatrava's work for some time, and he was especially eager to see the architect produce something at Ground Zero. Carrachiola had helped to convince Joe Seymour of the potential value of a serious act of architectural patronage, and he made certain that Calatrava was on the authority's short list. Calatrava's extravagant, curving structures of metal and glass are exceptionally graceful, and they could not be more different from the conventional and often heavy-handed buildings that the Port Authority's own in-house architects and engineers generally produce. Often, the authority's veteran architects and engineers have blocked innovative designs, but this time Carrachiola managed to overcome his own agency's bureaucracy. In July, the Port Authority announced that Calatrava and his American-based partner firms, DMJM + Harris and the STV Group, would be hired to design the permanent new transit station at Ground Zero.

Westfield, the enormous mall operator that had leased the trade center's retail space, was not coming around as quickly as the Port Authority. The company continued to put pressure on everyone else in the planning process to allow it to build a huge, sprawling suburban-style mall that would preclude the reopening of several of the streets that Libeskind, Garvin, and the local community board had all agreed should be put back. Westfield claimed that its lease gave it the right to build retail space in the configuration it wanted, whatever the master plan specified, and Westfield did not seem to care that it had no particular allies. Indeed, David Childs continued to be firmly against the company's demands, believing them to violate all of his own instincts about urban design, and Silverstein seemed to be trying to distance himself from Westfield as well.

Despite the fact that the LMDC had fully accepted the Libeskind plan, a couple of members of the agency's board, Carl Weisbrod and Madelyn Wils, who represented the Lower Manhattan business and residential communities, decided to take on the plan anyway, on different grounds from Westfield. They complained that Libeskind's sunken memorial space would make it inconvenient for many of their constituents to get from Battery Park City to the subway. They thought the memorial should be moved to ground level, which would have eliminated the key symbolic aspect of Libeskind's plan. The Civic Alliance issued a strong denunciation of the notion, which led Madelyn Wils to resign from the alliance, claiming that it had not shown downtown residents "the slightest bit of respect, empathy, or understanding." Rampe, Higgins, and the rest of the board did not yield to Weisbrod and Wils, however, and this attempt to eviscerate the master plan to satisfy the narrow concerns of a few of

Ground Zero's neighbors was beaten back fairly quickly. Rampe made it clear that the final design of the memorial area would be up to whatever designer was eventually selected for the memorial, but that anything chosen would have to conform to the Libeskind plan.

It would not be as easy to hold on to Libeskind's vision of the Freedom Tower and the other office buildings proposed for the site. Despite all of his effusive public praise for Libeskind, Larry Silverstein was working behind the scenes to assure that architects of his choice, not the LMDC's, actually designed the buildings. Libeskind could locate the buildings, Silverstein felt, but it was not up to him to design them. Silverstein started out not even accepting Libeskind's location for the Freedom Tower, which he wanted to move closer to the transit station; putting the tower at the far northwest corner of Ground Zero, Silverstein felt, isolated it somewhat. The LMDC insisted that the tower had to be built at Libeskind's preferred portion of the site, however, and Silverstein and David Childs, whom the developer wanted to design the building, soon backed down. They could give in on the site, perhaps, because they had gotten a more important concession: the Port Authority and the LMDC negotiated a new memorandum of understanding in mid-June that confirmed Silverstein's wish that architects other than Libeskind be hired to design the individual office buildings and that all designs for office buildings and retail space would be completed in cooperation with Silverstein and Westfield.

The Civic Alliance was the only group to speak out strongly in support of Libeskind, but it may have not been the kind of friend Libeskind wanted at the moment, since this time Rampe and the LMDC did not take the alliance's protest kindly. The Civic Alliance's report, Rampe said, "evinced no understanding of what we're doing in the process. We've engaged in what is the most open and transparent planning process ever, at least for a project of this size. The LMDC has stood for architectural excellence from the beginning." Libeskind, not wanting to bite the hand that fed him, told *The New York Times* that he knew there would be many architects working on the site but that his design "will be at the nexus, at the core of the project," so that there was presumably nothing to worry about.

Rampe did not directly address the specific issue the Civic Alliance raised, however, which was the possibility—indeed, the likelihood—that if Silverstein and Westfield's wishes were followed, the site was likely to lose the special aura that Libeskind had envisioned for it. The alliance produced a series of computer-generated architectural renderings that showed what Ground Zero might turn into, and they were devastating. In one image, a huge shopping mall sits adjacent to the "sacred ground" of the memorial site, dominated by advertising billboards like Victoria's Secret and a huge Westfield logo. In another image, the office buildings that Libeskind had envisioned as being all of a piece, like Rockefeller Center, and spiraling up, building by building, to the high point of the Freedom Tower are replaced by a series of banal, developer-style buildings looking down on the memorial site. In a particularly sly gesture, the site of the Freedom Tower is occupied by a building that looks very much like David Childs's Bertelsmann Building, a dreary, commercial tower on Broadway near Times Square, and the rest of the buildings look far worse—Ground Zero remade as a cacophonous, discordant Third Avenue. These images may have been something of a scare tactic, but they showed how fragile many people in the civic community believed the master plan was and how uncertain they were that Libeskind's design could survive political reality.

CHAPTER 13

An Unnatural Hybrid

The Collaboration of Childs and Libeskind

WHILE PATAKI'S ANNOUNCEMENT that he wanted the design and construction of the Freedom Tower to move forward immediately gave the planning process a certain exuberance in the spring, it had all but evaporated by the beginning of the summer. In May, Larry Silverstein made it clear that whatever positive things he may have said about Daniel Libeskind, he expected Skidmore, Owings & Merrill—which meant David Childs and his partner T. J. Gottesdiener—to design the tower, not Libeskind. Daniel Libeskind was not an architect of skyscrapers, and for a developer like Silverstein that would normally be enough to close the matter. "Danny, you've never designed a skyscraper. If I'm going to have heart surgery, I don't want a surgeon who's never done heart surgery before," Silverstein told him. This position should not have been surprising, since Silverstein had always chosen his words carefully when he spoke publicly about Libeskind; he may have referred to him as a genius, but Silverstein never described Libeskind's total design for Ground Zero as anything other than a site plan. The Skidmore, Owings & Merrill tower would "reflect the spirit of Daniel's site plan," Silverstein said in May, and that, to him, fulfilled any obligation he might have had to the LMDC and Libeskind's master plan.

Libeskind saw it differently. "I'm going to design the Freedom Tower," he told Silverstein. The banner that had hung behind the governor when he announced his intention to build the Freedom Tower was based on his rendering, not David Childs's, Libeskind said, and he believed that the public had come to expect that it would be getting a Libeskind building, not a building by another architect that had no connection to Libeskind other than its general placement on the sixteen-acre site. And it should not just be a Libeskind building but one that looked more or less like the design that had been unveiled the previous December in the Winter Garden, Libeskind felt. To do anything less in his view would be to break faith with the public and with the entire planning process. He said he would be happy to work in tandem with a firm that had more experience in skyscraper design, but the basic concept of the building had to be his.

The problem was complicated by the fact that if Libeskind was to have a partner, David Childs and Skidmore, Owings & Merrill were not the most logical candidates to join forces with him, despite the firm's considerable experience in skyscraper design. Childs had ideas of his own for the tower, and they did not resemble Libeskind's at all. Indeed, Childs had been working on a tall tower for Ground Zero since 2001, long before the LMDC's competition brought Libeskind into the process. In some ways, it had seemed like Childs's job from the beginning. Even though he had been neither a consultant to the LMDC like Beyer Blinder Belle and Peterson and Littenberg, nor a successful participant in the LMDC master-plan design competition, his role as Larry Silverstein's architect had always kept him closely involved in the planning process—closer to it, in some ways, than some people who had more official roles. Childs had always hovered in the background, close to power, and ready to assume a more conspicuous and formal role the moment others faltered.

Several of Childs's early designs for Ground Zero skyscrapers were for office towers of sixty or seventy stories with symbolic spires above, and Childs had worked with the structural engineer Guy Nordenson on a plan for a torqued tower that would taper as it rose. Nordenson proposed such a scheme as part of *The New York Times Magazine*'s design effort in September 2002, and while that was not precisely the same as the building he was assisting Childs with, it bore a close resemblance. What was most important to Childs—and to Nordenson, for that matter—was the notion that the high point of the tower rise out of the center of the building, so that it could be supported by the whole structure. Childs and Nordenson came up with numerous versions of the tower, and all of them culminated in a central spire.

Even though the tower Libeskind envisioned as part of his master-plan design combined, like Childs's, a medium-height office tower with a much taller spire, the difference between the two architects' approaches was enormous. Libeskind's design called for the spire to be on the west side of the tower and for the entire structure to be asymmetrical, which meant not only a different kind of appearance but an altogether different kind of structural system. In his first exhibited version, Libeskind envisioned that the spire would be almost distinct from the office tower, like a vast antenna joined to the side of a skyscraper; it would have been partially enclosed in glass and would have contained gardens. (Libeskind called the original scheme the Gardens of the World.) The office tower itself would have had a sharply sloping roof, so that from a short distance away it would have almost appeared like a diamond in the sky. The idea of a nearly freestanding spire proved impractical, however, and as Libeskind adjusted his master plan to respond to the LMDC's comments in February, he redesigned the tower to fuse the spire into the main structure, as well as to make the skyscraper itself somewhat bulkier. While the building became more practical, it did not lose the general shape that Libeskind had sought from the beginning: a profile that would echo the uplifted arm of the Statue of Liberty. Turning Frédéric Bartholdi's figure into an abstraction was the key aesthetic idea behind Libeskind's Freedom Tower in all of its versions.

Childs did not share Libeskind's fondness for crystalline forms, and he certainly had no interest in evoking the Statue of Liberty, although he did observe that the torqued form of his tower could be interpreted as an evocation of the slight twist in the Statue of Liberty's figure as she turns toward the harbor. In general, Childs does not like to think in terms of the analogies that Libeskind so loves, and he would much rather talk about his buildings in terms of their materials, their functions, or their relationship to their surroundings, which is a particular concern of his. Childs takes pride in thinking of himself as much more than a nuts-and-bolts architect, and he has always put great stock in urbanism, trying to connect his buildings both to the street and to their neighbors.

Skidmore, Owings & Merrill has long been viewed as the preeminent corporate architecture firm in the United States, and it rose to prominence largely on the basis of several classic postwar skyscrapers, such as Lever House and 500 Park Avenue in New York, and the Inland Steel Building, the Sears Tower, and the John Hancock Center in Chicago. These were all done long before David Childs's time, but at Skidmore skyscraper design is still seen as a serious and highly rational undertaking, and it was hard not to think that Childs felt that he and his firm had been cast in the role of the adults at Ground Zero, forced to share authority with Libeskind as the errant child.

Both Childs and Nordenson believe that the design of a skyscraper begins with its structure, not with a pictorial idea. They believe that the starting point is a structural form, which the architect crafts into a beautiful and visually appealing object. Some of Skidmore's most famous skyscrapers, such as the Sears Tower and the John Hancock Center, were produced by the team of Bruce Graham, a Skidmore design partner, and Fazlur Khan, a partner in the firm who was a celebrated structural engineer, and it occurred to Childs that he and Nordenson could function in a similar way at the Freedom Tower, even though Nordenson, an independent structural engineer, is not officially connected with Skidmore. Libeskind's Freedom Tower design, however, began not with a structural idea but with a visual goal, to create an abstract form that would suggest the profile of the Statue of Liberty; to Libeskind, the job of the structural engineer is to make the architect's visual idea possible.

The two architects have differences, then, that are quite literally more than skin-deep. They go to the heart of what skyscrapers are and how they are designed. As the design work for the Freedom Tower was beginning, Childs felt so strongly about the rightness of his concept that he could not envision himself functioning as Libeskind's corporate arm, providing the technical expertise and backup to enable Libeskind to get his design built. He felt he had earned the right to design the building himself or with Nordenson. After all, he was not only Larry Silverstein's architect of choice, having already designed the new 7 World Trade Center; he had produced the AOL Time Warner Center at Columbus Circle; a widely acclaimed design for the new Pennsylvania Station that was to be built within the shell of the old main post-office building; and a new headquarters building for Bear Stearns in Midtown Manhattan. He had been the architect for the new headquarters tower that had been planned for the New York Stock Exchange as well, and while that project did not survive September 11, it further confirmed his role as the architect who could speak the language of business yet who had stature in the design world as well.

In fact, Childs had tried very hard to maintain an existence in two distinct worlds, the world of practical architecture and the more theoretical, academic world of high-design architecture. It was not always easy to stake out that turf at Skidmore, especially given his own history at the firm, where he had taken charge during a severe economic downturn that threatened the firm's survival, became the first person to hold the title of chairman, and laid off more than half the employees. Childs's manner is soft-spoken, but in his years as Skidmore's chairman he proved he could be cold-blooded, and he is every bit as ambitious as Daniel Libeskind. He has had great success in the civic realm—he has long been sought after as a board member of prominent organizations, and he was recently appointed chairman of the Commission of Fine Arts in Washington, D.C., which passes judgment on public architecture in the capital. In many ways, Childs is a contemporary equivalent of Daniel Burnham, the eminent Chicago architect at the turn of the twentieth century who was noted as much for his civic work as for his actual buildings. What has so far eluded him, like Burnham, is a roster of completed buildings that will ensure that he will be known to posterity mainly for his architecture.

Twice, Childs teamed up with Frank Gehry to design skyscrapers for New York—once in the 1980s when they did a scheme for a pair of towers to rise on the present site of Madison Square Garden, and then in 2000 when they produced an entry in an invited competition to design a new headquarters for the New York Times Company. They withdrew from that competition when Gehry decided that he could not work for a client that was making as many demands as the Times Company appeared to be, but Childs and Gehry got along well and served each other's needs comfortably. Childs enjoyed being a partner with one of the great form makers of the age, and Gehry liked learning about skyscrapers from Childs. Each seemed to respect the other's turf, and the collaboration was genuine and positive. It did not hurt that Childs is a decade younger than Gehry, which might have put a slight brake on his general inclination to control most situations in which he is involved.

It did not take long to make clear that almost nothing about the Gehry-Childs collaborations could serve as a model for any collaboration between Childs and Libeskind. This time, Childs was the older partner, and he had no desire to defer to Libeskind, whom he viewed as pushy and aggressive and not as talented as Gehry. Libeskind, for his part, was not inclined to think of collaborating on a skyscraper as something of an adventure, the way Gehry did; he had the biggest job of his career riding on it and much of his reputation. To hitch his wagon to Childs's star seemed wrong to Libeskind—after all, he had won the Ground Zero master-plan competition, and Skidmore, Owings & Merrill had not even placed. He had been anointed by the governor, not Childs. Didn't that count for something?

But the real reason that Childs and Libeskind could not work together as smoothly as Childs and Gehry did is that unlike the earlier collaboration, when both Childs and Gehry came to their joint projects without any preconceived notions of what the buildings should be and embarked on the creative process more or less in tandem, at Ground Zero both architects had already decided what they wanted the building to be like. Each had a design of his own, and those designs were very different, not only in appearance but in underlying principle. About the only things the Libeskind and Childs schemes had in common were great height and the presence of a spire that stretched higher than the office portion of the building. Everything else, from the underlying structural system to the overall look and shape, was different. And each architect was deeply invested in the belief that his way of approaching the building was right, and the other architect's was wrong.

By the beginning of July, the Freedom Tower situation was at something of an impasse. For all intents and purposes, there were two parallel design efforts progressing, and each could stake some claim to being the "official" design—Childs's because it was sanctioned by Larry Silverstein, and Libeskind's because it emerged from the master plan sanctioned by the governor. The situation was an embarrassment, and it threatened to disrupt the already ambitious schedule that Pataki had set for construction. The governor urged Kevin Rampe to force Libeskind and Childs to figure out a way to work together. On July 15, Rampe asked the architects to meet with him at LMDC headquarters at 1 Liberty Plaza. Childs brought Gottesdiener and Janno Lieber, Larry Silverstein's executive in charge of the Ground Zero project, who had taken over from Geoffrey Wharton. Libeskind came with Edward Hayes, a lawyer he had recently hired who is well-connected politically—he is a close friend of Pataki—and was the model for the colorful attorney Tom Killian in Tom Wolfe's novel *The Bonfire of the Vanities*.

Hayes's presence gave the meeting the air of a crisis negotiation, and it offended Childs, who later said he had not known that the meeting was to have anything more than a routine agenda. The architects and their entourages sat in separate conference rooms at opposite ends of the twentieth floor, and Rampe and Matt Higgins shuttled between the two camps. After five hours of this, neither man had budged from his original position, which was that he should be the architect of the building.

"The Libeskinds are afraid of being chewed up by the Skidmore, Owings & Merrill machine," Rampe told Childs.

"Well, I'm afraid of being chewed up by the Libeskind machine," Childs replied.

Sometime after nine in the evening, Higgins sent out for pizza, and not long after that Rampe suggested that it might be helpful if Libeskind and Childs discussed things face-to-face, away from everyone else. The two men went into a third room. Childs was firm. He was willing to collaborate, he said, but not if Libeskind's design was the starting point. "Only if this is a blank slate can I work with you," he said.

"This is not a tabula rasa," Libeskind replied. "The Freedom Tower is an image, a basis."

"I have my own image," Childs said. "I appreciate and respect what you do, but it is not what I do."

Libeskind began to sketch his design on a piece of paper. "I have an idea how we can develop it," he insisted, but Childs continued to demur. Libeskind said that he would agree to a fifty-fifty sharing of authority. Childs said that was impossible, that one architect had to be in charge. "Someone has to be the writer of the Constitution," he said. Libeskind later recalled the marathon negotiating session as "grueling—it felt like the Grand Inquisitor scene in *The Brothers Karamazov.*"

Shortly before eleven o'clock, they came out of the room and announced that they had agreed that Skidmore, Owings & Merrill would be the official architect of the Freedom Tower and Libeskind would "meaningfully collaborate" on the design. Childs left, saying he had to get to Washington for a meeting the next day of the Commission of Fine Arts, and Libeskind remained until 12:45 A.M., when the final wording of a press release announcing the collaboration was worked out.

For the LMDC, it seemed as if Rampe and Higgins had pulled off a stroke of architectural diplomacy, averting a crisis later in the week. Childs and Libeskind appeared together at a press conference to announce the collaboration. Childs, who is more than six feet tall, stood beside the much shorter Libeskind and joked that their joint profile resembled the asymmetrical silhouette of Libeskind's version of the Freedom Tower. It was one of the few times they engaged in friendly banter. In fact, the agreement to collaborate turned out to have little effect, except to relieve the tension that had been building up over the preceding few weeks. Childs and Libeskind and their staffs were supposed to meet regularly over the summer and to set up a joint studio in the Skidmore, Owings & Merrill offices at 14 Wall Street, but the meetings took place only sporadically, and they were hardly productive. By the end of the summer, there was still no consensus on a design and little cordiality between the collaborators. Childs later described Libeskind's method of skyscraper design as "shaping a clay block and sticking a sword on one side of it."

Things were only to get worse. For all that Pataki, Rampe, and Higgins prided themselves on their skills at orchestrating a negotiation, their premise at bringing Libeskind and Childs together was flawed, since it reflected so little understanding of how architects work. Complicated buildings are often produced by architectural teams, but in almost every case there is a clear design leader. The designer in charge may be a practitioner such as Libeskind, without a large office and with relatively little commercial experience, or it may be a large firm, but generally the design architect has sole authority for aesthetic decisions and for the basic concept of the building. The associated firms, even if they are much larger, have the responsibility of executing the design architect's vision.

Libeskind and Childs could not work together in this kind of arrangement, and it made little sense to have asked them to. Both Libeskind and Childs saw themselves as entitled to be the primary design architect, and for different reasons both of them were correct. Putting them together was akin to asking Balthus and Ellsworth Kelly to collaborate on a painting. What was needed was not a forced collaboration between two architects but a determination by the client—who was really Governor Pataki and the Port Authority, not Larry Silverstein—that one of the architects should have full authority over the design of the Freedom Tower and the other should withdraw. But Pataki was unwilling to offend either architect or Silverstein, and he appeared to believe that creative differences could be as open to negotiated solutions as political issues could.

. . .

The friction between the architects increased through the autumn of 2003, and it played out at all levels. Childs and Libeskind did not even agree on where the building should be. Libeskind's master plan set it at the northwest corner of the site, but Childs wanted it further east, closer to the transit station. "It would have been on hard land, not fill, and it would have been better for the composition of the skyline," Childs said. But Pataki stepped in and said he wanted the tower built where Libeskind had envisioned it, and Childs gave in.

Some of the Libeskind staff members who were assigned to the Freedom Tower team complained that the Skidmore architects treated them more as unwelcome intruders than as colleagues; some of the Skidmore people, for their part, thought that their Libeskind counterparts were inexperienced and arrogant. According to *The New York Observer,* Daniel Libeskind himself was asked not to appear in the project office unless David Childs was also there. Meetings broke up in anger, and in mid-October Libeskind walked out of one design meeting, unsure of whether he wanted to continue on the project at all.

Libeskind had made a genuine effort at compromise. His office prepared simple models of the designs the two architects were working on before the "collaboration" officially began—Childs's original torqued, tapered design and Libeskind's more angular design from the master plan—and then Libeskind and his team produced models of several other versions that incorporated various elements of both in a progression, so that each model would show a step in an evolution from Childs's design to Libeskind's. Libeskind decided he could live with one of the designs in the middle. He felt that it contained enough of the visual elements he wanted his skyscraper to have, and yet it still had Childs's twisting and tapered shaft as its basic form. He presented it to Childs, who rejected it outright. Childs continued to maintain that he was the architect and that he had no obligation to Libeskind beyond conforming to the master plan.

After the October blowup, the tensions between the architects became more public. Pataki was forced to address the problem, and he made a statement saying he would "call upon all parties in the rebuilding effort to place the public's interest above self-interest, and I will chart a course to make it happen." He concluded: "I'm confident the Freedom Tower will eclipse anything either of them has produced before. That's typical of so many great artistic collaborations throughout history—Michelangelo and Pope Julius II made the Sistine Chapel, Philip Johnson and Mies van der Rohe made the Seagram Building—just think what Libeskind and Childs will make."

Pope Julius, of course, was Michelangelo's patron, not his artistic collaborator, and Philip Johnson was Mies's very junior colleague, so neither analogy really applied. In fact, they proved the opposite point to the one Pataki wanted to make: to create a great piece of architecture, you need one creative force in charge, not two.

Pataki continued to pressure the architects to cooperate, however, and so did Silverstein. At one point, the architects were called to a meeting with the developer and told that they had to make a greater effort to work together. Skidmore's technical work had to be the basis for a joint design, Silverstein said, but he wanted the design to conform to four principles Libeskind sought: that it reach 1,776 feet, that it be asymmetrical, that it line up with the slurry wall in the foundation of the original trade center, and that it be the culmination of a spiraling group of towers across Ground Zero. Childs, aware that Silverstein was speaking for the governor, did not refuse. He produced a revised design in November with a shape that seemed to be a hybrid of his own ideas and Libeskind's. The building also had some other elements: a top made up of a cable structure devised by Guy Nordenson and a windmill farm to provide the building with power, which had been suggested by Guy Battle, another engineer. Libeskind's huge spire had been reduced to a relatively small punctuation mark, not unlike the spire Childs himself had used to crown the Bertelsmann Building, the glass-sheathed office tower he had designed in Times Square in the late 1980s.

Both Pataki and Silverstein liked the compromise design. Libeskind, however, noted that the antenna went all the way up to two thousand feet, 224 feet higher than he had intended. (The superstructure stopped at 1,776 feet.) He worried that the tower was now too big and that the cable structure at the top in particular seemed disproportionately large and might overwhelm the rest of the building. He had been communicating with the governor and his chief of staff, John Cahill, frequently through Ed Hayes, and at the beginning of December Libeskind decided he had to play that card yet again.

Unfortunately, all of the computer renderings and photographs of the latest version were in the Skidmore, Owings & Merrill office on Wall Street, not in Libeskind's office two blocks away on Rector Street. Libeskind thought he needed these materials to make a case to the governor, so some members of the Libeskind team tried to remove copies from the Skidmore office. The Skidmore architects refused to let them be taken away, and not long after the *New York Post,* always eager to fan the flames of anti-Libeskind sentiment, reported that there had been a "Watergate-style break-in" at Skidmore, Owings & Merrill. "The fight over the Ground Zero Freedom Tower has spiraled completely out of control," the paper said, under a headline that read "Madhouse: Ground Zero Designers at War."

The governor's staff agreed with Libeskind's objections, and Childs was told to reduce the tower somewhat, to 1,600 feet. By then, there was no longer any pretense of a collaboration. Childs and his team were doing the work, and Libeskind was simply evaluating it to determine whether it met the constraints of his master plan and therefore could win his approval. There were no more Libeskind staff members working in the Skidmore office. Libeskind worried that the 1,600-foot superstructure was still too big, since it would push the entire building, including the antenna, beyond 1,776 feet, and he said he would not endorse it as consistent with the master plan.

Childs refused to budge, and on Friday, December 12—three days before the day Pataki had said he wanted to have a finished design to show the public—Childs, without Libeskind but with Janno Lieber of the Silverstein organization, was called to a meeting with Charles Gargano in the governor's Manhattan office on Third Avenue. Childs presented his scheme. Gargano listened respectfully, then excused himself and returned a few minutes later with Pataki. Pataki and Gargano began to discuss the building's shape with Childs and Lieber and suggested that the sloping top, which Libeskind had wanted but which had been eliminated when the cable structure was added, be restored to the main structure, where it would be slightly obscured within the cable crown.

A committee of political figures working with several different architects and engineers was an odd group to design any building, let alone the world's tallest skyscraper on the world's most carefully watched site. The next day, Saturday, Pataki called Childs on the phone from Bermuda, where the governor was spending the weekend at Mayor Bloomberg's vacation house, and told him that he wanted to see the tower scaled back another hundred feet to win Libeskind's approval. Childs indicated to the governor that he thought the cut might damage the proportions of the building, but Pataki made it clear that he needed this concession. The architects could have another few days to revise their plans, since the governor was willing to delay the public unveiling to Friday, December 19. The time was useful, not only because it could take several days to prepare the elaborate models needed for a press conference but also because there was yet another design issue to negotiate: Libeskind had also said that he felt that his spire had been given short shrift, and he wanted it increased in size.

Childs and his team worked all weekend and into the beginning of the week and came up with a further revision, which was discussed at a lunch Pataki had with the two architects, Charles Gargano, and John Cahill at 101 Park Avenue, not far from his office, on December 17. The lunch was supposed to mark the successful completion of the design, but the event was strained. Childs remained unhappy about the fact that one hundred feet had been lopped off, and Libeskind was irritated that he had not yet seen the final models of the completed design, which he felt that Childs and Silverstein were keeping from him to avoid further complications. Libeskind was finally invited to see the models the following morning, December 18, and he agreed to accept the design. Childs was unhappy about the Libeskind spire—he would later refer to it as "the toothpick" and, worse, as "the bayonet"—but officially both sides were in agreement. The war was over, and the press conference was on for the next morning, which made it one year and one day after the first presentation of all of the plans, including Libeskind's, in the Winter Garden.

The frantic rush and the incessant fighting had hardly been worth it. The "final" Freedom Tower design was better than some of the versions that had been worked on over the preceding weeks, but it could hardly be called distinguished. The tower had neither the simple clarity of some of Childs's and Nordenson's early versions nor the visual power of Libeskind's design. The proportions, which everyone had worried about so much, still were not right. The handsome web of cables at the top occupied so much of the building that it seemed more than a crown but less than a full structure in itself—and no one had seemed to notice that the open trusswork of cables, while potentially quite beautiful, bore a certain relationship to the open latticework of Rafael Viñoly's design, which the governor had rejected because he felt it was too much like a skeleton. The cable structure was lighter and more graceful visually, but it was still a skeletal top set above a more conventional skyscraper bottom.

At the very top, the spire Libeskind had so wanted still looked tacked on, even though it had been given a bit more heft late in the game at Libeskind's insistence. As a complete work of design, the Freedom Tower had all the defects of an unnatural hybrid. It showed its multiple parentage, and it seemed to be trying to do everything at once, which meant that it could not communicate either Childs's or Libeskind's aesthetic ideas with much precision. They were all watered down by being forced together.

Putting a tall structure of some sort at Ground Zero was a critical idea because repairing the skyline meant so much to so many people who felt that they had lost not only friends and fellow citizens on September 11 but the physical form and shape of the city itself. But it was urgent that the building be extraordinary, and this building was not. A truly great tower at Ground Zero was an opportunity to stake a claim for the future of the skyscraper—the greatest of all American building types and the most important contribution American culture has made to world architecture—in the city best known for skyscrapers, on the very piece of land on which that

American culture was attacked. The Freedom Tower tries to do all this, but weakly and tentatively. It may turn out to be innovative from an environmental standpoint, but that is far from certain. It is certainly not a retrograde piece of aesthetics, but it hardly seems to break the new ground that was hoped for, either. And it does not even seem up to the level of some of the more exciting projects that were presented in the LMDC's competition, such as the United Architects design or Norman Foster's evocative pair of joined towers.

The Freedom Tower unveiling took place in Federal Hall, on Wall Street, the same room in which Beyer Blinder Belle's ill-fated designs had been announced in the summer of 2002. As if to erase the memory of that event or perhaps to change the karma in the room, this time the presentation was made from a platform on the west side of the rotunda, not from the east side. But turning everyone 180 degrees did not obscure the reality of the situation: the press conference was a political event organized to announce a political compromise, not the presentation of a great work of architecture. It was unlikely that very many of the hundreds of people present failed to realize that the building being presented was an awkward hybrid, the product of two architects who did not like each other, did not want to work together, and who each believed that the best features of his own design had been compromised by the other.

The press conference was led by Pataki, who said that "today is a celebration of the successful collaboration of two great architects." Childs and Libeskind sat on the platform, looking slightly uneasy, as Pataki went on to call the new building "a symbol of our confidence in our freedom and our belief in tomorrow. Everyone will look at this building and think of the heroes we lost—we will build it and show the world that freedom will always triumph over terror." Mayor Bloomberg said a few words after Pataki, and then the two men pulled a string to rip open a curtain in front of a model of the tower that was as tall as Pataki himself. The tower lit up, and David Childs was introduced. It was a moment of some triumph for Childs, who had done what many observers of the planning process had predicted from the beginning: he had become the architect of the biggest and most important skyscraper at Ground Zero not by winning the LMDC's competition or through any aspect of the official planning process at all but because he and Larry Silverstein had remained on the sidelines, preparing their plans and waiting out the official process as much as participating in it. Childs had been through gruesome battles not only with Libeskind but also with public officials that left his building seriously compromised, but at least he was the architect, not Daniel Libeskind.

Childs spoke for several minutes and avoided the self-congratulatory rhetoric of the day in favor of putting the focus back on architecture. He presented an eloquent and extended defense of the building as an urban symbol, and he talked about his desire to have the building make a distinctive mark in the sky and be integrated into the grid of the city at ground level, and he wove together issues of symbolism, environmentalism, structure, history, and urban design. It was a virtuoso performance—the only problem being that the building itself did not seem up to Childs's description of it. He ended with a minor, slightly condescending, reference to Libeskind, whom he referred to as "Danny." "We will continue our discussions with Danny to assure that we work with his master plan as we go ahead," Childs said.

Libeskind followed, and he said nothing specifically about the building at all. "Working with Skidmore, Owings & Merrill has not been easy—but a civic process is about people," he said. "I want to say how much I appreciate the governor's efforts here—he is a visionary." Libeskind said a few words about his ideas for the master plan and about his determination that the tower echo the Statue of Liberty's shape and that it rise to a height of 1,776 feet, which he called "a global symbol of optimism. God bless America."

Larry Silverstein followed Libeskind. "Working with talented, brilliant architects is a challenge in itself," he said, in a remark that was as close as anyone came that morning to being candid. Silverstein quickly reverted to standard press-conference rhetoric. "What we see today is beautiful, it is spectacular, it is also very practical," he said. "It will be the new icon of the New York skyline." He told the audience that he would meet the governor's request to lay the foundations for the building by the third anniversary of September

11, and he mentioned that Pataki had also asked him to commit to topping out the steel structure by September 11, 2007, the sixth anniversary of the terrorist attacks. He was less sure about meeting this deadline. "I said, 'Governor, there are hard commitments and soft commitments,' " Silverstein said, "and this commitment will have to be a softer commitment."

Silverstein was right to be cautious, since the symbolic start of construction in September 2004 would be no more than a ceremony, and it could take place without every aspect of the design being completed. But few people believed that the building would be ready to begin actual construction soon enough to permit the entire steel structure to be completed three years later. This was, after all, to be the tallest tower in the world, and it presented numerous engineering problems that were far from solved, including the viability of the windmill farm at the top. There were no doubts about Nordenson's cable structure, which David Childs likened to the Brooklyn Bridge, but whether it made sense at the scale that was contemplated remained to be seen. And of course, the design itself was still evolving. Silverstein had indicated that he did not want to pay for all of the elaborate top, and no one had begun to figure out how it otherwise would be financed. Taking it off might solve the financial problem, but then Ground Zero would be left with not much more than an ordinary office building, which would start the political problems all over again. The governor could not afford to have the building stalled, but it would not help him much if two years of effort brought forth an ordinary tower that no longer could lay claim to being the world's tallest.

Once the design became truly final, it could still take a year or more to complete plans and construction and engineering drawings for the building. And much also depended on the resolution of Larry Silverstein's legal dispute with Swiss Re, the lead insurance company for the trade center. In Silverstein's ideal scenario, as outlined by his attorney Herbert Wachtell, he would have nearly seven billion dollars at his disposal for rebuilding. But that depended on the courts agreeing with Wachtell and Silverstein's contention that certain types of insurance documents, which had not been finalized by September 11, nonetheless were in effect, and also that the two planes hitting the two towers constituted two separate occurrences, not one single event, and that Silverstein was therefore entitled to a double payment on his claim.

With only a single payment, Silverstein did not have as lavish a budget as many people thought. He was, after all, still obligated to pay the Port Authority $120 million per year in ground rent, and by late 2004 that tab alone would have reached $360 million. In the five years it might take to get the building completed and ready for occupancy, that total would approach one billion dollars. Constructing the building would cost one billion dollars or more, and then there were all the costs for architects, engineers, and other consultants to be figured in. And then there were Silverstein's lawyers, who cost much more than architects. By mid-2004, his legal fees were reportedly $100 million. By the time the building was finished, all of the costs connected with it could use up much of Silverstein's insurance payment, with little left to build the other office structures called for in the master plan.

But what else could be done? There was no other way to pay for the building other than the insurance funds. Conventional sources of real-estate financing were not likely to step in, for an important reason: there was relatively little in the way of an assured market for the building, and the financial institutions that normally finance commercial office buildings do not do so on a whim but only on the basis of commitments from tenants who agree to pay market rents. There were no such tenants for the Freedom Tower, and it was not likely that any would be found quickly, given how much empty office space still remained downtown. Much of the World Financial Center across the street, which had been badly damaged in the attack, remained vacant at the end of 2003; even though American Express and Merrill Lynch, the major tenants, returned and some new tenants arrived, there was still lots of available space. Silverstein's own 7 World Trade Center building would be finished long before the Freedom Tower, and it was going to add a significant amount of new office space to the neighborhood also. Was it really possible that the demand for first-class office space in Lower Manhattan would continue to grow at a sufficient rate to make the Freedom Tower profitable? Perhaps, but it was not surprising that banks and financial institutions did not want to count on it.

The only tenant who had indicated any interest in moving into the building was Pataki himself. Of course, where the governor goes, other state offices can certainly follow. There is, it need hardly be said, a precedent for erecting a very tall building—indeed, the tallest skyscraper in the world—on a particularly large site on the west side of Lower Manhattan, and having that project be enthusiastically supported by an ambitious governor of New York State who wanted the building to be seen as a hallmark of his administration and who chose not to worry about the fact that it put a huge amount of office space into the marketplace for which there was relatively little demand, such that in the absence of enough tenants the huge building would be filled up at the governor's behest largely by state and Port Authority offices. Perhaps the most disturbing aspect of the entire saga of planning Ground Zero was the possibility that the Freedom Tower might turn out to be less a symbol of renewal than of how little had been learned from the troubled history of the original World Trade Center. In mid-2004, the Freedom Tower seemed less to signify innovation than history repeating itself.

CHAPTER 14

The Memorial Competition

A MEMORIAL TO THE 2,800 PEOPLE who died in the attack on the World Trade Center was always going to be an essential part of the rebuilt Ground Zero—for many people, a memorial was the only thing on the sixteen acres that mattered. As September 11, 2001, receded into the past, the voices clamoring to turn the entire site into a memorial largely faded away, replaced by a general acceptance of the concept that Ground Zero would have a mix of commercial development and cultural centers and transportation facilities. But that did not diminish the belief that the memorial would somehow stand above those everyday things and be a place apart. The memorial was sacred ground, whatever happened elsewhere on the site, and as such it had to be planned differently.

This would not be like any memorial ever created in the United States before. It was not marking a terrible event that took place far away, like the monument to the battle at Iwo Jima outside of Washington, D.C., or the Vietnam Veterans Memorial. In a sense, it would be more like Gettysburg, because the place of commemoration is the very place in which the event being commemorated occurred. But the center of New York's financial district is hardly a rural battlefield or the relatively sparsely populated center of Oklahoma City. Density was its hallmark, and as people believed that Ground Zero was sacred, they also began to accept the notion that, paradoxically, its sacred nature might be best expressed by celebrating the joy and the potential of everyday urban life. That is the real design dilemma, and the one for which no other memorial prepares us: the extent to which it is impossible, conceptually, to fully separate the symbolic memorial from everything else that would be done on these sixteen acres.

There were other issues that faced the designer of a memorial at Ground Zero, as memorials are not only for those with memories and for people in need of healing. But at Ground Zero, the priority of the memorial-planning process was the concerns of victims' family members, and that led to pressure to find and execute a design quickly. Concern about helping people who had suffered losses in the trade-center attack was a legitimate and even urgent priority for society, but it was not always consistent with the creation of a memorial that would have meaning for those who did not live through September 11, the generations yet to come.

Everyone brings some kind of experience, which is to say some kind of memory, to any memorial, even if it is not the awful, searing experience of having lost someone on September 11 or of having lived through that day in some other way. Memory can come in other forms. It can mean knowledge, and feeling, that come from other things—in the case of the Holocaust, from studying history, or having Jewish identity, or being sensitive to the inhumanity of fascism; in the case of Gettysburg or the Lincoln Memorial, the history we have learned throughout our lives is the memory we bring to these places. Would they mean as much if you had no memories, no knowledge? Probably not. But then again, no one could go to the Lincoln Memorial, even without knowing of Abraham Lincoln and the Civil War, or read a word of the Gettysburg Address carved on the wall yet think the memorial was an ordinary place. There, the physical form of a place does, in and of itself, instill profound feelings, a sense of awe, even if you come with no memories at all. The truly transcendent memorials are not limited by our memories and are able to inspire a powerful emotional response whatever experience we bring to them, but they are rare.

Henry Bacon's Lincoln Memorial possesses grandeur, clarity, purity, and an absence of both fussiness and pettiness—the things that define nobility, at least in architecture—and they contribute to its ability to communicate to people who have no direct memory of Lincoln and the Civil War, which is to say everyone who has seen this memorial for at least the last half century. Bacon's building is certainly the greatest Greek temple ever constructed in the United States, but it is not the classical style itself that makes it extraordinary but Bacon's ability to distill it to a certain clear, almost abstract essence.

Daniel Chester French's statue of the seated Lincoln has a great deal to do with the inspiring nature of this memorial, of course, but not everything by any means, since one of the things that makes the Lincoln Memorial so remarkable is how completely it transcends Lincoln as an individual and makes you think about the implications of his vision and about what it still means to us today. This is exactly what John Russell Pope was unable to do a short distance away in his Jefferson Memorial, even though Jefferson, as a figure, had a vision as sweeping as Lincoln's, perhaps more so, and full of relevance for today. Yet the Jefferson Memorial is just a statue inside a round colonnade; by trying to focus so much on Jefferson the man, it limited him. You feel awe at Jefferson's achievements when at Monticello or the University of Virginia but not here. A dull, flat place cannot be redeemed by the earnestness of its intentions or by the deservedness of its subject—even if you bring lots of knowledge-memory to the Jefferson Memorial, you leave feeling almost nothing at all.

At the Washington Monument, Robert Mills's great obelisk, not only are there the qualities to be found at the Lincoln Memorial—grandeur, clarity, and purity—and an absence of fussiness and pettiness, there is also an exquisite, subtle kind of symbolic rightness to this design. It is a singular object for the first president, a figure like none other. It stands literally as tall on the landscape as he stands on the landscape of history. Washington the city revolves around it, as the nation at its beginnings can be said to have revolved around George Washington. But it is understated and simple, and it never says any of these things directly.

At the Vietnam Veterans Memorial by Maya Lin, the most widely admired memorial of our time, the message is also abstract and understated but subtle in a way that the Washington Monument is not—it goes down into the ground, not up, to symbolize the anguish and pain of that war, but it is open to the sky, to symbolize hope, and the arms of the wall are on axes with both the Lincoln Memorial and the Washington Monument, to connect to the larger stream of American history. Everything is abstract except one thing: the names, and they are absolutely, powerfully, horrifically, and beautifully real. Never, ever, have the things that cannot be put easily into words—the great and painful issues—been presented with such abstraction, while at the same time the things that can be put into words—the names—been presented with such blunt, direct, powerful force.

None of that was understood, of course, by the people who forced a mediocre sculpture of soldiers into this memorial. But it is worth noting now, many years later, how extraordinary it is that the part of the memorial that was so controversial, that was denounced as abstract and uncommunicative to the public has become a beloved icon, while the statue has been all but forgotten. There is a lesson in that, and it is to let great artists do their work and trust that the public, in time, will get it.

It is not an accident that the Vietnam memorial loomed large as people began to confront the question of the memorial at Ground Zero. It manages to do what the families of those who died wanted most, which was to pay tribute, while at the same time inspiring a sense of awe even in those who did not lose loved ones in the war. Not the least aspect of the genius of its design is how much Lin understood that the memorial does not exist only for those who have lost loved ones and that tribute, and healing, are only the beginning of the goals of any memorial. The meanings of memorials change over time, and each generation brings a new interpretation to what it sees. If Lin was lucky as well as brilliant, it was in the fact that the architectural competition in which her design was the winner was not held until some years after the end of the Vietnam War, and the emotional wounds, while real, were less raw. The rush to move quickly at Ground Zero forced a different and much more short-term set of priorities on the planning process.

Almost all of the great memorials were designed and built years after the events that they mark. Lincoln had been dead for more than fifty years when the Lincoln Memorial was completed, Washington for almost one hundred (although much of that delay was the result of political and financial problems in getting the memorial finished, not a conscious desire to take time to ponder Washington's significance). Sir Edwin Lutyens's Monument to the Missing, in Thiepval, France, the greatest of all World War I memorials, was completed in 1932 in the battlefields of the Somme, more than a dozen years after the end of the war. It is an enormous and complex structure that, like Bacon's, uses the classical vocabulary to extraordinarily powerful emotional effect, although here it is twisted, deliberately, almost perversely, as if to show us the horror of war. It is an assemblage of arches, facing in all four directions, mounting toward a high center with something of the massing of a setback skyscraper from the 1920s, and it looms, ominously. Vincent Scully has written of this that "it is an enormous monster: its tondi are eyes; its high arch screams. It is the open mouth of death. . . . [T]here is no path for us. We must violate the grass. Closer, we are enveloped by the creature's great gorge. One sarcophagus like a palate lies within it, under the arch. We must go left or right up the diagonal stairways to approach it. The white stone panels are covered with the names of the dead"—more than seventy-five thousand of them. And then, beyond and through the biggest central arch, is a cemetery. To quote Scully again: "We descend from the monument, approaching the graves. Now they seem to be facing the arch, advancing across the open space toward it . . . the terrible courage of human beings advancing in the open toward the monster, who is absolute—absolute pain and nothingness. He is emptiness, meaninglessness, insatiable war and death. There is no victory for the dead. All that courage wasted. But there they stand, the men, unbroken."

Here, the power of architectural form is absolute, and it is not static—it works, like so many great pieces of architecture do, as an experience of procession, of movement through it in real time. But the thing for us to remember is how powerfully this architectural object makes us feel tragedy and emptiness and futility—a solid makes us feel the void.

A solid to make us feel the void—that is the final paradox, maybe, that all monuments must address. The success of a monument comes, in part, from a designer who is skillful enough to understand the depths of our experience of architectural form and to think, as Lutyens and Bacon and Lin so obviously did, about why certain kinds of form and space can inspire the most profound emotions. The experience of a great memorial, like great religious architecture, is not a fully rational thing, and it has very little to do with the more practical aspects of architecture. It does not feed people, it does not fix what is broken, it is not necessary in the sense that shelter is necessary. Jeannette Winterson has quoted a conversation between a woman and Ezra Pound in which the woman asked Pound what he thought art was for. Pound replied, "Ask me what a rose bush is for."

From the beginning, John Whitehead and other officials of the Lower Manhattan Development Corporation had believed that an international design competition, open to anyone, would be the best way to find an appropriate memorial design. A competition was how the extraordinary design by Maya Lin for the Vietnam Veterans Memorial had been found; Lin was a Yale undergraduate when she submitted her design, and no one in the architectural world had ever heard of her before. The unusual success of Lin's design, which both jump-started her career and influenced the design of an entire generation of memorials elsewhere, has come to make architectural competitions seem like the only way in which to find architects for large-scale, symbolic civic projects of this sort. The design for the memorial to the Oklahoma City terrorist bombing of 1995, the domestic event that most resembled the attacks of September 11, was also determined through an architectural competition, which further underscored the notion that a competition would be the natural way to proceed at Ground Zero.

Not only did a competition hold forth the possibility of revealing another brilliant and unknown talent like Maya Lin, it would also be a way in which the public could feel some sense of active engagement. The outpouring of emotion about the destruction of the World Trade Center led to literally thousands of designs for the rebuilding of the site by average citizens. Some were sent to the LMDC; some to CNN, which held an open call for designs; and others to newspapers and magazines that were covering the story. (My own files bulged with unsolicited designs for new skyscrapers, for "peace gardens," for new neighborhoods, and for every which kind of memorial.) Most of these submissions were earnest but mediocre at best and of little use to the planners or to anyone except their creators, for whom they presumably offered some therapeutic benefit. But the feeling that these unsolicited designs represented was genuine, and an open competition for a memorial would allow other ideas from citizens anywhere in the world to get a real hearing by the planning authorities. Holding a competition was, in a way, an opportunity to make the Ground Zero planning process more truly public than it had been at any other stage. If another Maya Lin turned up, so much the better, but at least anyone who wanted to participate in this part of the process could do so by presenting his or her own creative work, an opportunity that, for many people, was far more meaningful than showing up at a meeting or a public hearing.

Many of the unsolicited designs from the public in the months following the terrorist attack were, if not literally memorials, commemorative in nature. If there is anything that can be said to characterize the bulk of them, it is that they started with the belief that the entire site was to be treated as sacred and that even the biggest and most commercial structures that might be built on it should not appear ordinary or conventional. The designs seemed to share a certainty that even if Ground Zero was to have commercial activities, it should still not look like any other part of the city. A great many of the public's designs tried to integrate a huge skyscraper that would replicate the iconic role of the twin towers with a memorial to the people who died in the buildings. There were plans like the submission from a pair of designers from Beverly Hills who proposed build-

GETTY IMAGES

The Lower Manhattan skyline before September 11, 2001

AP PHOTO/BOB CHILD

Alexander Garvin discusses redevelopment with the architect Frank Gehry

GETTY IMAGES

Daniel Libeskind presents his winning design to Mayor Michael Bloomberg and Governor George Pataki at a press conference in February 2003

GETTY IMAGES

Mayor Bloomberg congratulates Libeskind on his design as John Whitehead looks on

AP PHOTO/BEBETO MATTHEWS

David Childs, Daniel Libeskind, and Larry Silverstein at Ground Zero in July 2003

Joseph Seymour (left), executive director of the Port Authority, Governor George Pataki, and Larry Silverstein at Ground Zero in April 2003

AP PHOTO/KATHY WILLENS, POOL

GETTY IMAGES

From left: LMDC President Kevin Rampe, former senator George Mitchell, Governor George Pataki, Daniel Libeskind, Nina Libeskind

Larry Silverstein and Nina and Daniel Libeskind applaud as they view the eight final memorial designs at the Winter Garden in December 2003

AP PHOTO/KATHY WILLENS

A model of the Freedom Tower is unveiled on December 19, 2003. From left to right are George Pataki, Daniel Libeskind, Larry Silverstein, and David Childs

GETTY IMAGES

David Childs (center) speaks about the just-unveiled model for the Freedom Tower. Looking on, from left, are Charles Gargano, Jospeh Seymour, Larry Silverstein, Governor George Pataki, and Daniel Libeskind

AP PHOTO/GREGORY BUL

Daniel Libeskind's original plan for rebuilding at Ground Zero, which he presented at the Winter Garden in December 2002

The Freedom Tower (as conceived by Studio Daniel Libeskind during the Innovative Design Study) and the Statue of Liberty as seen from the west

ing one tower in more slender form than the originals, a second tower in lower form, and a huge, undulating American flag, visible from the sky, atop the site—"The Ultimate Iconic Retaliation," their proposal claimed. A Pennsylvania designer suggested a seven-hundred-foot tower in the shape of a star, and a New York architect and urban designer suggested a series of towers around what he called Monument Circle, one of which would have been a sixty-story skyscraper-memorial. There were pyramidal towers and torqued towers and skyscrapers of every imaginable shape and configuration, the designers of which tried, earnestly but generally with little success, to combine the idea of an office tower with the symbolic power of a memorial.

The Port Authority's determination to restore the ten million square feet of office space that the original twin towers had contained and Governor Pataki and the LMDC's decision to support this effort all but guaranteed that none of the unsolicited designs would ever get much of a hearing, even if they had been more sophisticated. Commercial development was going to dominate Ground Zero, which meant that a commercial plan was needed. The commemorative aspect of the site and the commercial aspects began to be viewed as essentially separate undertakings. Paying respect to the dead and honoring the lives lost were one effort, and rebuilding the city was another. No longer was a tower itself the memorial or the memorial aspects scattered through the site. The memorial was to be thought of as a distinct district, a portion of the sixteen acres set aside for the purpose of honoring the dead, and the rest of the site was to be seen as being much more like the rest of the city.

It was a critical decision to conceptualize the site as having two distinct parts, and it was little noticed at the time. The Beyer Blinder Belle schemes and the LMDC competition entries were not the first plans to make a rigid distinction between the memorial area and the other parts of the site; the private Cooper Robertson and Skidmore early site plans for Brookfield Properties and for Larry Silverstein also set aside a memorial quadrant, with the city restored around it on the rest of Ground Zero. But those schemes had no official status, and when they were being drawn up in late 2001 and early 2002, the public had barely begun to consider the notion that commemoration and renewal would be expressed in separate and distinct parts of the site.

In most of those early plans, the footprints of the original twin towers were the centerpiece of the memorial district. In some of them—most notably David Childs's first schemes for Silverstein, which called for a performing-arts structure in the southwest corner of the site overlapping much of the footprint of the south tower, and a couple of Peterson/Littenberg's early studies for the LMDC—portions of the footprints were covered by buildings or streets, and the memorial section shifted slightly. The reason was not disrespect for the symbolic role of the footprints, but urban design—it turned out that Minoru Yamasaki had located his towers with some precision, placing them on the axis of major north-south streets and roughly in line with the Manhattan street grid. When urban designers began to work on a plan to restore some of the streets, they found that blocks laid out more easily if the edges of the footprints could be traversed.

As the planning process went on, however, it became clear that keeping the footprints free of any kind of new construction was a political necessity. To many family members, the footprints were resonant with a deeper meaning than any other part of Ground Zero. They *were* the twin towers, in a kind of spiritual sense; they represented the space in which their wives or husbands or children or parents had died, and the survivors were adamant that there be no new construction there. At one point relatively early in the planning process, Governor Pataki announced that he agreed with the families, and he promised that the footprints of the original towers would remain forever vacant. "We will never build where the towers stood," the governor said. His statement took many planners at the LMDC by surprise, since there had not yet been an official recommendation about that. But it was good politics on Pataki's part, since by preempting that decision the governor probably helped convince many family members who had been opposed to construction anywhere on Ground Zero to mute their opposition to other uses on the site. After they knew that the footprints were to be protected, they could begin to accept the idea of commercial buildings on other portions of the site.

Once the sixteen acres of Ground Zero were split into two distinct parts—commemoration and renewal—it was probably inevitable that the planning process would break into two parts as well. The planners tended to speak of this as just a matter of putting things into a logical order: first you design an overall master plan, and then you can design a memorial to fit into its assigned piece of the site. It sounds reasonable enough, but accepting this order of things had a subtle effect on the entire planning process, since it implicitly downgraded the memorial. The needs of commercial development, rather than the commemorative aspects of the site, appeared to be the driving force behind the design. If the memorial were truly the most important thing, it would have been designed first, and everything else would have been organized around it.

Whether right or wrong, this aspect of the process surely reflected the realities of the situation. Commercial development *was* primary, at least in the view of the Port Authority and Larry Silverstein, and while the planners at the LMDC tried hard to suggest that their agency's official position was otherwise, there was little that they could do to change the priorities. The master plan would leave a space, and the memorial would be fit into it.

One of the reasons that Daniel Libeskind's plan was so appealing both to many of the families of people who died at the trade center and to architects and planners was that Libeskind skillfully blurred the distinction between commemoration and commercial development. Libeskind's decisions to leave the bathtub excavated to a depth of thirty feet and to leave exposed a large portion of the slurry wall were officially just his solutions for a setting for the memorial. But they contained such powerful memorial components that they were seen by many people as being tantamount to a memorial. Libeskind extended the commemorative aspect of the plan to other portions of the site with ideas such as his Wedge of Light plaza, his Park of Heroes, and his suggestions about inscribing lines in the pavement that would contain the names of fire and police rescue squads, set in such a way as to indicate the direction from the heart of the site to the companies' home bases. Libeskind's plan contained all of the commercial components that the Port Authority required, as well as a skyline element and a transit station, but its commemorative aspects seemed to dominate. The same could be said, in some ways, about what Rafael Viñoly, Frederic Schwartz, and their colleagues in the THINK team had produced. But Viñoly and Schwartz's latticework towers, while certainly a civic structure of commemoration, were not as attuned to memorialization as Libeskind's work, and they left even less leeway than Libeskind had for a future memorial by some other designer.

If the design of a memorial was going to proceed on a separate track from the rest of the planning, the desire of the families to get it moving made it clear that the LMDC could not wait until the master plan was settled to get the memorial process started. In the summer of 2002, as the agency was struggling to revive public interest in a planning process badly shaken by the negative reaction to the six Beyer Blinder Belle schemes, the LMDC hired Anita Contini, a well-known curator, to oversee the planning of a memorial and cultural facilities at Ground Zero. Contini, who had founded a Lower Manhattan arts group called Creative Time and later served as a vice president of Merrill Lynch in charge of sponsorships and events marketing, was a longtime resident of downtown who was widely respected both by established, uptown arts institutions and by younger, more cutting-edge arts groups and artists themselves. She was comfortable working within a large organization, and she had proved herself adept over the years at creating projects that could win widespread community support.

Contini started work in August, shortly before the master-plan competition was launched. Her first job was to work with the LMDC's Families Advisory Council, made up of members of the victims' families, to create a mission statement and a set of overall guidelines for a memorial, which she hoped could be finished by the end of the year. Then she would have to organize and direct the architectural competition for the memorial, which would be a much bigger effort, since it would involve helping to select a jury, working with the eventual winner of the master-plan competition to determine the architectural parameters of a memorial, issuing a call for entries, receiving and processing them, and setting the guidelines for evaluating them. Contini had no idea how many entries there would be, but at the very least there would probably be one hundred times more than the nine schemes the master-plan evaluators had to look at. The competition was organized to have two stages: an initial, anonymous one, open to anyone who registered, and a second one, which was planned to consist of a handful of finalists who would be invited to work with Contini and the LMDC to develop their concepts further, after which they would be made public and a final decision made.

When she first arrived, Contini said, she was overwhelmed by the level of public interest in the challenge she faced. Everyone, she observed, had an idea for a memorial or the desire to talk about it. "It's almost as if the world has to do this for their own therapy—like when something happens to someone in your neighborhood, you show up with food, and now, the whole world is making offerings," she said. "How do we respect the fact that the whole world feels like it is the family? We've never seen anything like this. But I think it's a great opportunity, and it's comforting for me and for the families."

Contini's first order of business was to take the advisory-council members on tours of existing memorials to help them in the effort to create a mission statement. Under the guidance of Kenneth Jackson, the president of the New-York Historical Society, the group toured numerous memorials in New York City, such as the memorial in Tompkins Square Park to the victims of the *General Slocum* disaster in the East River, the Prison Ship Martyrs Memorial in Fort Greene Park in Brooklyn, the *Maine* Memorial at Columbus Circle, and various other statues and civic monuments around the city. Many are all but forgotten or, like the *Maine* Memorial, viewed more as general works of civic sculpture than as commemorations of a particular historic event. The *Maine* Memorial is a rather triumphant piece of Beaux Arts statuary, but it is all but impossible to derive from it any knowledge of the event and the war it marks, let alone any sense of emotional connection to the dead it honors. Contini observed how little historical explanation many of the memorials contained, and she wondered how meaningful many of them would be in the future, as the events they marked receded into history. Contini did not pretend to have any answers, but she asked exceptionally thoughtful questions. "Maybe they shouldn't have long-term relevance—not everything should be remembered forever," she said. "Do we want to celebrate the culture of death, instead of the culture of the living?

Do we want to have so much reminding us of the terror and the tragedy, or more of a living memorial about our culture? And how do we give families respect without taking it away from the other people in the community and other needs?"

Contini also took the advisory council on a longer trip, along with Alex Garvin and some other LMDC officials. The group visited Washington, D.C., where they saw the Holocaust Museum, the Vietnam Veterans Memorial, the Franklin Delano Roosevelt Memorial, the Pentagon, the Lincoln Memorial, and Arlington National Cemetery; they went to Shanksville, Pennsylvania, the site of the downed plane on September 11; the Civil Rights Memorial in Montgomery, Alabama—like the Vietnam Veterans Memorial a Maya Lin design; and they spent time in Oklahoma City, where they visited the memorial and museum that commemorated the terrorist attack in 1995 and met with the citizens' group that had grappled with similar design and political issues to the ones that they were preparing to face.

Following their travels, the advisory council turned to the creation of a mission statement, a task that filled much of the rest of 2002. It was the first step in laying the groundwork for the memorial competition, which Contini and her colleagues at the LMDC hoped to be ready to launch not long after the master plan was set early in 2003. The group's initial attempt at a mission statement was notable for its cautious, even hesitant language and sense of propriety. It read as follows:

> We create this memorial to honor the 3,042 innocent lives lost in the terrorist attacks that occurred on September 11, 2001, when American Flight 11 and United Flight 175 crashed into and destroyed the World Trade Center Towers, American Flight 77 crashed into the Pentagon in Washington, D.C., and United Flight 93 crashed in Shanksville, Pennsylvania, and when the World Trade Center was bombed on February 26, 1993. Those were attacks on our loved ones, our cities, our nation, our way of life, and our very freedom. We respectfully honor those who died and those who survived and carried on, those who came to help

> and those who risked their lives to save others, and those brave and compassionate citizens from around the world who stood with us in our time of need.
>
> For all who come to learn and understand, we dedicate this memorial to the unfulfilled dreams of those lost, to our country and the strength of our democracy, to our resolve to preserve an open, diverse and free society, to our determination to remain ever vigilant in order to safeguard our nation, and to those peoples around the world who united with us in a joint quest to end hatred, ignorance, intolerance, and strife and promote peace.

The final version was not nearly so genteel. It was shorter, simpler, and blunter:

> Remember and honor the thousands of innocent men, women, and children murdered by terrorists in the horrific attacks of February 26, 1993, and September 11, 2001.
>
> Respect this place made sacred through tragic loss.
>
> Recognize the endurance of those who survived, the courage of those who risked their lives to save others, and the compassion of all who supported us in our darkest hours.
>
> May the lives remembered, the deeds recognized, and the spirit reawakened be eternal beacons, which reaffirm respect for life, strengthen our resolve to preserve freedom, and inspire an end to hatred, ignorance, and intolerance.

It was not merely the substitution of the word *murdered* for *died* but the direct and clear quality of every part of the final statement that marked it as different and significantly better. The ideas were essentially the same as in the first version, but the mode of expression was entirely different. It was as if the drafting committee, having been fearful of expressing its feelings too directly at first, had to tiptoe toward them in its preliminary statement. Once that first draft had been made public, the committee members could feel released from the obligation to be so well mannered and allow themselves to say what they truly wanted to.

The program for the memorial was also devised with the help of the families, and it did not undergo much change at all. It consisted of two sections, "guiding principles" and "program elements." The principles were not much more than a kind of stepping-stone from the mission statement, a series of preliminary thoughts intended to guide participants in the competition toward a design. There were nine principles, and some were as bland as the requirement that designs "embody the goals and spirit of the mission statement." Others stated that memorial designs had to "convey the magnitude of personal and physical loss at this location"; "respect the sacred quality of the space that will be designated for the memorial"; "encourage reflection and contemplation"; and "create an original and powerful statement of enduring and universal symbolism."

The actual program elements, however, were more specific. They required that the memorial recognize each individual who was a victim of the attacks; provide space for contemplation, including separate areas for families of victims and a space to serve as a resting place for unidentified remains from the site; "make visible" the footprints of the original twin towers; and convey historic authenticity, either by including original elements that had survived the attack or by preserving existing conditions of the site. The guiding principles and the program elements were both thoughtful. They contained, however, a striking omission: neither document specified that the memorial design had to conform to the master plan. The plan was not, of course, fully set at the time the principles and program elements were being drafted, but Libeskind had been chosen and his plan adopted by the time the memorial competition was formally launched in the late spring of 2003, so the absence of any mention of it was curious. The closest the program came to the issue of the rest of the site was a statement that competitors had to "include appropriate transitions or approaches to, or within, the memorial," which could be taken to mean almost anything at all. The decision not to make any explicit mention of the master plan was to turn out to have significant ramifications months later, as the competition drew to a close.

CHAPTER 15

Reflecting Absence

WITH THE MISSION STATEment and program done, the next order of business was to create a jury. Given how politicized the planning process had been from the outset for the commercial side of the site, it was notable that there seemed to be little political pressure on the choice of a memorial design. Indeed, politicians seemed at pains to show how willing they were to isolate the memorial from the forces that they themselves had brought to bear on the rest of the process. "You can't have a memorial designed by politicians," Pataki said much later, after the process had been concluded, but he and the LMDC had been true to that ideal from the beginning.

Not only was the jury largely free of political figures—it contained only two: Patricia Harris, one of Bloomberg's deputy mayors, and Michael McKeon, a public-relations executive who had formerly been Pataki's director of communications—more striking still, it had only one representative of the victims' families: Paula Grant Berry, a publishing executive whose husband, David Berry, had been killed in the south tower. She had been active on the committee that drew up the mission statement and program. The presence of only token representation by the families made the New York process considerably different from that in Oklahoma City, where family members demanded the majority of votes on the jury, and politicians were loath to turn them down.

What made it different in New York, where things are usually more, not less, contentious than in the midwest? The very complexity of the planning process and the enormity of the events of September 11 probably made it clear from the beginning to most family members that this would be a vastly more public and less intimate memorial than the one in Oklahoma City, which for a time seemed to belong to the families of the 168 people who were killed there. Surely many families in New York saw Ground Zero in similarly personal and private terms, but they were always aware that the world felt a sense of ownership, too, and that it was watching with an intensity that had not been present in Oklahoma City for more than a few weeks after the bombing there.

New York is also, of course, one of the great art capitals of the world and the most culturally sophisticated city in the United States; even those family members who did not consider themselves a part of the city's cultural community probably had some degree of awareness that there would be pressure to name a jury with significant artistic credentials. And however uncertain the success of the LMDC's master-plan competition was at the point at which the memorial jury was being selected, there was no doubt that the public had shown plenty of interest in sophisticated, visionary architecture. If the memorial competition was to aim toward the same standards, it needed a jury capable of knowing the difference between good design and bad.

And thus the majority of the jurors were people from the city's arts community. Vartan Gregorian, the president of the Carnegie Corporation and the former president of both the New York Public Library and Brown University, was the jury's chairman. Maya Lin, whose Vietnam memorial would have made her a prominent presence in the jury's minds under any circumstances, agreed to serve on the panel, as did Michael Van Valkenburgh, a distinguished landscape architect who teaches at Harvard; Martin Puryear, the sculptor; Enrique Norten, an architect and professor of architecture at the University of Pennsylvania; Susan K. Freedman, president of the Public Art Fund; Nancy Rosen, an independent art adviser; Julie Menin, a downtown restaurateur who had helped to draft the mission statement; Lowery Stokes Sims, director of the Studio Museum in Harlem; and James E. Young, a professor at the University of Massachusetts who has written extensively about memorials and who served as an adviser to the competition to create a Holocaust memorial in Berlin. David Rockefeller, the philanthropist and arts patron—and, not incidentally, the banking executive who was deeply involved in the creation of the original trade center—served as an honorary member of the jury.

It was a stellar panel. The group was unpaid, and it was promised both complete autonomy and a relatively limited time commitment. The first promise was kept, and the jurors returned the respect accorded them by the politicians by keeping their deliberations strictly confidential; there were virtually no leaks throughout the months during which the jury was evaluating the entries, which made the competition altogether different from the rest of the planning process, throughout which supposedly private details were continually ending up in the papers. The second promise, however, could not have been more wrong. "He told me it would take a couple of weeks," Vartan Gregorian said of John Whitehead, who had recruited him to the jury, after the panel finished what turned out to be more than six months of work.

Actually, the labor of reviewing the final total of 5,201 entries, while gargantuan for the jury, turned out to be less than originally feared. When the LMDC issued its call for entries in the spring, 13,683 people responded and paid a twenty-five-dollar registration fee, which got them a packet of information about the competition and the right to submit an entry. When the deadline for entries arrived on June 30, 2003, it turned out that somewhat less than half of the registrants had actually sent in a design. But the 5,201 who did made the LMDC's memorial competition the largest architectural contest in history.

The designs were stored in a warehouse on West Thirty-sixth Street, far from Ground Zero, and they were so voluminous that it was difficult to assemble them all at once, a problem that was to vex the LMDC once the competition concluded, since there would be considerable pressure to exhibit all 5,201 entries publicly. (The LMDC solved the problem by mounting a virtual exhibition, putting all of the entries online in late February 2004, at which point the public could see a proposal for a memorial consisting of two white airliners with victims' names inscribed on the seats; a monumental red question mark; a glowing apple; and 5,198 other designs, many of which were considerably more convincing.)

The jury did much of its work in a sealed-off office space on the thirtieth floor of 120 Broadway, an old building owned by Larry Silverstein that offered such good views of Ground Zero that in the weeks following September 11 it was the location of a camera providing a twenty-four-hour live television feed showing the ongoing work of clearing the site. The rules of the competition required all of the entries to be submitted anonymously on a single thirty-by-forty-inch display board. The boards were trucked from the warehouse and placed on easels around the twenty-thousand-square-foot office. (The entries were identified by coded numbers, which is common practice in competitions of this sort.) To tighten security, the jurors agreed to leave all of their notes at 120 Broadway. They then decided to require that every juror look at every entry, at least giving it a passing glance, and they decided that they would allow no formal deliberations unless all of them were present. For an entry to remain in the competition, ten of the thirteen jurors had to be in favor of it.

The deliberations began in late summer and stretched through the fall. The sophistication of the jury meant that there was easy agreement on dispensing with entries that were literal or excessively kitsch—there were not going to be any representations of airplanes or angels or firemen rescuing people—but beyond that, there was no easy consensus. Maya Lin's manner is quiet, but she is forceful, and she and the other designers, Michael Van Valkenburgh and Enrique Norten, quickly emerged as influential jurors. Given the influence of her work, even had Lin never spoken at all, she would have been among the jury's strongest forces.

Lin, as well as several other jury members, was not fond of Libeskind's master plan, particularly the way in which he treated the footprints. Not only did his large excavated area preempt the memorial design in the minds of many of the jurors, they resented the way in which Libeskind's scheme called for a cultural building to be cantilevered out over the north end of the sunken area, including a substantial portion of one of the footprints. It was, in their view, pretentious structural exhibitionism, not reasonable planning, and in any event it tied the hands of the memorial designer far more than it should. Most of the jury members did not consider themselves under any formal obligation to honor the terms of the master plan—so long as the best designs met the requirements of the memorial guiding principles and program elements, they would be satisfied.

Once it had eliminated the entries it considered vulgar, tasteless, or trite, the jury still had several hundred entries left, and its job got harder. The group met for hours, day after day, struggling not only with the aesthetic concepts behind the remaining designs but with issues such as how easily they could be built, how appropriate their natural features would be to the New York City climate, and how well they would handle the crowds the memorial will attract, perhaps as many as ten million visitors per year. Finally, the group whittled the number down to nine, four more than its original goal. The LMDC staff prepared to find out the identities of the designers and contact them.

At that point, it turned out that one of the nine finalists, a design called "Twin Piers," which had actually been created some months before the competition by Fred A. Bernstein, an architect and writer, had been submitted by Bernstein's partner, Charles Upchurch. Bernstein himself had chosen to enter a more recent design that he thought would have a greater chance of success because it was more compatible with the master plan, and the rules prohibited anyone from submitting more than one entry. "Twin Piers," which called for a memorial to consist of a pair of pierlike constructions extending out into the Hudson River that would have reproduced the outline of morning shadows of the World Trade Center towers on September 11, was disqualified on the grounds that it was a violation of the one-entry rule. Bernstein and Upchurch sued the LMDC, saying there was nothing in the rules that prohibited Upchurch from claiming the design was his, and lost.

Eight finalists remained. They were contacted in September and told to keep their selection confidential while they reworked their designs and made use of a $130,000 budget to produce computerized animations, more elaborate drawings and models, and videos in which they described their designs. The models were all manufactured by the same company both for security reasons and to ensure that they would all be uniform in size and presentation style. A press conference was scheduled for November 19 in the Winter Garden. Only a few days before did the jury get to learn the identities of the finalists and meet them.

The press conference was elaborate and oddly anticlimactic. Like all of the Ground Zero press events, it was full of pomp and self-congratulatory references to the glories of the public planning process. This time, of course, while the competition had been more public than any other aspect of Ground Zero planning because anyone had the right to participate, it had also been much less public because the jury had operated in total secrecy.

It could not, of course, have been otherwise. The LMDC had said it would treat the memorial as a serious artistic endeavor apart from political meddling, and it kept its word. If the jury had been required to deliberate in public, it would have been impossible for it to have kept its focus on pure quality. Indeed, so determined was Anita Contini to avoid anything that remotely resembled the spectacle of celebrity architects that had colored the master-planning competition that it was decided that none of the memorial finalists would even appear at the press conference. Their work would speak for itself. The jury, too, was kept away (except for Gregorian, who made a statement on behalf of his colleagues), the better to avoid having the press ask awkward questions about the deliberations—which, after all, were far from finished. The plan was for the eight designs to be exhibited in the Winter Garden for several weeks and for the jury to use that time to take a breather, gather its thoughts as the public weighed in, and then reconvene and make a final selection by the end of the year.

The eight designs proved how conscientious the jury and Contini had been and how open they had been to the work of unknowns, but there was no Maya Lin among the finalists, to be sure.

The most impressive design appeared in many ways to be the least feasible, an austere scheme by Michael Arad, a thirty-four-year-old architect who worked for the New York City Housing Authority, called "Reflecting Absence," which all but defied Libeskind's master plan as well as much of the underground infrastructure that was already being built. Arad decided to fill in Libeskind's bathtub, obscuring the exposed slurry wall. He depressed only the footprints, which he wanted to fill in with reflecting pools. He planned a stark plaza at ground level, some contemplative space underground, and a cultural building that would have been a narrow wall along West Street, replacing Libeskind's cultural buildings and all but walling off the site from the west.

The most inventive design, after Arad's, was called "Passages of Light: Memorial Cloud," by Gisela Baurmann, Sawad Brooks, and Jonas Coersmeier. It would create an awe-inspiring space by means of what its authors described as "ten thousand vertical conduits of light," encouraging people to look up as well as inward. Another strong design, "Inversion of Light," by Toshio Sasaki, called for the footprint of the south tower to become a reflecting pool above a circle of lights. The floor plan of the north tower would be illuminated from below, and a blue laser light would shine into the sky, in a manner reminiscent of the much-admired temporary memorial of 2002, "Towers of Light," that consisted of twin beacons of light representing the destroyed towers. The five other schemes were well meaning, but they were marred by no small degree of hokeyness, beginning but hardly limited to their sappy names. Each light in "Garden of Lights" represented a victim of the attack, and there would be an "offering path" where people could place flowers. The victims' names would appear on alabaster cylinders that the designers called altars. In another scheme, "Dual Memory," there would be a gallery with pictures of victims projected onto glass. And in "Votives in Suspension," lights, one for each victim, would hang in an underground space—shimmering stars that could make the place feel a bit like a fancy contemporary restaurant in Dallas.

Almost all of the schemes seemed to have a somewhat generic quality, as if they were more concerned with encouraging feelings of warmth rather than emotions more directly connected to the trade-center tragedy. They seemed soft, if not kitschy, like the interiors of all too many contemporary suburban churches. Curiously, none of the schemes chosen preserved the twisted and burned shards of steel from the facade of the twin towers, which are powerful almost beyond words. The remnants of steel had always seemed like the ideal focus of a memorial since they are both startlingly graphic and utterly specific, but it seemed as if they were too painful and too much of this place alone. Instead, most of the designers opted for schemes that could commemorate any sadness, not the particular horror of the World Trade Center events, and most of the finalists' projects had the bland earnestness of a well-designed public plaza.

The public was underwhelmed by the designs, and there were suggestions that maybe the process should start all over again or that the jury should reject all of the finalists and look back at the others one more time, as if there were some gem that had been overlooked. Governor Pataki admitted that he "didn't see one that just jumped out and struck me as the perfect, appropriate memorial," and he spoke of the process as "discouraging," but he was not prepared to risk the political backlash that would inevitably have followed any move to withdraw the jury's independence. In early December, Michael Kimmelman, the art critic of *The New York Times,* wrote a scathing critique of the whole competition process in which he denounced the idea of allowing the public to submit entries and suggested that it was a route to certain mediocrity. The solution, Kimmelman declared, was to be proudly elitist and to have the courage to commission a great work by a great architect. As an example, he cited a public monument he admired, the great arch in St. Louis designed by Eero Saarinen.

Actually, the Saarinen arch was chosen in an architectural competition in 1948, so it proved the opposite point. But Kimmelman's piece nevertheless had the curious effect of galvanizing the jury and of making them more determined than ever to prove that the competition had not been a mistake and that it could yield something worthwhile. The rules permitted the jury to communicate with the designers at this point and to help them strengthen their schemes; to that end, the jury prepared a series of questions for each of the finalists that it called "jury concerns." Maya Lin believed that there was only one finalist strong enough to be chosen, Michael Arad. Michael Van Valkenburgh liked Arad's scheme also, and so did several of the other jurors who were influenced by Lin. The concern the jury had expressed about Arad's scheme was the absence of any kind of landscape element. Trees and gardens, as James Young had reminded his colleagues throughout the process, not only provide visual softening but can serve as symbols of renewal and regeneration as well. (At one point when the jury had narrowed the field down to about twenty-five designs, Young noticed that none of them had gardens, and he urged Van Valkenburgh to talk to the group about the value of landscape. After that, the finalist group was adjusted to include several designs with gardens.) The jury understood that austerity was fundamental to Arad's memorial design, but it worried that the memorial would be too stark for the public to accept, and several members of the jury believed it was possible to add some landscaping without destroying the integrity of Arad's concept. Arad was encouraged to join forces with a landscape designer to soften his design somewhat. He formed an alliance with Peter Walker, a distinguished, Berkeley-based landscape architect who is known for his minimalist designs. Although Walker himself had submitted an entry to the competition that did not make the finalist group, his restrained aesthetic made him an ideal partner for Arad, and he quickly set about adding trees to Arad's design.

Since the finalists were now known and the jury was in communication with them, the process was no longer so leakproof. Rumors began to spread that there were two schemes under serious consideration, "Memorial Cloud" and "Garden of Lights," both of which were praised in an editorial in *The New York Times*. In fact, there were three possibilities remaining on the table. Maya Lin remained committed to "Reflecting Absence," especially as Arad and Walker continued to refine the design, and Lin encouraged her fellow jury members to join her. Over the Christmas holidays, she spoke to friends of her hope that she would be able to sway the jury when formal deliberations, which had been postponed until the first week of January, resumed. Among the designers, Enrique Norten was not committed to "Reflecting Absence." Norten had a different favorite, "Memorial Cloud." As the jury resumed its meetings on

January 5—this time gathering in Gracie Mansion—it was deadlocked. There was a "Reflecting Absence" cadre, led by Lin and Van Valkenburgh, a "Memorial Cloud" group led by Norten, and several jurors in favor of "Garden of Lights." But the group was disappointed by the follow-up presentation by the designers of "Garden of Lights," who had not made the refinements the jury suggested, and that design went off the table, leaving the other two memorials under serious consideration.

Norten continued to argue for "Memorial Cloud," but there were concerns that it would not be practical to build, or would be too flamboyant visually. Much of the final discussion centered on the question of connection to the site, and Young and Lin both argued that Arad's design, with its preserved footprints as the central idea, was integral to the particulars of the World Trade Center, whereas "Memorial Cloud" could have been anywhere, and its soft, gentle environment could have commemorated anything, not just loss and sadness. "It seems strange to say that something has an intrinsic memorial logic, but that's what it came down to, in the end," Young said. "Arad's design had an intrinsic memorial logic to it, and the cloud didn't. The debate was between a spectacular, eye-catching aesthetic object, and something that was more logically a memorial. I felt that the cloud was, in the end, all about itself."

Gradually, convinced by Young's memorial rationale and Lin and Van Valkenburgh's repeated belief that Arad's was the most aesthetically powerful design, a few jurors who had favored other schemes moved toward "Reflecting Absence." The debate stretched through dinner at Gracie Mansion and numerous bottles of wine, with still no resolution after multiple ballots, like an old-time political convention. Seven votes would not close the matter, and neither would eight or nine—the one thing the jury agreed on from the beginning was that it would not change its rules, which required ten of the thirteen to vote yes. Eventually, at about eleven o'clock at night after a full day of meetings, "Reflecting Absence" received ten votes, and the decision was made.

When Daniel Libeskind learned of the vote, he was horrified. This was the scheme that paid the least heed to his master plan, and he saw it as a deliberate slap in the face. Libeskind told Kevin Rampe and Matthew Higgins that the jury had undermined two years of his work. There was no way, Libeskind thought, that Arad's memorial design could be made compatible with his master plan; that had been clear from the beginning, when the finalists were first revealed in November. The mess with David Childs over the Freedom Tower had been trouble enough, Libeskind felt; wasn't he entitled now to some respect, to an easier situation? It almost seemed as if the jury just wanted to assert its independence from the rest of the planning process, at Libeskind's expense.

Rampe and Higgins were not so thrilled themselves. Asserting its independence from the master plan was precisely what the jury wanted to do, and Rampe could not reverse the jury or even complain publicly about it. At the same time, he had no desire to alienate Libeskind. He had worked hard to hold the fragile Freedom Tower coalition together, and while that had not been a complete success, at least Libeskind had endorsed David Childs's final design, and the two men had appeared onstage together with the governor to unveil the tower just before Christmas. What if the memorial situation turned out to be even worse, and he could not patch together an agreement? Rampe could not afford to have Libeskind walk off in anger—if nothing else because Pataki would be furious—and yet he did not want to force Libeskind to swallow something that changed the fundamental aspects of his plan.

Rampe began to negotiate. He told Arad that his awkward slab building along West Street had to go, and he asked Arad to agree that he would not have any say over the location or the design of cultural buildings at Ground Zero, to preserve some more authority for Libeskind. The day after Arad's designation was announced, Libeskind, with a sheaf of drawings for the master plan under his arm, flew to California to spend a day working at Peter Walker's office with Walker and Arad, trying to find some common ground. It was hardly an easy session—Walker and Libeskind had recently clashed over landscaping plans for the Denver Art Museum that Libeskind is designing, and Walker had been replaced as the museum's landscape architect—but the three men emerged with at least some degree of willingness to work together. It was only at that meeting, Libeskind said later, that he realized that Arad and Walker had not understood that certain things in the master plan, like the location of train tracks, service areas, and so forth, were already fixed. "I said, 'Michael, you can't just change a ramp, because it affects so many things that are already set underground, like the concourses, the width of streets, the stations,' " Libeskind said. "It became clear that they had talked to no one but the jury."

Libeskind had put his finger on the problem with the competition. It was admirable to have isolated the jury from political pressures. But the jury was so independent of the rest of the planning process—and so determined to exert its own will on the memorial—that its members felt little obligation to respect decisions that had already been made. Since any communication between officials of the LMDC and the finalist architects was viewed as political interference, when Andrew Winters, the LMDC's head of planning and design, reviewed the eight finalists to determine how compatible they were with the master plan, he was not permitted to report his findings directly to the designers but only to the jury. It was up to the jury to pass along Winters's comments to the architects. But since many of the jury members had little interest in the master plan and little wish to protect it, it is not clear how many of Winters's observations, including some reservations he had about the inconsistencies between Arad's scheme and the master plan, ever reached the architects—or if they did, what form they took.

After his initial rage subsided, Libeskind decided to go along with Arad's plan, partly because the design had improved significantly thanks to Walker's involvement—among other things, Walker added clusters of deciduous trees in a subtle geometric pattern—and partly because Libeskind decided he could ill afford to be perceived as everyone's adversary. Libeskind, after all, still had no building at Ground Zero to design himself, and the museum structure was likely to be assigned to an architect before long. He did not want to end up as only a master planner. So Libeskind agreed to Arad's desire to remove the cantilevered museum building from the northeast corner of the memorial portion of the site; although he kept the museum in the same general portion of the site, not on the south end as Arad had proposed, it was no longer going to be cantilevered over the footprints of the towers. (One of the jurors called the cantilever "an aggressive dagger" and said "it was encumbering the footprints, and our job was to open them to the sky"—an implicit admission that the jury openly encouraged the competition entrants to break with the master plan if they wanted to.) More important, Libeskind ultimately gave up on the large excavated pit for the site, even though that had been a hallmark of his original master plan, and he agreed to endorse Arad's proposal to excavate only the footprints of the towers. It was a significant concession, although Libeskind did not want to view it that way. He now claimed that he had never meant to present his large excavated area as anything other than a starting point for the memorial architects, "a space that could be used and interpreted in any way the competitors chose to use it."

That was quite different from Libeskind's position a few months earlier, when Madelyn Wils and Carl Weisbrod had complained that the huge depressed area would be an inconvenience for the neighborhood residents and businesses and tried to get it changed. Not a chance, Libeskind had said back then; it was integral to the master plan. But that was then, and this was now. The memorial design had been chosen. It violated Libeskind's plan as much as any suggestion Wils and Weisbrod had ever made, but now there were other things to consider. The design Arad and Walker had produced was strong, clearly the toughest and the least sentimental of all of the finalists, and it would not be an easy thing to take on either the memorial plan itself or the serious and independent jury that had chosen it. And so Libeskind fell into line, and an element that he had described as a vital part of his overall design for Ground Zero and which had been defended by the LMDC over many months, was suddenly gone, eliminated in an instant because it was incompatible with Michael Arad's memorial.

A week after the announcement that Arad had won the competition, the LMDC held an elaborate press conference, once again with Pataki presiding at Federal Hall on Wall Street, to present Arad and Walker's revised design. It was less than a month after the Freedom Tower unveiling, but the LMDC wanted to make at least as big a splash with this event. The memorial would be the last of the major elements of the Ground Zero design that the LMDC would be showing, which meant—astonishingly for the journalists who had been covering the story for nearly two years—that after this there would probably be no more big events for the LMDC to hold. Once Libeskind had agreed to accept Arad's design, only one thing seemed to threaten the general air of goodwill that the LMDC hoped would prevail, which was the unhappiness of some city firemen, policemen, and emergency medical workers that their colleagues who had died at the trade center would not be recognized in a separate memorial or in distinct portions of the main memorial. Putting the names of all who died together on a single list, in random order, was a principle that the LMDC did not want to change, but by the time the press conference began it looked as if everyone, including Michael Arad, was comfortable with what can be described as a Solomonic solution. The shields or emblems of the fire department, police department, or emergency medical team would be included beside the names of their members who had died, thus marking them as distinct from office workers who, in the view of the rescue workers, had died under different circumstances. It was a subtle way of denoting the rescue workers who entered the trade center to save lives while still maintaining the overall principle that the dead would not be listed in any kind of hierarchy. To some family members, though, the tiny shields were a hierarchy, and later in the winter, Thomas Johnson—a board member of the LMDC whose son, Scott, had been a worker in a brokerage firm who was killed in the south tower—objected strongly to the plan. Kevin Rampe, caught between the family members of police and firefighters who wanted an even more separate form of recognition than the shields and other family members who thought the shields were too much, stood firm.

The event at Federal Hall was held on an exceptionally cold mid-January morning, and it began in the usual way, with a line of men in dark suits walking onto the platform: Rampe, John Whitehead, the mayor, the governor, and Daniel Libeskind. Vartan Gregorian was also on the platform. There were two less familiar faces. They were Peter Walker, a professorial-looking man of medium height who seemed younger than his seventy-one years, and Michael Arad. Arad was tall and thin, almost like a Giacometti figure, and he wore a suit without a tie. He and Walker sat together with the governor, the mayor, and Rampe; Libeskind sat on the other side of the platform with Whitehead, Gregorian, and an assistant secretary of the Department of Housing and Urban Development, who was representing the federal government.

"A short while ago we were here to unveil the Freedom Tower," Pataki said, and he pointed to the tower in a new model of Ground Zero that also included the memorial. "You don't unveil a memorial," he continued, and then he talked about how the memorial had to be "a powerful remembrance" and "consistent with the master plan." Pataki then praised the jury, which was present this time, seated together in the front row. "I won't try to explain it," the governor said of the memorial design itself, and then he proceeded to do exactly that. "This is a powerful memorial that above ground will allow us to have some concept of what we have lost—and then you will descend, past the slurry wall, which Daniel Libeskind in his original concept had preserved, to the memorial center, where we will tell the story. We will be able to see and feel and touch the twisted steel from the tower itself. And then, around the reflecting pool, will be inscribed the names. Our goal was to allow the jury to make its best professional judgment, and you have done that," Pataki concluded, facing the jury.

Bloomberg's comments were unusual, at least from a political figure. He seemed to grasp the point of Arad's abstract design immediately, and he summed up its essence clearly. "A memorial makes you think, it makes you question," he said. "You don't want to tell everybody our version—a memorial should leave people room to imagine in their own ways. It is going to be a thoughtful place."

Gregorian then introduced Arad, who embraced him and walked up to the lectern. Arad seemed earnest and slightly uncomfortable, like a bright student invited for the first time to address his professors. "It is a very difficult task I have been entrusted with, and I will do my best to rise to this occasion," he said. "What happened on September 11 influenced me greatly, but my own sense of loss is insignificant compared to family members', and I know their hopes are very high. I will do my best not to disappoint them." Arad seemed genuinely frustrated by the difficulties of pleasing everyone, and his modest and somewhat callow tone was a contrast to the all-too-polished rhetoric of most speakers at LMDC events. Arad then went on to explain the genesis of his design, which he conceived of not long after September 11 as two square, open boxes in the Hudson River—the footprints of the towers as voids with the water flowing past them. Eventually, he explained, he took his initial concept and merged it into the requirements of the competition, moving his symbolic footprints onto the Ground Zero site. An essential part of his plan, he explained as he walked over to the model, was to bring visitors down from the street: "Slowly, the sights and sounds of the city disappear and you enter into darkness, and you see a reflecting pool, two hundred feet by two hundred feet, surrounded by ribbons of names, and then, eighty feet below, at bedrock, you see a deep fissure."

Arad did not mention Libeskind's name, but it was clear that his rationale for bringing visitors down into the earth was not very different from Libeskind's own, however different the form of his design ended up being, and the experience he described sounded remarkably like the one Libeskind had envisioned for his original design. Libeskind, who had sat almost stone-faced through Arad's speech, came later to the platform and started out by taking the role of architect as elder statesman. "First, I want to congratulate Michael Arad for a very bold, simple idea and a profound design," Libeskind said. "This is a proof that not only is the process working, but it is creating a unity." And then Libeskind began to sound more like his old self. "Nowhere but in New York, a beacon of hope," he said, and his energy level mounted. "We are presenting to the world something that is optimistic—something that will allow us to move forward."

CHAPTER 16

Commerce and Culture at Ground Zero

THE MEMORIAL DESIGN WAS NOT quite as settled as it appeared to be at the press conference, despite Libeskind's agreement to support it. The problems with getting Michael Arad's design to align with the underground infrastructure proved more daunting than expected, and it turned out that Arad had not actually replicated the footprints of the towers in their actual size and precise locations but had reduced their size and shifted them slightly to accommodate the demands of his own design. In a less emotionally charged situation, this might not have mattered—it was a not unreasonable amount of artistic license for an architect to take, and the idea of the memorial, as James Young put it, should certainly not be to elevate a pair of destroyed buildings over the symbolic evocation of lives lost. But this was Ground Zero, where reason did not always prevail, and the Lower Manhattan Development Corporation was especially sensitive to the feelings of family members who felt that the footprints were not a flexible symbolic concept but a hard, tangible reality. The agency insisted that Arad provide drawings that showed the exact variation in his design from the actual footprints and study the implications of shifting his scheme so that his square cuts into the earth would coincide exactly and unequivocally with the footprints of Minoru Yamasaki's towers.

The one architect in the entire planning process at Ground Zero who seemed immune from criticism was the one with the least connection to the United States, Santiago Calatrava. Although he had decided to settle part-time in New York before he was invited to work at Ground Zero, Calatrava was Spanish by birth and had spent most of his professional life commuting between Spain and Switzerland, where he maintained the headquarters of his large practice. For the first several months after the Port Authority's July announcement that he would be the architect to design the transportation center, little was heard from Calatrava, in contrast to Libeskind, Childs, and the other Ground Zero architects, who seemed perpetually in the news. Calatrava's design was largely complete by the end of 2003, and the Port Authority, true to form, kept it solidly under wraps. There were no leaks, in part because the press was so unaccustomed to significant news coming from the Port Authority that few reporters were even trolling for gossip. Then, in late January, after the LMDC had finished its series of announcements about the Freedom Tower and the memorial, the Port Authority held a press conference of its own to unveil Calatrava's design. This time, the praise of public officials seemed not to be an attempt to put a favorable gloss on a difficult situation but a reflection of the response of the broader public, since almost everyone—even architecture critics—liked what Calatrava had wrought. It was telling that the Museum of Modern Art, which ignored the Libeskind plan despite the participation of Terence Riley, the head of its architecture department, on the LMDC's screening committee at the start of the design study, decided to present Calatrava's design in a special exhibition in the summer of 2004.

The transportation-center design bears some resemblance to Calatrava's one major completed American building, his entry pavilion to the Milwaukee Art Museum, which in turn shows the influence of one of New York's great buildings from the 1960s, Eero Saarinen's TWA Terminal Building at Kennedy Airport, as well as

Saarinen's Ingalls Rink at Yale University. Calatrava takes the swoops and curves of Saarinen's concrete buildings and makes them lighter, higher, thinner, and more tensile in feeling; it is Saarinen updated for an age of advanced technology, with lots more glass, lots more sunlight, and a sense of verticality. The major aboveground hall holds forth the promise of being one of New York's most exhilarating public interiors, although it also seems to suggest some of Calatrava's shortcomings. His buildings tend often to be overly symmetrical and do not always deliver space that is as engaging as his striking exterior shapes promise. Calatrava is an engineer, and he is as gifted in the translation of structural ideas into dramatic form as any architect alive, which is why his buildings are deservedly popular. They are exciting, however, more than they are profound. Calatrava has a fairly limited design vocabulary, and it relies on the exaggeration of some relatively simple forms, such as big, swooping curves, for effect.

But no architect could be a better symbol of the Port Authority's willingness to try playing architectural patron and to demonstrate that its engineering heritage could yield something new and different that would be a suitable symbol of the authority's good intentions, not to mention its own learning curve since September 11. Calatrava is courtly and gracious, and he communicated his passion for his architectural mission, as well as for New York City in general, with a sincerity that made him a refreshing presence amid the politicking of Ground Zero. He was a new face moving onto the public stage at just the moment when the public was coming to find the old faces—which is to say, Libeskind, Childs, Silverstein, and Pataki—a little too familiar. Calatrava was also helped by the fact that from a programmatic standpoint, his project was probably the only thing at Ground Zero that no one was against. Everyone seemed to like the idea of a transportation hub that would bring a kind of monumental grandeur to the PATH trains that run between Lower Manhattan and New Jersey, would pull together the confusing mess of subway lines in the area, and could also serve as a ceremonial vestibule for this entire part of the city. Unlike the memorial, which provoked deeply conflicting feelings from different parties and thus made it difficult for Michael Arad or Peter Walker to be perceived as a heroic figure, the idea of a "Grand Central Terminal for downtown" was seen as a universal good by people on all sides of the other Ground Zero issues. The warm enthusiasm with which Calatrava's design was received certainly affected the image of the Port Authority, which for much of the time since September 11 had been viewed as an obstacle to progress. Now, it seemed almost enlightened and self-assured.

The acclaim for Calatrava was a mixed blessing for Daniel Libeskind. On the one hand, it created a certain aura of good feeling around Ground Zero in general, which could only help in the larger planning effort. The sense that this key part of the project was in good order would surely have some spillover effect on perceptions of everything else, especially since Libeskind and Calatrava had worked smoothly together from the beginning, a fact that Libeskind had not hesitated to mention when people wondered whether his conflicts with David Childs meant that he could not comfortably get along with any other architect. He saw his easy relationship with Calatrava as proof that he was more than happy to meet another strong architect halfway.

But Calatrava had also succeeded in creating the first clear architectural icon for Ground Zero, a role that Libeskind had very much wanted for himself. He still hoped for the museum commission, but that would not be awarded until the LMDC decided the tenant of the museum building, since any institution would obviously expect to have some say in who its architect would be. The process of overseeing the cultural complex at Ground Zero, like the memorial competition, fell to Anita Contini, and she and her staff had been so preoccupied by the complications of the memorial that they were forced to move more slowly on the question of the cultural facility. In mid-February the LMDC issued a paper entitled "Report on the Memorial Center and Cultural Complex at the World Trade Center Site" that seemed intended mainly to remind people that the agency had not forgotten its plans to build a range of cultural facilities at Ground Zero, including a museum of September 11, a performing-arts center at the corner of Greenwich and Fulton streets, and one or more other museums and institutions that would "recognize and complement the historical and cultural significance of the World Trade Center site" or would "diversify the cultural opportunities downtown." These last institutions would be placed in one or two buildings at the southwest corner of Greenwich and Fulton streets—the buildings that Libeskind had originally wanted to cantilever over the footprints. The report was intentionally quite general as to what kinds of cultural institutions would fulfill its broad mandate, since it also said the LMDC would consider educational institutions, civic organizations, and fine-arts institutions—in short, almost any valid cultural program. The LMDC continued to evaluate proposals from various cultural institutions over the winter and early spring, as Contini, Rampe, and the board tried to navigate between pressures from major, established arts institutions such as the New York City Opera and the New York Hall of Science that actively hoped to move to Ground Zero; organizations such as the Ninety-second Street Y on the Upper East Side that had no desire to relocate but saw a Ground Zero branch as a way to extend their audience; entirely new institutions that had the possibility of significant funding such as the Museum of Freedom, a project led by Tom Bernstein, Roland Betts's longtime business partner in Silver Screen, Chelsea Piers, and other ventures; and smaller, locally based arts organizations.

Culture served an essential purpose at Ground Zero. It would be a kind of leavening force, an intermediary between the all-out commercialism of the main program, with its huge amount of office and retail space, and the commemorative aspects of the site. Coming to Ground Zero to visit a museum or to hear an opera would not be the same as going there to mourn, but it would not be the same as going there to make money, either. It seemed to blunt the opposing ways that people viewed the site and to provide an opportunity for genuine civic purpose.

Still, however valid the cultural effort would turn out to be—and however significant its architectural expression might end up being—it would still be a sidelight, not the main event. Ground Zero was not going to be Lincoln Center, any more than it was going to feel like the row of memorials on the Mall in Washington, D.C. It would be a commercial place, first and foremost. And while it was possible to justify this as representing the resumption of the kind of life that was lost when the World Trade Center was destroyed and thus as a valid, even necessary, response to the terrorist attack, rebuilding Ground Zero largely as a commercial site meant, inevitably, that it would be subject to largely commercial pressures.

As the cold winter of 2004 gave way to spring, things at Ground Zero grew harder, not softer. Governor Pataki advanced the groundbreaking for the Freedom Tower to July 4, separating it both from the anniversary of September 11 and from the Republican National Convention at the end of August. Pataki's decision was not the result of any rapid progress on the design of the tower; the design was still unresolved, and little progress on it had been made over the winter and spring. There was no longer any likelihood of a final design in August or September, and officials may have decided that they were better off tying the groundbreaking to Independence Day than risking criticism by holding it during the Republican convention or on September 11. The groundbreaking itself turned out to be something of an anticlimax, notable mainly for the enormous, twenty-ton block of granite quarried in upstate New York and brought down to the site to serve as a formal cornerstone. The graphic design firm Pentagram, along with Skidmore, Owings & Merrill, designed the stone, on which was carved a simple text: TO HONOR AND REMEMBER THOSE WHO LOST THEIR LIVES ON SEPTEMBER 11, 2001 AND AS A TRIBUTE TO THE ENDURING SPIRIT OF FREEDOM. The dignity and brevity of the inscription at least seemed in accord with the reality of the situation, which was that the groundbreaking was nothing more than a symbolic gesture. It was a chance to pretend that construction was starting on a building whose design was not entirely certain, whose construction documents had not yet been finished, and into which no one had expressed any intention to move other than the governor himself.

There was, however, money to build the tower. Unlike most commercial skyscrapers, which require loans from financial institutions who expect to see commitments from paying tenants before turning over any money, the Freedom Tower could be erected with the money Larry Silverstein was getting from the trade center's insurance policies. Or at least most of it could; Silverstein was still not happy about paying for the elaborate top, which would contain no rental space. But the spire of the Freedom Tower was the least of the financial issues Silverstein faced over the summer. In early May, Herbert Wachtell's ambitious legal gamble to get his client double payouts from all the insurers failed utterly, which meant that Silverstein would not get the money he had hoped to use to build the other skyscrapers called for in the Ground Zero plan. The courts rejected Silverstein's claims that insurance documents that would have committed all the insurance companies to the double payout were in effect at the trade center, and decided that the developer was entitled only to the minimal amount from most of insurers. It was a huge setback for Silverstein. It was clear that he would have been much better off had he listened to his former colleague, Geoffrey Wharton, who urged him after September 11 to negotiate a settlement with the insurance companies, which would have allowed both him and the insurers to avoid the cost and delay of litigation and to appear statesmanlike in the bargain. A settlement would almost surely have yielded Silverstein more money than he ended up with after deciding to go for broke.

Now Silverstein would have to seek conventional financing for the other buildings, and that would take years. In some ways, of course, it was not a bad outcome, since it meant that the buildings could not be constructed on the developer's or the Port Authority's whim, but would have to await genuine market demand. Silverstein tried to make the best of it, and in a television interview at the end of May he talked about how he wasn't getting any younger—he turned seventy-three on May 30—and how for him, the most important goal was getting to complete the entire project during his lifetime. His favorite line was that he wasn't of an age where he could buy green bananas, and he tossed it off everywhere, from television interviews to meetings with the executives of the LMDC. Losing the insurance case, Silverstein said, was just another complication, just another delay, but one that he would surmount as he had surmounted the others that had come before him.

In fact, it was much worse, since it threw into question whether Silverstein could ever build the other buildings called for in the master plan. Perhaps the market would require all that office space in another decade or two, but it was hard to believe that it could happen any sooner, and it might not even occur then. Silverstein would be completing 7 World Trade Center in the next couple of years, and presumably the Freedom Tower a few years after that, neither of which yet had any tenants to speak of. Those buildings—and many of the vacant floors in the World Financial Center across the street from Ground Zero—would probably have to come close to filling up before financial institutions would choose to lend money for the other skyscrapers. And in the meantime, the terms of Silverstein's lease with the Port Authority required him to continue to pay rent of ten million dollars a month, regardless of whether he built anything at all. If it took until sometime in 2008 to finish the Freedom Tower, Silverstein would by then have paid the Port Authority between seven and eight years' worth of rent, or as much as $960 million, before he had earned a penny from the trade center site. On top of construction costs, which were expected to approach $2 billion, this meant Silverstein would have spent close to $3 billion of insurance proceeds before the Freedom Tower opened. He also had to use the insurance money to pay his lawyers—whose billings reportedly exceeded $100 million—and the architects, planners, and engineers who were working on his portion of the site.

The architects' fees were considerably smaller than the lawyers', but they were also the subject of more contention. Silverstein and Libeskind battled over Libeskind's $800,000 bill for work on the Freedom Tower. Silverstein said that since Libeskind had a contract with the LMDC for more than $2 million for his master planning work, that should be sufficient to cover his contribution to the Freedom Tower, and offered a token payment of $125,000. Ed Hayes, Libeskind's lawyer, accused Silverstein of trying to punish Libeskind for taking issue with David Childs's design. By early summer, the dispute had escalated to litigation.

Libeskind's diminished role was underscored in late June when *The New York Times* titled an update on Ground Zero "The Incredible Shrinking Daniel Libeskind: How Ground Zero's Visionary Architect Went from Master Planner to Minor Player." The thrust of the piece was that Libeskind had become all but irrelevant, and while the article's judgment was exaggerated and its presentation almost gleefully cruel—above the headline was a picture of a tiny Libeskind figure in empty space—it was impossible to deny that there was some degree of truth to the observation. Libeskind no longer seemed central to the process, and he had been boxed into a difficult situation. If he fought, as he had with David Childs and later with Michael Arad, he ran the risk of appearing selfish and demanding. But when he went along with compromises to his plan, he appeared to lack authority.

While Silverstein squabbled over money and the legalities of insurance payouts, Michael Arad continued to struggle with the LMDC over the memorial. Arad, despite being in his thirties with relatively little experience, believed that winning the memorial competition entitled him to be treated with the authority of an established architect. Kevin Rampe, Andrew Winters, and other officials at the LMDC had no desire to undercut the competition, which had caused them enough trouble already, and they were impressed with the progress that Arad and his landscape architect partner, Peter Walker, had made. But they drew the line at letting Arad control the memorial project himself. They insisted on an established architecture firm, and after considering several, they settled on Davis Brody Bond, which made its reputation in the 1960s and '70s with socially conscious housing, and which now designs primarily academic and cultural institutions. It was a good enough fit that shortly after the alliance was announced, Arad accepted an invitation to join the firm himself, while continuing his direct relationship with the LMDC.

Paying for the memorial was not going to be easy. The LMDC decided to set up an independent foundation to seek private funds to underwrite the bulk of the costs of both the memorial and the cultural facilities that would be constructed at Ground Zero, and several of the city's most prominent figures, including Sandy Weill, chairman of Citigroup, and Jerry Speyer, the real-estate developer and arts patron, turned down the request to head the new organization. John Whitehead and the board wanted a prominent citizen to lead the fundraising effort, but a great many of the city's leaders who were in a position to do the job were already tapping their fellow citizens for other causes, and the memorial, unlike the humanitarian effort in the immediate aftermath of September 11, didn't seem so urgent. There was also a problem with the breadth of the new foundation's mission, since it encompassed not only the memorial designed by Arad but new cultural institutions that had not yet even been chosen, let alone designed. Whitehead rejected the idea of splitting up the fundraising effort, however. He felt strongly that it should be conducted by a single foundation, since he didn't want solicitations for the formal memorial to be competing with solicitations for the cultural buildings. They were all of a piece, all part of the public face of Ground Zero, Whitehead felt. The cultural institutions had a de facto commemorative role, and the whole idea of the master plan was to weave it all together. Keeping all of the fundraising together in a single foundation would underscore this point—and it would also assure that the LMDC would retain control of how funds were divided between the memorial and the cultural institutions.

Deciding which cultural institutions would end up at Ground Zero was a complex process in itself, and like the design of the Freedom Tower and the memorial competition it took far longer than anyone expected and revealed deep divisions of opinion among officials, planners, and the public. Here, too, there was little agreement about anything, except the basic idea that it was a worthwhile thing to have some cultural facilities in the mix. But should they be new ones, created especially for Ground Zero, or established ones that were resettling downtown as a gesture of support? Should the emphasis be on performing arts or on visual arts? What role should the history of September 11 itself play? And should the new cultural facilities be designed primarily to serve tourists, who after all had plenty of other cultural institutions to visit in the rest of the city, or should they be designed to serve the needs of the relatively culturally starved Lower Manhattan neighborhood?

John Whitehead felt strongly that the neighborhood was not the priority, and that as Ground Zero was getting a memorial that would be an international tourist attraction and would presumably have a tower that would be of international stature, it needed cultural facilities on the same level. He was especially pleased that the board of the New York City Opera, which had been hoping to build a new opera house for several years, had indicated a desire to move downtown and had made an aggressive play for designation as the primary performing arts organization. Early in the process the opera company had indicated a willingness to consider working with Daniel Libeskind, and its director, Paul Kellogg, felt strongly that a downtown location could bring in significant numbers of new, younger operagoers that the company was not attracting to its present home in the New York State Theater at Lincoln Center. To counter the argument that its performance schedule would not create enough constant activity to justify giving over the key intersection of Greenwich and Fulton streets to the company, the opera agreed to expand its programming, to bring in a dance company as a partner, and also to make its hall available to other organizations for daytime events.

But an opera house of the size the City Opera required would still have more than two thousand seats, and with backstage facilities would take up a lot of space—more space, some people thought, than could easily fit on the corner, given the size of the Freedom Tower next door. There was some discussion of sliding the opera house into the base of Freedom Tower, but that created further complications and delays, and even the strong support of the LMDC chairman did not make the opera company's designation a certainty. To Whitehead's dismay, pressure grew to designate a smaller arts organization, the Joyce International Dance Center, as the main performing arts tenant at Ground Zero. The Joyce needed only a thousand seats, and along with the Signature Theater Company it proposed a theater cluster that would include a couple of smaller houses that would be occupied by a number of different performing arts groups. The Drawing Center, a small, nonprofit exhibition space, would add a visual arts component. *The New York Times* editorialized in favor of the consortium, stating that the City Opera "seems to us too unwieldy for the setting. It is not so much a question of the wrong art as the wrong space." The newspaper that had constantly argued for the highest ambitions in every aspect of planning at Ground Zero seemed to have decided that, in the cultural arena, smaller and more modest was better.

In early June, the Arts & Leisure section of the *Times* weighed in with a symposium of the paper's critics on the subject of culture at Ground Zero, and no one but Anthony Tommasini, the music critic, had anything good to say about the City Opera proposal. Tommasini reminded readers that the company had been called the "people's opera" by Fiorello La Guardia, and urged that Paul Kellogg consider a somewhat smaller hall as a compromise with those who viewed the City Opera plan as too grand. Michael Kimmelman, the art critic, called for a casual, free-form mix of temporary exhibition space and artists' studios, and A. O. Scott, the film critic, offered an earnest but somewhat naïve plea for building storefronts instead of institutions so that the city's natural culture might arise from the streets. The general tone was one of skepticism about the official proposals, and the more established the institution, the more dubious the critics (Tommasini aside) were about its appropriateness for Ground Zero. Herbert Muschamp, for his part, rejected culture altogether, saying "opera house, museum, and so on: these proposals are signs of cultural failure." He then argued for "abandoning the flawed ground zero design process altogether in favor of reconstructing the twin towers more or less as they were."

Unfortunately, once again the *Times* had published a major statement at a time when the decisionmaking process was all but complete. Four days after the Arts & Leisure feature, the LMDC held a press conference in the Winter Garden to make public its final decisions about the cultural makeup of Ground Zero—the December and January events at Federal Hall having turned out not to be the final big announcements after all. The news this time was that the "smaller is better" group had carried the day. The consortium of the Joyce International Dance Center, the Signature Theater, and the Drawing Center was offered space in the undesigned cultural buildings, along with the Freedom Center, the new, less institutional-sounding name for Tom Bernstein's still-unformed museum project. The decision was a victory both for Anita Contini, who had favored the notion that Ground Zero should be a home for somewhat smaller, more nimble cultural organizations than the City Opera, and Richard Schwartz, chairman of the New York State Council on the Arts, who had been equally unenthusiastic about the idea of putting the opera at Ground Zero. As usual, John Whitehead had only positive things to say in public about the decision, but he was deeply disappointed at his failure to convince his colleagues that the opera company was the logical tenant for Ground Zero.

In the end, the decision was less a matter of Whitehead's failure than it was the result of a groundswell of doubt about the value of large, established cultural institutions, or at least about their appropriateness at Ground Zero. If Anita Contini and her colleagues were unwilling to endorse the view of some of the *Times* critics that the best culture is noninstitutional culture, they did believe that there is greater energy and freshness in smaller, more nimble organizations than in larger ones, a view that was only strengthened by the highly publicized problems that had bedeviled both Lincoln Center and Carnegie Hall over the last few years. To many people the very word "opera" seemed to connote a kind of elitism that they hoped the Ground Zero project would be able to avoid.

But whatever the motivations behind the decision, the LMDC had surely not compromised standards of excellence with the Joyce–Signature–Drawing Center combine. While the Freedom Center was still an unknown quantity, the other three organizations had lists of achievements that put them among the best of the city's smaller arts groups, and together they made up a diverse and lively combination. The LMDC staff clearly had little sympathy with Whitehead's view that the symbolic role of Ground Zero demanded an established institution of national or even international stature. As a result, the Queens-based New York Hall of Science, among the city's major science museums, was another big loser in the cultural stakes, since it had hoped to establish a Manhattan beachhead at Ground Zero, and it, too, was rejected—like the City Opera, it was thought to be too big and too set in its ways to bring the innovation that was hoped for.

That neither the City Opera nor the Hall of Science is a conservative institution—in fact, compared to such established predecessors as the Metropolitan Opera or the American Museum of Natural History, they are both scrappy upstarts—merely added a layer of irony to the whole business. For many people in the city's cultural community, Ground Zero overall was looking like far too established a development, given the weight that Larry Silverstein and the Port Authority carried, and they wanted to shift the balance of power. In many ways, the decision to give smaller, younger cultural institutions preference was a way of making the entire project feel more populist, or less like it was fully controlled by established forces of power. The City Opera lost out, at least in part, because Larry Silverstein and the Port Authority had remained the dominant forces in the rest of the project, and because culture was the only realm of Ground Zero in which populism and diversity still seemed to carry significant weight.

Epilogue: The Limits of Architecture

It is true to say that planning at Ground Zero began with a sense of a unique mission, and ended up being far more like other large-scale building efforts than anyone had expected. But the story does not end there. It is important to remember, first, how much was accomplished, and second, how much this may mean for the way in which cities are planned everywhere. When the process first began, in October 2001, I spoke at a forum organized by the Gotham Center for New York City History at the City University of New York, and called for a tower that would be an unconventional skyscraper, a symbol on the skyline as well as a commercial building—"an Eiffel Tower for the twenty-first century," I called it, and that, in some form or another, is what the architects of the Freedom Tower have tried to do. A few months later, at a conference in the spring of 2002 sponsored by Regional Plan Association, I developed this idea further, saying that the mission at Ground Zero is to build "a tower that will use the technology of our time as aggressively and inventively as Eiffel used the technology of the nineteenth century, and use it to produce a tower that I hope will be as beautiful. I can imagine that the design of such a tower would be the greatest architectural commission of our time." This, of course, was long before the epic battle between Daniel Libeskind and David Childs was envisioned. I also said that I hoped that we would "move gradually toward thinking that there are ways in which we can respect the lives of those who died there and at the same time respect the future of the city and build toward it, that honoring the lives lost and building anew need not be entirely incompatible." And then I added the following:

> I hope that we build ambitiously, and daringly. If we respond with the conventional, then we have failed to grasp the meaning of this moment, and the depth and resonance of its challenges. But I think there is a deep contradiction here, and we have to be honest enough to address it. We want to build a conventional neighborhood here, in part because we want to fill this part of the city with vibrant life, embracing what we have lost, and reasserting the value of that everyday urban life that was so brutally taken away. But we also know that to make what we build too conventional, to make it too much like other places, is to deny the enormity of what happened, to deny the reality of history.
>
> Another way to say this is to say that all of the things that we like about neighborhoods and cities, the pleasant, relaxed, traditional urbanism that makes, say, Battery Park City so appealing to so many people, are not the kinds of things that express the enormity and the power and the depth of what happened on September 11. The problem we face, in short, is that if we express the tragedy of September 11 in its full magnitude, it is hard to imagine that we will be making a neighborhood that is as easy and comfortable to live and work in as we want it to be. But we cannot trivialize the events of September 11, and the lives lost, by turning the neighborhood into just a pleasant theme park, either. It is not a mall, and it is not a festival marketplace. It has to show some scars. There has to be some sense of the extraordinary. I do not believe that the greatest thing we can do here is like perfect plastic surgery, obliterating any trace of a scar.

Daniel Libeskind's master plan understood this challenge, and even though it has been compromised, the goal of balancing commemoration and renewal, of combining the awesome and the everyday, still remains. It has often seemed slanted rather more toward the everyday than a lot of people would want it to be, but even at its worst moments, Ground Zero has never been just a commercial project.

What does it mean for other times, other places, other cities? No one wants any city to suffer through the tragedy that befell New York on September 11, but cities will always build at large scale, whatever the reason. Indeed, today commercial pressures often push cities toward vast megadevelopments, even if social pressures do not always support them. By mid-2004, Ground Zero was not the only enormous development planned for New York. Mayor Bloomberg and Daniel Doctoroff had turned their efforts to a proposal for a huge rezoning of the far west side of midtown Manhattan that would include a football stadium for the New York Jets, which would also be the centerpiece of a hoped-for Olympics in 2012. Bloomberg and Doctoroff had become so entranced by the possibilities of this project that they became less engaged in Ground Zero as it moved ahead, perhaps welcoming the opportunity to plan for an area in which they did not have to engage in political struggles with either the state government, the Port Authority, or a private developer. But—and this is the point—they could hardly proceed as they wished. There was significant public opposition to the city's plan, which called for numerous new office towers and a subway extension as well as the stadium, and its advocates could hardly operate as the creators of the original World Trade Center had, or as Robert Moses might have with one of his neighborhood renewal schemes. They had to embark on a long effort to convince skeptical citizens as well as many of the same civic groups that had been active in Ground Zero of the merits of their plan.

As we move more fully into what we might call the populist planning age of Jane Jacobs, and more definitively away from the autocratic planning age of Robert Moses, there will be more attempts to convince citizens that large, ambitious plans will enrich city life, not diminish it. Many of the efforts to sell the public on New York City's plan for the stadium and other projects on the far west side have involved claims that the stadium will enhance urban activity and street life. This may or may not turn out to be so; the striking thing is the extent to which public presentations intended to win support for the project have focused on the restaurants and shops that will accompany the stadium, as well as on the public amenity of a nearby riverfront park. Advocates of huge projects now seem to feel that the best hope they have of winning public approval is to convince people that big things are good because they strengthen and enable little things. Whether one needs a huge stadium to get a sidewalk café is debatable—but it says a great deal that today, one appears to need a sidewalk café to sell a huge stadium.

Public involvement in planning will not go away. Government officials and private developers have all recognized this, and it is now a common occurrence to have new urban projects marketed to the public in the manner of the New York football stadium proposal, as their supporters try to make the case that huge developments embody the small-scale values of traditional urban neighborhoods. Sometimes they may actually do so, but they can also be Trojan horses, containing not the seeds of renewal but of destruction. We may well be living in the age of Jane Jacobs, as opposed to the age of Robert Moses, but we also live in the age of marketing, and it is common today to see large projects presented as if they epitomized the small-scale, naturally occurring urban values Jacobs espoused.

The challenge, as we move forward from Ground Zero, is twofold, and it requires a willingness to do things that do not seem to go together. The first is to keep public involvement meaningful and not allow it to be restricted, as it was at Ground Zero, to issues of design, but rather to assure that the public has the opportunity to say something about what a block or a neighborhood or a riverfront should be used for in the first place. There never was such an opportunity at Ground Zero; that, more than anything else, was where the process failed. The public was only invited into the dialogue to talk about what the place would look like, not to share in the earlier decisions about what use this land would be put to.

The second challenge, paradoxically, is not to think of public involvement as a panacea, and to remember that planning is not something best done by referendum. Planning and building cities involve difficult choices that often require long-term vision, and sometimes they involve being willing to take risks. Putting plans up for a vote is no guarantee of a mandate for greatness and daring. In design, the public voice is often a cautious one. Cities—for all that they need the loving serendipity of neighborhoods and the vital energy of streets—flourish also in boldness and a willingness to embrace the new. At Ground Zero, the public moved closer to a bold vision than it has in a long time, and the greatest legacy of the process will be to inspire even more confident alliances of private imagination and public passion.

In many ways the story of rebuilding Ground Zero has been a story of the struggle of a certain kind of idealism against the pressures both of money and of time. When the planning process began, it was buoyed by an overwhelming tide of emotion. It seemed, for at least a short while, that the usual rules of building in New York would be suspended in light of September 11 and that one positive effect of the tragic destruction of the World Trade Center would be a different way of looking at Manhattan real estate—indeed, a different way of looking at the entire idea of the city. Rebuilding Lower Manhattan after September 11 was the first chance New York had in a very long time to produce an ambitious piece of civic planning. It was an opportunity for the most creative architects and planners in the world to turn their attention to the challenge of Lower Manhattan and to make use of the best design ideas that the last generation had produced. Everyone knew that it was already a very different neighborhood from the one into which the original World Trade Center had been inserted, vastly more interesting and diverse, and this could be a chance to make it better still, so long as decisions were made on the basis of what kind of uses, what kind of buildings, and what kind of public spaces would make the best twenty-first-century city for everyone—not on the basis of what would make for the best short-term return for real-estate developers and investors.

That did not happen, in large part because the person with the most power in the planning process, Governor Pataki, did not choose to step in at the beginning and wipe the slate clean so that planning could truly have started from zero, not from the point at which the Port Authority and Larry Silverstein wanted it to start. That would not have been easy. But as the events of September 11 were unprecedented in American history, so, too, should the response have been unprecedented. After all that happened in the aftermath of the terrorist attacks and the destruction of the most powerful symbol of the American skyline, it is hard to believe that the public would have objected to a decision to take over these sixteen acres of land for public purpose, and to use public funds to purchase the land from the Port Authority or to buy out Silverstein's lease.

Still, it is wrong to think of the planning process, however much it may have failed to achieve its potential, as business as usual. Larry Silverstein's initial attempt to rebuild the site according to his and the Port Authority's wishes was firmly rebuffed. Even the most pragmatic politicians knew that Ground Zero could not be treated as if it were a normal real-estate project, and Pataki had started the LMDC in part to ensure that the planning process was at least somewhat more open to public review. Later, after the gubernatorial election of 2002, Pataki became more assertive, but it was far too late for a completely fresh start or for any radical rethinking of the site. All that was possible was to make the best of the conflicting forces that swirled around Ground Zero.

Those forces could be summed up as political power, money, and architecture and planning. The first two are always part of life in New York and have always played a critical role in shaping the urban landscape. It should not be a surprise that they have continued to be potent factors at Ground Zero. The surprise would be if politics and money had become irrelevant. The third force—design—has risen and fallen and risen again in significance in the history of New York, but it has rarely, if ever, been the dominant force. Even the greatest works of architecture of New York, from Central Park and the Brooklyn Bridge to the Woolworth Building, Rockefeller Center, and the Seagram Building, reflect economic and political forces and not solely aesthetic ones.

But design meant more at Ground Zero than it has for most of New York's history, and there are several reasons. The first has nothing to do with the events of September 11. Architecture has played a larger role in the culture for much of the last generation, thanks to a higher level of visual literacy and the increasing presence of notable, iconic buildings, not to mention the celebrity status of their architects. The relationship between architecture and political power and money was changing even before September 11, as architecture became, for better or for worse, a marketing tool for museums, civic buildings, apartment buildings, and even commercial office buildings and stores. Daniel Libeskind's Jewish Museum was drawing huge numbers of tourists to Berlin long before September 11, just as Frank Gehry's Guggenheim Museum brought an onslaught of visitors to Bilbao. More to the point, office buildings by Norman Foster and Fumihiko Maki and Jean Nouvel (the three architects selected by Larry Silverstein to design the other three office buildings at Ground Zero, should they ever get built) were very different from the kind of banal commercial boxes created by developers a generation ago.

This is the cultural background against which the architectural campaign of Ground Zero was set: architecture was poised and ready, in a sense, to fulfill a new set of cultural obligations that the overpowering emotions of September 11 set before it. To many people, the very idea of design seemed to embody the idealism that was sought in the reconstruction of the sixteen acres. We would respond to this tragedy by showing the world the very best we were capable of, the most advanced and creative architecture we could produce.

It was a laudable goal, and what was particularly striking was the extent to which it was shared not only by architects and planners but by a wide range of citizens. After September 11, architecture seemed to have acquired a seat at the table of power, based on the belief that ambition of design could confer a depth and seriousness to whatever was built at Ground Zero. This belief not only inspired such disparate events as Max Protetch's gallery show in January 2002 and *The New York Times Magazine*'s architectural beauty pageant the following September, it had a direct connection to the public's negative reaction to the initial schemes by Beyer Blinder Belle and the LMDC's subsequent attempt to turn around the planning process by initiating its master-plan competition. And it led to the extraordinary event with which this book opened, the presentation of serious and mostly avant-garde architectural proposals for Ground Zero before an audience of New York's leading politicians, civic leaders, and real-estate executives, and later to the celebrity of Daniel Libeskind, to Larry Silverstein's willingness to work with Libeskind, if not to give him authority over the design of the Freedom Tower, and to the selection of Santiago Calatrava to design the transportation center. In each instance, there was a shared belief that architecture was capable of being a force for good—or, more to the point, that aesthetics might have some tangible effect on the quality of life and on the statement that New York City wished to make to the world.

The mistake many people in the design world made was in believing that the forces of power in New York, once they had decided to use architecture as a kind of calling card for the renewed city, would actually cede any significant degree of power to aesthetics. If architecture was given a seat at the table that it had never before had, that seat was not, as many critics and architects had expected, at the head of it. "Our goal was to build a twenty-first-century city—theirs was to reelect George Pataki," a planner active in the process said, looking back on the events of 2002. The judgment may be harsh, but there is no question that political and economic forces remained in control. What played out through 2002 and 2003 was the use of architecture for political ends, not the use of politics for architectural ends—that is the key moral of the story, to the extent that anything in this saga can be called a moral. However difficult it may have been for many architects, planners, and critics to accept this, the key political and economic decisions in the planning process remained more or less the same as they had been before architecture was elevated to the status of a political tool.

Architecture's power, then, was limited. This is not to say that design was mere window dressing, although there were discouraging moments when it certainly appeared to be no more than that. But at many of the most important junctures of the long process, architecture and the ambitions that quality design represents were a serious factor. So, too, was the role that various civic groups, such as New York New Visions and the Civic Alliance, played in trying to keep both the public and the official planners mindful of the notion that Ground Zero was not supposed to be business as usual.

The LMDC's master-plan competition, for all its flaws, represented an earnest attempt to marry the ambitions of serious design with political realities. But it was a marriage that was fated always to have two partners on unequal footing. The political and economic forces that prevailed at Ground Zero—the state government, the LMDC, the Port Authority, the Silverstein lease, and the program requiring ten million square feet of office space and enormous amounts of retail space as well—combined to all but overwhelm the abilities of talented architects to shape the site to its highest potential. The idealism of good design could not, in the end, mitigate the harshness of this extreme commercial program.

Architecture almost always reflects power, and it can never obscure it. Great architecture over time can take on its own reality, and its beauty can sometimes even render moot the circumstances of its creation—no one thinks of Central Park in terms of the agonizing political struggles that went into its creation, for example, or of Rockefeller Center as a huge economic risk embarked on almost by accident by the son of the nation's richest industrialist. But when the works of architecture are as fraught with political compromise as the buildings at Ground Zero appear likely to be, it is hard to believe that time will turn this effort into a triumph. Libeskind's master plan has been whittled away, the Freedom Tower represents neither Libeskind's nor David Childs's ideas in their strongest forms, and the other office towers are so far in the future that it is difficult to imagine what forms they will take. Silverstein's decision to name three architects of international renown to design the other towers seemed to suggest that the developer had undergone an architectural epiphany of some sort, but given the absence of a market for these towers or the money to build them it is probably better thought of as an architectural publicity stunt. (Maki, Foster, and Nouvel met with David Childs in the winter of 2004, which could be taken as a sign that some work is being done on their buildings, but Libeskind was not present at the meeting, which made it clear that the process of trying to weaken the master-plan architect's control over the entire project was continuing unabated.)

The disappointment of Ground Zero is in part a failure of time. If the original architecture of the World Trade Center demonstrated a great fallacy of America in the 1960s—the fallacy of size, the beliefs that bigger was always better and that American might and power could solve any problem—the planning process since September 11 demonstrates the fallacy of America in the 1990s and beyond, which is the fallacy of speed, the belief that faster is always better. Faster is not better when you are trying to get beyond tragedy, because it denies the reality of mourning and of human nature, which is that psychological wounds take as much, if not more, time to heal than physical wounds and that you cannot rebuild a city successfully when you do not know entirely what you want it to be and when the wounds are still fairly raw. We have demonstrated many things in the rebuilding process, but patience is not one of them. We rushed into it, desperate to renew, as if building quickly would prove to the terrorists that our culture was strong and able and still on top of the world. But the pressure to build quickly was also, in part, a pressure to avoid rethinking the site from the beginning and to consider what alternative uses might, in the long run, serve the city better.

New York City is resilient, and so is Lower Manhattan, which will survive whatever happens at Ground Zero. Indeed, Lower Manhattan was in the middle of a remarkable transformation before September 11, as it evolved from being almost entirely an office district into a richly diverse neighborhood, with residences, restaurants, stores, and cultural facilities, many of which took over former office buildings. It is all but certain that the ultimate future of the neighborhood lies less in what is done in response to September 11 as in the continuation of all of the positive forces that were at play on September 10. These forces are continuing to strengthen. In some cases they have been reinforced by the LMDC itself, which has funded numerous improvements to parks and public spaces outside of Ground Zero. The one thing that is beyond doubt at this point is that Lower Manhattan will be an increasingly vibrant and diverse neighborhood, whatever form the sixteen acres of Ground Zero ultimately take.

Of course, those sixteen acres will symbolize New York's future, and if they turn out well, they will have the potential to raise Lower Manhattan from a lively and good downtown to one of the great urban centers of the world. Rebuilding Ground Zero is the first great urban-design problem of the twenty-first century, and for all that has gone wrong, for all that the planning process has often seemed weak and lacking in the clear, bold vision that we had hoped for, there have been plenty of times when it has brought forth waves of optimism and hope of a sort that New Yorkers had not seen in generations. Most of the time, idealism plays a role in planning in New York that is so small as to be barely worthy of mention, but on the sixteen acres that once contained the World Trade Center, it has counted for much more. If nothing else, the planning process has reflected the realities of New York at the beginning of the twenty-first century. Idealism met cynicism at Ground Zero, and so far they have battled to a draw.

Sources and Acknowledgments

Every writer would like the world to believe that he does it all himself, but in the case of a book like this one, there are far too many people who know otherwise. I have interviewed almost all of the people who are mentioned in this book, and many of them have been exceptionally generous with their time, graciously meeting with me numerous times as the long planning process unfolded. I owe a debt of thanks to John Whitehead, Roland Betts, Lou Tomson, Kevin Rampe, Matt Higgins, Anita Contini, John Hatfield, Andrew Winters, and Alex Garvin, all of whom are or were a part of the Lower Manhattan Development Corporation. Joe Seymour of the Port Authority has been generous with his time, as have Charles Gargano of the Port Authority and the Empire State Development Corporation, Deputy Mayor Daniel Doctoroff, and City Planning Commission Chair Amanda Burden.

Many architects, including some whose designs I have had less than flattering things to say about, have kindly made themselves available to talk, time and time again. I owe particular thanks to Daniel Libeskind, Nina Libeskind, David Childs, and Rafael Viñoly for numerous interviews, some of them conducted in their offices, some at public meetings, and many others over leisurely and pleasant meals. But other architects have been generous with their time as well, including T. J. Gottesdiener, Marilyn Jordan Taylor, Guy Nordenson, Frederic Schwartz, Santiago Calatrava, Steven Peterson, Barbara Littenberg, Roger Duffy, Peter Walker, Greg Lynn, Jesse Reiser, Richard Meier, Charles Gwathmey, Norman Foster, Stanton Eckstut, John Belle, David Rockwell, Robert A. M. Stern, Bartholomew Voorsanger, and Christopher Choa.

Robert Yaro and Tom Wright of the Regional Plan Association have been especially helpful, and I must also thank two of the most articulate of the many relatives of those who died on September 11, Nikki Stern and Tom Roger. Diana Balmori organized a dinner that helped me focus my thinking on the complex memorial issue, and I remain grateful to Mike Wallace, the great historian of New York, for inviting me to participate in what I believe was the very first public program about the future of the site, held at the Graduate Center, City University of New York, in October 2001. I thought it was too soon after September 11 to have much to say, but as I look back at my notes, I see that several of my ideas began to take shape then, and they were further refined at a symposium organized by Henry Wollman for the Steven L. Newman Real Estate Institute at Baruch College early in 2002, where I was privileged to share the platform with James Young, whose ideas many months later became critical to the successful completion of the memorial competition. Later, Robert Ivy, the editor in chief of *Architectural Record,* organized several programs that gave me the opportunity to explore other aspects of this topic in public forums. So did the filmmaker Ric Burns, in an interview he and James Sanders conducted with me as part of their ambitious film about the World Trade Center. Both James Young and Maya Lin, his colleague on the memorial jury, have been helpful, particularly after the conclusion of the memorial competition freed them to speak. My thanks go also to Larry Silverstein and his former colleague Geoffrey Wharton, as well as to Kent Barwick, Ray Gastil, Kenneth Jackson, and Edward Hayes for their time. Jennie Sheehan has provided help in organizing research material. Edward Novotny has been a source of behind-the-scenes assistance, and the public relations departments of both the LMDC and Skidmore, Owings & Merrill have graciously allowed the use of images of the design that they controlled.

Any writer who is chronicling a major news event as it happens must rely not only on his own reporting but on that of others, and I have learned from the work of many of my colleagues who have written about aspects of the rebuilding of Ground Zero, including Ada Louise Huxtable, Michael Sorkin, Robert Ivy, Philip Nobel, Christopher Hawthorne, James Russell, Suzanne Stephens, Peter Slatin, Blair Kamin, and Nicolai Ouroussoff. While readers will note that I have been critical of some of the coverage of the rebuilding effort in *The New York Times,* that newspaper's voluminous coverage has nonetheless been an essential tool, and it is important to cite the work of James Glanz, Eric Lipton, and David Dunlap, which has consistently represented newspaper journalism at its very finest.

Glanz and Lipton's book, *City in the Sky: The Rise and Fall of the World Trade Center,* which combines their excellent reporting on the physics of the collapse of the towers with a strong history of the buildings' construction, is now the finest all-around history of the World Trade Center. It was a useful source for me, as were two earlier books: Angus Gillespie's *Twin Towers,* which is far too forgiving of the Port Authority and the overbearing intentions of the original design, and Eric Darton's *Divided We Stand,* which is perhaps not forgiving enough. Michael Sorkin has produced two important books in the aftermath of September 11: *After the World Trade Center,* a collection of essays which he edited along with Sharon Zukin, and *Starting from Zero,* a collection of his own writings on the planning process. I was both informed and inspired by Mike Wallace's concise and passionate book on rebuilding, *A New Deal for New York City.* Max Protetch has assembled the various schemes for the World Trade Center site produced by architects for his gallery exhibition of January 2002 in a book entitled *A New World Trade Center.* The full texts of the reports of the civic groups that were influential in the planning process, particularly New York New Visions and the Listening to the City project sponsored by the Civic Alliance are available online at www.newyorknewvisions.org and www.civic-alliance.org. Among numerous other websites on which documents I found useful were posted were those of two online publications, the Gotham Gazette (www.gothamgazette.com/

rebuilding_nyc), which has chronicled the rebuilding process from the beginning, and the Slatin Report (www.theslatinreport.com), a real-estate newsletter with a strong bias toward enlightened planning. The Regional Plan Association (www.rpa.org) and the New York chapter of the American Institute of Architects (www.aiany.org) also provided useful links.

For background on New York City, the planning issues discussed early in this book, and the cultural forces that have led to the new political power that architecture has come to possess, there are numerous sources, and I will mention only three of the most critical. Jane Jacobs's classic *The Death and Life of Great American Cities* and Robert Caro's *The Power Broker: Robert Moses and the Fall of New York* together tell much of the story of the view toward cities that brought us to the original World Trade Center. Alexander Garvin's *The American City: What Works, What Doesn't* is important not only as a post–Jane Jacobs document, but for the insights it offers into the thinking of the planner who played a significant role in the evolution of the Ground Zero rebuilding process.

This project was helped in other ways by people who had nothing themselves to do with the challenge of rebuilding. I owe a special debt to two editors at *The New Yorker,* David Remnick and Sharon DeLano. David asked me early in 2002 to track the progress of planning at Ground Zero; the result was my first long piece on the subject, "Groundwork," which appeared in May 2002. He then extended a more or less open invitation to stay with the story and continue to report it for the magazine. Eventually, I wrote eight pieces for *The New Yorker* on aspects of rebuilding the World Trade Center site, and while I have used only a few short portions of these pieces in the text of this book, the research I did to write them has truly made the larger labor of this book possible. Without the support of David Remnick and *The New Yorker,* this book would not have come to be. And without Sharon DeLano, this book would not have the form that it does. Sharon did not edit this book, but her skillful editing of all of my pieces at *The New Yorker* has formed the foundation for it, shaping my sense of this complex subject, and—

as she always does—sharpening my awareness of the difference between facts that matter and facts that do not.

At Random House, Kate Medina has championed this project almost from the beginning, with consistent energy, goodwill, and good ideas. Her commitment and enthusiastic support has made working with her a consistent pleasure, and I can say the same for her assistant, Danielle Posen. Carol Schneider of Random House made an early contribution to this project that turned out to be crucial. I am grateful also to Evan Camfield, Carole Lowenstein, Molly Lyons, Tom Perry, London King, Gene Mydlowski, and Beck Stvan of Random House. I must also thank Ann Godoff, no longer with Random House but the editor who first suggested this book and who worked to give it shape at the outset. My agent, Amanda Urban, was of course a part of this project all along. As she always does, she has made all kinds of potentially difficult problems magically disappear.

My wife, Susan Solomon, has been a constant and critical reader of this text, and she and my sons, Adam, Ben, and Alex; my parents, Edna and Moe Goldberger, and my mother-in-law, Ruth Solomon, have supported this project in the best possible way—with enthusiastic interest, frequent questions, and gentle reminders that they would like me to get it done. They remind me, continually, where architecture ends and real life begins.

PAUL GOLDBERGER
May 2004

Index